TEACHER'S ANNOTATED EDITION

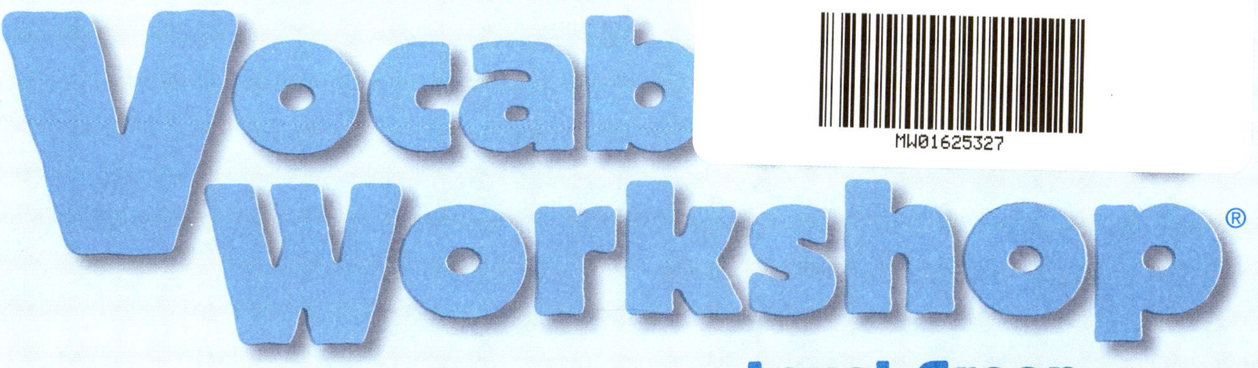

Vocabulary Workshop®

Level Green

Enriched Edition

with iWords™ Audio Program

Jerry L. Johns, Ph.D.
Senior Reading Consultant

Distinguished Teaching Professor Emeritus
Department of Literacy Education
Northern Illinois University

Consultants

Joseph Czarnecki, Ph.D.
Faculty Associate, School of Education
Johns Hopkins University
Baltimore, MD

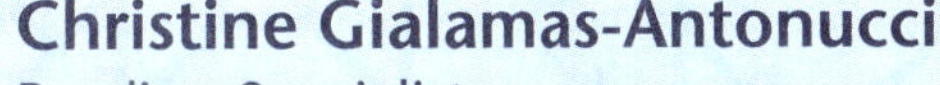

Christine Gialamas-Antonucci
Reading Specialist
Chicago Public Schools
Chicago, IL

Lucy Lugones
Technology Consultant
St. Luke's School
New York, NY

Helen Wood Turner, Ed.D.
Reading Specialist
Turning Point Academy
Lanham, MD

Sadlier

TEACHER'S ANNOTATED EDITION

Vocabulary Workshop®

Enriched Edition

with iWords™ Audio Program

Advisers

The publisher wishes to thank the following teachers and administrators, who read portions of the series prior to publication, for their comments and suggestions.

Khawla Asmar
Assistant Principal
Milwaukee, WI

Ann Jennings
English Specialist
Rustburg, VA

Megan Mayfield
Teacher
Woodstock, GA

Carolyn Branch
Lead Charter Administrator
Kansas City, MO

Amy Cristina
Teacher
Panama City, FL

Cora M. Kirby
Reading Specialist
Washington, DC

Julie Cambonga
Assistant Principal/Teacher
Sierra Madre, CA

Tara M. Gaiss
Literacy Specialist
Kings Park, NY

Lisa Mayer
Teacher
Houston, TX

Nancy Wahl
Elementary School Teacher
New York, NY

Photo Credits: Cover: pencil: Used under license from Shutterstock.com/Pedro Nogueria; wood grain on pencil: Used under license from Shutterstock.com/Christophe Testi. Alamy/Big Cheese Photo LLC: T39; Punchstock/Blend Images: T5; Punchstock/Digital Vision: T7; Used under license from Shutterstock.com/Monkey Business Images: T12, T17

For additional online resources, go to **vocabularyworkshop.com** and enter the Teacher Access Code VWL11TXM72EN.

Address inquiries to Permissions Department, William H. Sadlier, Inc., 25 Broadway, New York, NY 10004-1010.

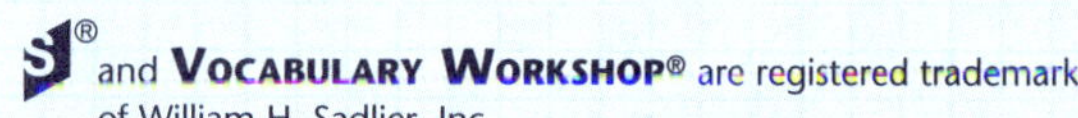

Printed in the United States of America.
ISBN: 978-0-8215-8023-3
11 12 13 14 15 BRR 24 23 22 21 20

Contents
TEACHER'S EDITION

Additional Resources

vocabularyworkshop.com

Student Resources Online new!
- Audio of Unit Passages
- iWords Audio Program
- Visuals of Unit Words
- Audio Glossary
- Flash Cards
- Interactive Games
- Practice Unit Worksheets
- Interactive Word Map

Teacher Resources Online new!
- Common Core State Standards
- Planning and Pacing Guide
- Graphic Organizers
- Family Games

Assessment Online new!
- Beginning-of-Year Diagnostic Assessment
- Interactive Unit Quizzes
- Test-Taking Strategies
- Final Mastery Test

Supplemental Components
*Test Booklet Forms A and B
*Online Assessment

*Optional purchase

Vocabulary Workshop is an engaging, multimedia program with a systematic approach to direct vocabulary instruction. Its blend of print and mixed media components helps to enrich and support instruction for all learners. **Vocabulary Workshop** Level Green is part of a comprehensive elementary-through-high-school series.

Level Green is:

- Aligned with the Grade 3 Common Core State Standards, Language Standards K–5, Vocabulary Acquisition and Use. (See page T18.)
- Enriched with audio and visual resources to support all learners, including English Language Learners. (See pages T8–T11 and T17.)
- Supported by best practices in current research. (See pages T6–T7.)
- Complete with opportunities to practice for vocabulary and writing-related sections of standardized tests.
- Designed to build student vocabulary and word learning strategies to develop literacy competencies as measured by given performance indicators. (See page T13.)

Instructional Approach

Vocabulary Workshop implements best practices in the areas of vocabulary development and vocabulary skills. The program provides both contextual learning and direct instruction of specific vocabulary words, and it explicitly teaches vocabulary building strategies. **Vocabulary Workshop** features:

- **Contextual learning** All Unit words are introduced through Lexiled passages that represent a variety of genres.
- **Systematic, direct instruction** Each Unit features direct instruction essential to help students learn words that are not part of the students' everyday experience.
- **Multiple exposures** Each core word appears at least five times per Unit, so students encounter words repeatedly in different and multiple contexts.
- **Writing exercises** Activities, including Completing the Idea and Write Your Own, ask students to demonstrate their understanding of the words.
- **Vocabulary building strategies** Each Unit includes a Word Study lesson that teaches how to implement strategies, such as using context clues.
- **Word relationships and meanings** Shades of Meaning lessons teach students about the nuances of word meanings.
- **Reviews** Vocabulary for Comprehension, Classifying, and Completing the Idea appear frequently and provide a review of words from previous units.

Assessment

Vocabulary Workshop Level Green provides several comprehensive ways to assess students' knowledge of Unit words. Multiple assessment tools available for formative and summative assessments can provide insight into students' understanding of the words. These assessments include:

- **Beginning-of-Year Diagnostic Assessment** Benchmark assessment of words to be taught provides insight into students' prior knowledge of words.
- **Interactive Unit Quizzes** and **Worksheets** Printable practice worksheets provide differentiated follow-up as needed, based on results of the Unit Quiz.
- **Ongoing Assessment** Systematic observation helps to provide insight into students' understanding of Unit words.
- **Final Mastery Test** A printable end-of-year test assesses students' knowledge of the words.
- ***Test Booklets** Two forms of Unit, Midyear, and Final Mastery Tests provide additional opportunities for retesting.
- ***Online Assessment** Preformatted or customized assessments can be administered online.

Word List

At the heart of **Vocabulary Workshop** Level Green are the 180 core Unit words. The list includes words that:

- Appear in a wide variety of texts, both academic and trade publications.
- Appear in written and verbal interactions with mature language users.
- Pertain to a broad spectrum of content areas.
- Apply to standardized tests.

The list of core Unit words for Level Green has been developed from many sources, including spelling and vocabulary lists; current content-area textbooks, glossaries, and ancillary materials (especially for general, nontechnical terms); and classic and contemporary fiction and nonfiction. University-level scholars and classroom teachers also played an integral role in generating this list. Both contributed to and approved the selection of words for the grade.

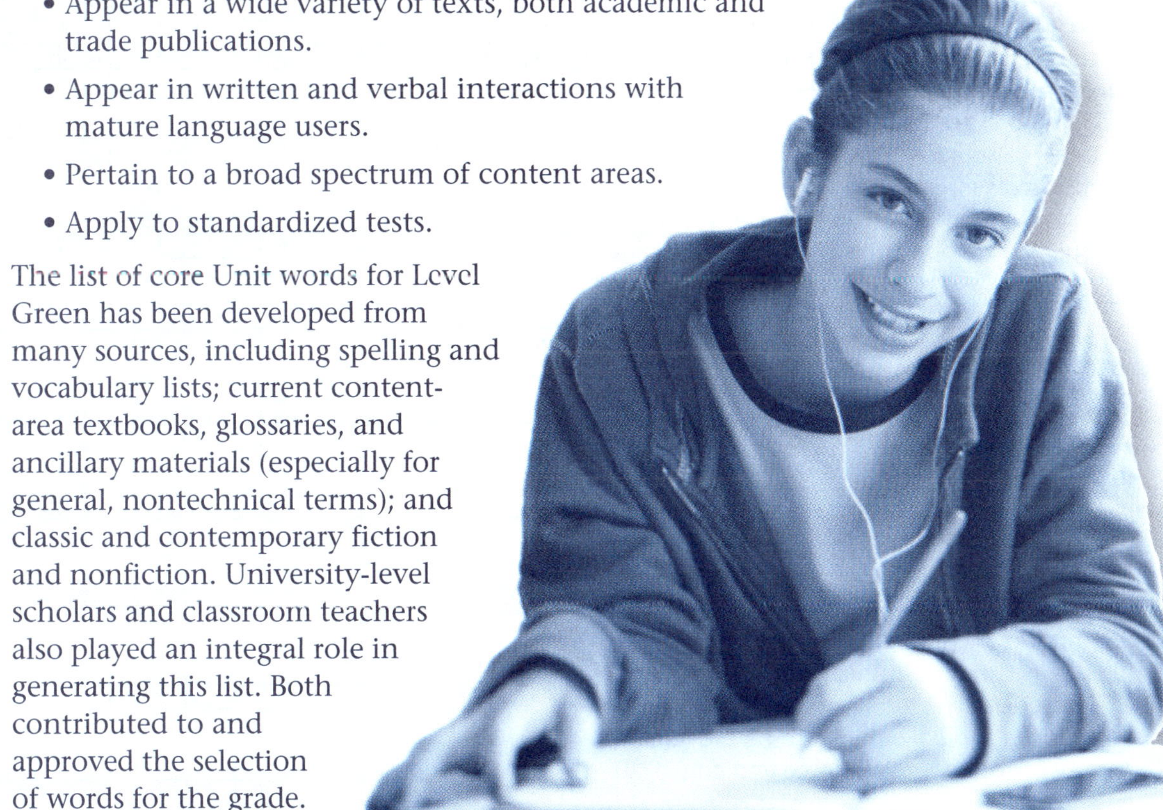

* Optional purchase

A Research-Based Program

VOCABULARY WORKSHOP Level Green is designed to promote language acquisition with an instructional approach that is supported by research and best practices as prescribed by vocabulary scholars. Research shows that vocabulary plays a critical role in learning to read and comprehend text (Biemiller, 2003; Stahl & Stahl, 2004). It also shows that a student's vocabulary is one of the best predictors in how well that student will understand text and be able to communicate in writing (Stahl & Nagy, 2006).

Research Shows:	Vocabulary Workshop
The Value of Direct Instruction	
Researchers agree that although extensive reading is important to vocabulary growth, direct instruction is more effective and more efficient than incidental learning in achieving deeper, richer levels of lasting vocabulary understanding (McKeown & Beck, 1988). Stahl and Fairbanks (1986) recommend using a definitional and contextual approach to direct instruction, and Nagy (1988) recommends including integration, repetition, and meaningful use. Beck and McKeown (2004) suggest that for direct instruction to be most effective, it should focus on useful words that students are most likely to encounter.	Level Green provides direct instruction for 180 carefully selected words. These words are introduced in Units that give concise definitions and examples of usage and then provide exercise sets in which students see and use the words in a variety of contexts. To promote retention, students must interact with each word five times over the course of a Unit.
The Value of Contextual Learning of Vocabulary	
Research has shown that for vocabulary instruction to be effective, it must not only provide definitions, but also demonstrate how words are used in natural contexts (Nagy, 1988). Many researchers also agree that much of vocabulary growth occurs indirectly through language exposure (Cunningham & Stanovich, 1998). Vocabulary development is enhanced when students are exposed to print-rich environments.	Level Green introduces the 10 taught words of each Unit in the natural context of a passage before students learn the dictionary meanings of the words. In the Reviews, students read additional passages with taught words in context. Here, the words are from the three previous Units. Students answer questions that assess word meaning and general comprehension.
The Value of Providing Multiple Exposures to Words	
If students are truly to gain ownership of new words, vocabulary instruction must provide multiple and varied encounters with those words (Daniels, 1996; Leung, 1992; Senechal, 1997; Stahl & Fairbanks, 1986). Research (National Reading Panel, 2000) also suggests other practices that should inform the way vocabulary is taught in the classroom; these include using multiple methods of instruction and actively engaging students in word learning. Any word that is introduced should continue to be provided in a variety of contexts to reinforce and enrich students' understanding (Beck & McKeown, 2004).	Level Green presents a variety of contexts that represent as fully as possible each word's semantic range and application. Level Green also provides activities in which students are active participants. They are encouraged to complete sentence starters with their own ideas and engage with words in writing and speaking activities.

Research Shows:	Vocabulary Workshop
The Value of Building Vocabulary Through Word Study	
According to *Put Reading First* (Armbruster, Lehr, & Osborn, 2001), children need to develop strategies that include using word parts to figure out the meanings of words in text and also using context clues. According to Aranoff (1994), word structure helps to determine the meaning of an unfamiliar word that is derived from the same stem as a familiar word. Many researchers promote teaching strategies that enable students to access the words they will encounter in school texts, including teaching morphemic and contextual cues in tandem (Baumann, Kame'enui, & Ash, 2003).	Level Green teaches word-learning strategies such as analyzing word parts (affixes and roots) and consulting references. Level Green also provides instruction on topics such as homographs and multiple-meaning words that can help students to build their vocabularies.
The Value of Exposing Students to Nuances of Language	
According to Beck, McKeown, and Kucan (2002), instruction that offers rich information about words and their uses enhances students' language comprehension and production. Effective instruction should integrate instructed words with other knowledge, including how words relate to one another and how words relate to real-world and personal experiences (Nagy, 1988).	Level Green provides students with opportunities to interact with word meanings on a deeper level in Shades of Meaning. Each Shades of Meaning page focuses on a specific strategy, including analyzing idioms, adages, proverbs, and figurative language. Pages also explore the nuances between word meanings, enabling students to recognize the importance of word choice.

For a Bibliography of References, go to **vocabularyworkshop.com/green**.

A fuller discussion of current research in vocabulary instruction and practices can be found in the Sadlier Professional Development Paper *Vocabulary Instruction in the Elementary Grades* at **vocabularyworkshop.com**.

A Blend of Print and Mixed Media for the Student

Vocabulary Workshop Level Green combines print, audio, and visual media to motivate students and enrich their vocabulary. This integrated approach delivers vocabulary instruction in a way that reaches a diversity of learners and helps all students truly "own" words in their growing vocabularies.

Student Book and Audio Components

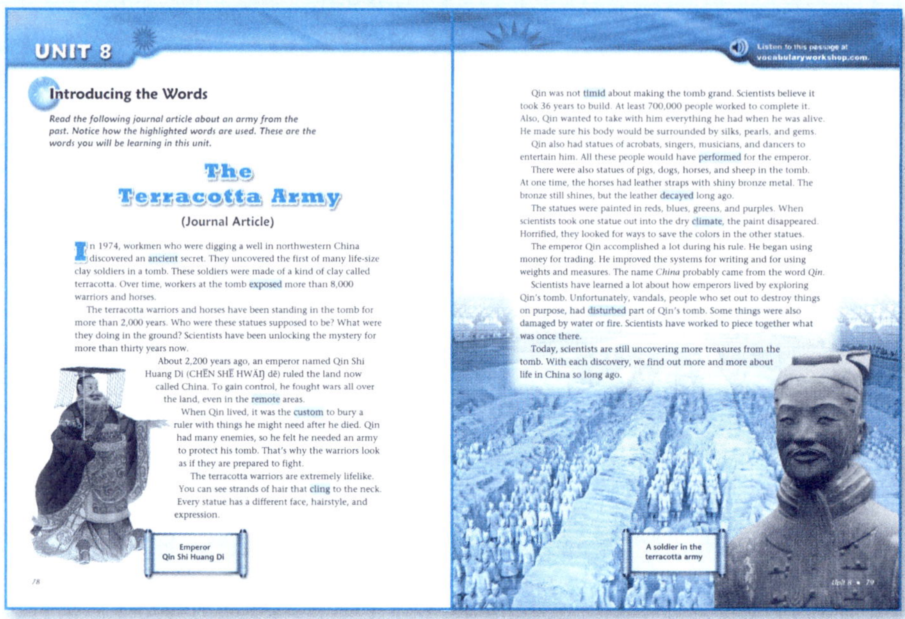

UNIT 8

Introducing the Words

Read the following journal article about an army from the past. Notice how the highlighted words are used. These are the words you will be learning in this unit.

The Terracotta Army

(Journal Article)

In 1974, workmen who were digging a well in northwestern China discovered an ancient secret. They uncovered the first of many life-size clay soldiers in a tomb. These soldiers were made of a kind of clay called terracotta. Over time, workers at the tomb exposed more than 8,000 warriors and horses.

The terracotta warriors and horses have been standing in the tomb for more than 2,000 years. Who were these statues supposed to be? What were they doing in the ground? Scientists have been unlocking the mystery for more than thirty years now.

About 2,200 years ago, an emperor named Qin Shi Huang Di (CHĒN SHĒ HWÄŊ dē) ruled the land now called China. To gain control, he fought wars all over the land, even in the remote areas.

When Qin lived, it was the custom to bury a ruler with things he might need after he died. Qin had many enemies, so he felt he needed an army to protect his tomb. That's why the warriors look as if they are prepared to fight.

The terracotta warriors are extremely lifelike. You can see strands of hair that cling to the neck. Every statue has a different face, hairstyle, and expression.

Emperor Qin Shi Huang Di

78

Listen to this passage at vocabularyworkshop.com.

Qin was not timid about making the tomb grand. Scientists believe it took 36 years to build. At least 700,000 people worked to complete it. Also, Qin wanted to take with him everything he had when he was alive. He made sure his body would be surrounded by silks, pearls, and gems.

Qin also had statues of acrobats, singers, musicians, and dancers to entertain him. All these people would have performed for the emperor.

There were also statues of pigs, dogs, horses, and sheep in the tomb. At one time, the horses had leather straps with shiny bronze metal. The bronze still shines, but the leather decayed long ago.

The statues were painted in reds, blues, greens, and purples. When scientists took one statue out into the dry climate, the paint disappeared. Horrified, they looked for ways to save the colors in the other statues.

The emperor Qin accomplished a lot during his rule. He began using money for trading. He improved the systems for writing and for using weights and measures. The name *China* probably came from the word *Qin*.

Scientists have learned a lot about how emperors lived by exploring Qin's tomb. Unfortunately, vandals, people who set out to destroy things on purpose, had disturbed part of Qin's tomb. Some things were also damaged by water or fire. Scientists have worked to piece together what was once there.

Today, scientists are still uncovering more treasures from the tomb. With each discovery, we find out more and more about life in China so long ago.

A soldier in the terracotta army

Unit 8 • 79

Introducing the Words

- 18 Units, 10 words each are provided.
- Introductory passages provide contextual learning in a variety of genres.
- Audios of Unit Passages are available online.

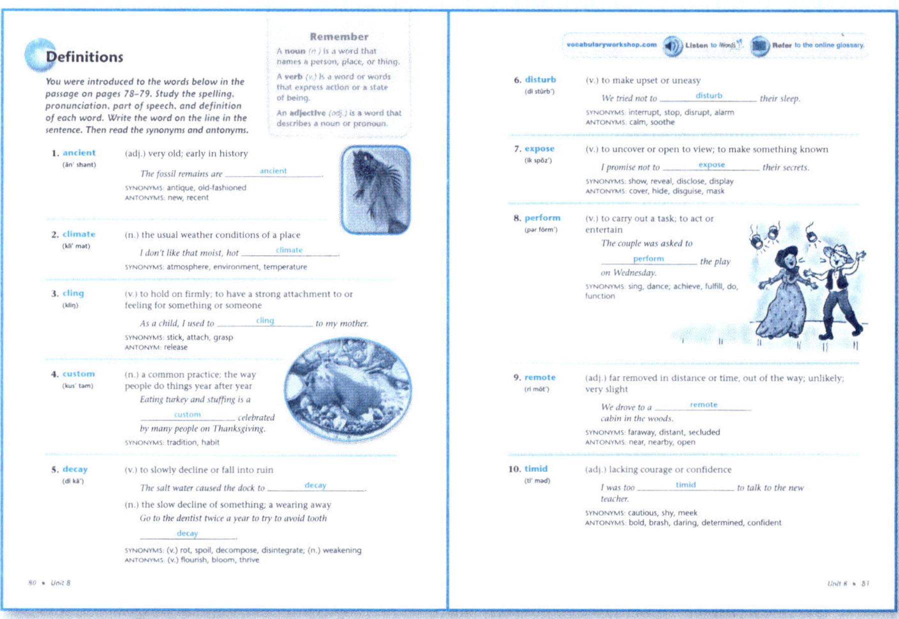

Definitions

You were introduced to the words below in the passage on pages 78–79. Study the spelling, pronunciation, part of speech, and definition of each word. Write the word on the line in the sentence. Then read the synonyms and antonyms.

Remember
A **noun** (*n.*) is a word that names a person, place, or thing.
A **verb** (*v.*) is a word or words that express action or a state of being.
An **adjective** (*adj.*) is a word that describes a noun or pronoun.

1. **ancient** (ăn' shənt) (adj.) very old; early in history
The fossil remains are ancient.
SYNONYMS: antique, old-fashioned
ANTONYMS: new, recent

2. **climate** (klī' mət) (n.) the usual weather conditions of a place
I don't like that moist, hot climate.
SYNONYMS: atmosphere, environment, temperature

3. **cling** (kliŋ) (v.) to hold on firmly; to have a strong attachment to or feeling for something or someone
As a child, I used to cling *to my mother.*
SYNONYMS: stick, attach, grasp
ANTONYM: release

4. **custom** (kus' təm) (n.) a common practice; the way people do things year after year
Eating turkey and stuffing is a custom *celebrated by many people on Thanksgiving.*
SYNONYMS: tradition, habit

5. **decay** (di kā') (v.) to slowly decline or fall into ruin
The salt water caused the dock to decay.
(n.) the slow decline of something; a wearing away
Go to the dentist twice a year to try to avoid tooth decay.
SYNONYMS: (v.) rot, spoil, decompose, disintegrate; (n.) weakening
ANTONYMS: (v.) flourish, bloom, thrive

80 • Unit 8

vocabularyworkshop.com Listen to iWords. Refer to the online glossary.

6. **disturb** (di stûrb') (v.) to make upset or uneasy
We tried not to disturb *their sleep.*
SYNONYMS: interrupt, stop, disrupt, alarm
ANTONYMS: calm, soothe

7. **expose** (ik spōz') (v.) to uncover or open to view; to make something known
I promise not to expose *their secrets.*
SYNONYMS: show, reveal, disclose, display
ANTONYMS: cover, hide, disguise, mask

8. **perform** (pər fôrm') (v.) to carry out a task; to act or entertain
The couple was asked to perform *the play on Wednesday.*
SYNONYMS: sing, dance; achieve, fulfill, do, function

9. **remote** (ri mōt') (adj.) far removed in distance or time, out of the way; unlikely; very slight
We drove to a remote *cabin in the woods.*
SYNONYMS: faraway, distant, secluded
ANTONYMS: near, nearby, open

10. **timid** (ti' məd) (adj.) lacking courage or confidence
I was too timid *to talk to the new teacher.*
SYNONYMS: cautious, shy, meek
ANTONYMS: bold, brash, daring, determined, confident

Unit 8 • 81

Definitions

- Word meanings and example sentences are featured.
- Grade-appropriate synonyms and antonyms expand vocabulary.
- Engaging visuals depict words and provide context.
- iWords Audio Program and Audio Glossary, available online, support all learners, including English Language Learners (ELL) and striving learners.

Preview print and digital components for a sample unit.

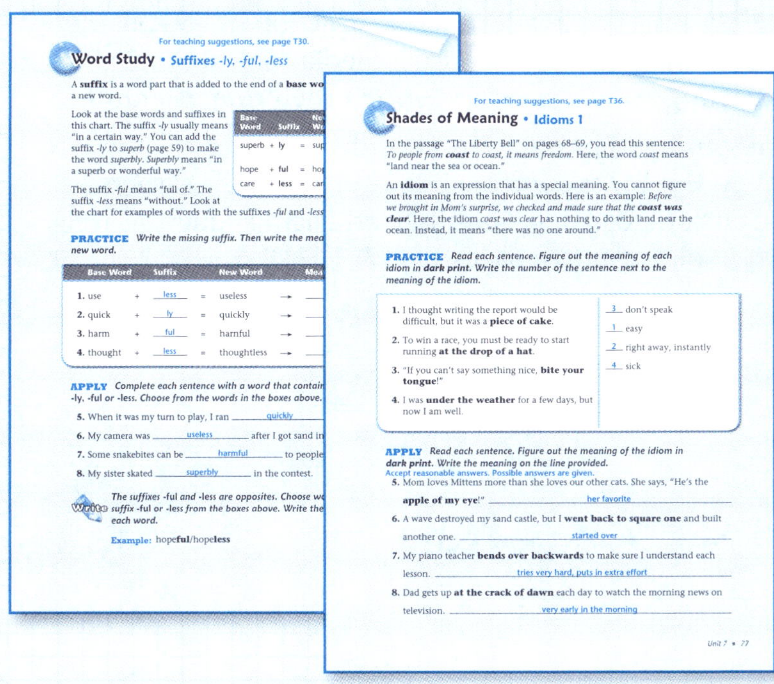

For teaching suggestions, see page T30.

Word Study • Suffixes *-ly, -ful, -less*

A **suffix** is a word part that is added to the end of a **base wo**
a new word.

Look at the base words and suffixes in this chart. The suffix *-ly* usually means "in a certain way." You can add the suffix *-ly* to *superb* (page 59) to make the word *superbly*. *Superbly* means "in a superb or wonderful way."

Base Word		Suffix		Ne We
superb	+	ly	=	sup
hope	+	ful	=	ho
care	+	less	=	car

The suffix *-ful* means "full of." The suffix *-less* means "without." Look at the chart for examples of words with the suffixes *-ful* and *-less*

PRACTICE *Write the missing suffix. Then write the mea* *new word.*

Base Word		Suffix		New Word		Mea
1. use	+	less	=	useless	→	
2. quick	+	ly	=	quickly	→	
3. harm	+	ful	=	harnful	→	
4. thought	+	less	=	thoughtless	→	

APPLY *Complete each sentence with a word that contai* *-ly, -ful or -less. Choose from the words in the boxes above.*

5. When it was my turn to play, I ran quickly
6. My camera was useless after I got sand in
7. Some snakebites can be harmful to people
8. My sister skated superbly in the contest.

Write *The suffixes -ful and -less are opposites. Choose w* *suffix -ful or -less from the boxes above. Write the* *each word.*

Example: hope**ful**/hope**less**

For teaching suggestions, see page T36.

Shades of Meaning • Idioms 1

In the passage "The Liberty Bell" on pages 68–69, you read this sentence: *To people from **coast** to coast, it means freedom.* Here, the word *coast* means "land near the sea or ocean."

An **idiom** is an expression that has a special meaning. You cannot figure out its meaning from the individual words. Here is an example: *Before we brought in Mom's surprise, we checked and made sure that the **coast was clear**.* Here, the idiom *coast was clear* has nothing to do with land near the ocean. Instead, it means "there was no one around."

PRACTICE *Read each sentence. Figure out the meaning of each idiom in **dark print**. Write the number of the sentence next to the meaning of the idiom.*

1. I thought writing the report would be difficult, but it was a **piece of cake**.
2. To win a race, you must be ready to start running **at the drop of a hat**.
3. "If you can't say something nice, **bite your tongue**!"
4. I was **under the weather** for a few days, but now I am well.

3 don't speak
1 easy
2 right away, instantly
4 sick

APPLY *Read each sentence. Figure out the meaning of the idiom in **dark print**. Write the meaning on the line provided.*
Accept reasonable answers. Possible answers are given.

5. Mom loves Mittens more than she loves our other cats. She says, "He's the **apple of my eye**!" her favorite
6. A wave destroyed my sand castle, but I **went back to square one** and built another one. started over
7. My piano teacher **bends over backwards** to make sure I understand each lesson. tries very hard, puts in extra effort
8. Dad gets up **at the crack of dawn** each day to watch the morning news on television. very early in the morning

Unit 7 • 77

Word Study

- Vocabulary strategies, such as using context clues and analyzing prefixes, suffixes, and roots, support word learning.
- Integrated speaking and writing activities expand word knowledge.

Shades of Meaning

- Words that have shadings of meaning and relationships to other words, as well as expressions with nonliteral meanings, are explored.

Additional Online Components

Use online components to support and extend the instruction in the student book. They are interactive whiteboard (IWB) compatible and available to students, teachers, and families. Students will enjoy these engaging activities while they learn and review vocabulary words.

vocabularyworkshop.com	
Online Component	**Purpose**
Audio of Unit Passages	Provides a recording of each Unit's introductory passage. English Language Learners can hear the passage being read as they follow along in their student books.
iWords Audio Program	Brings each vocabulary word to life with a recording of its definition and illustrative sentence. iWords™ provide oral models and oral practice for ELL students.
Visuals of Unit Words	Appears in the iWords™ Audio Program to provide visual context for the words and support for ELL students.
Audio Glossary	Lists all vocabulary words by alphabetical order and by Unit. The Audio Glossary models pronunciation for ELL students.
Interactive Games	Reviews the content of each Unit.
Interactive Word Map	Enables students to build a printable vocabulary concept map for each Unit word.
Interactive Unit Quizzes	Reviews definitions of each Unit's words and mirrors standardized tests. Quizzes are automatically scored.
Practice Unit Worksheets	Reviews each Unit's words in multiple-choice format and in passage-based, critical reading, multiple-choice format. They can also be used as a reteaching tool for ELL students.
Family Games	Presents the content of each Unit in a gamelike setting.

A Blend of Print and Mixed Media for the Teacher

Vocabulary Workshop Level Green presents systematic, direct instruction of vocabulary through an integration of print and online audio and visual media tools that help students "own" words in their growing vocabularies and enrich their understanding.

The Teacher's Edition contains resources to promote successful vocabulary instruction. These include research, tips for supporting English Language Learners, alignment with Common Core State Standards, a Planning and Pacing Guide, as well as teaching notes for the Student Book pages (see pages T6–T7, T17–T43).

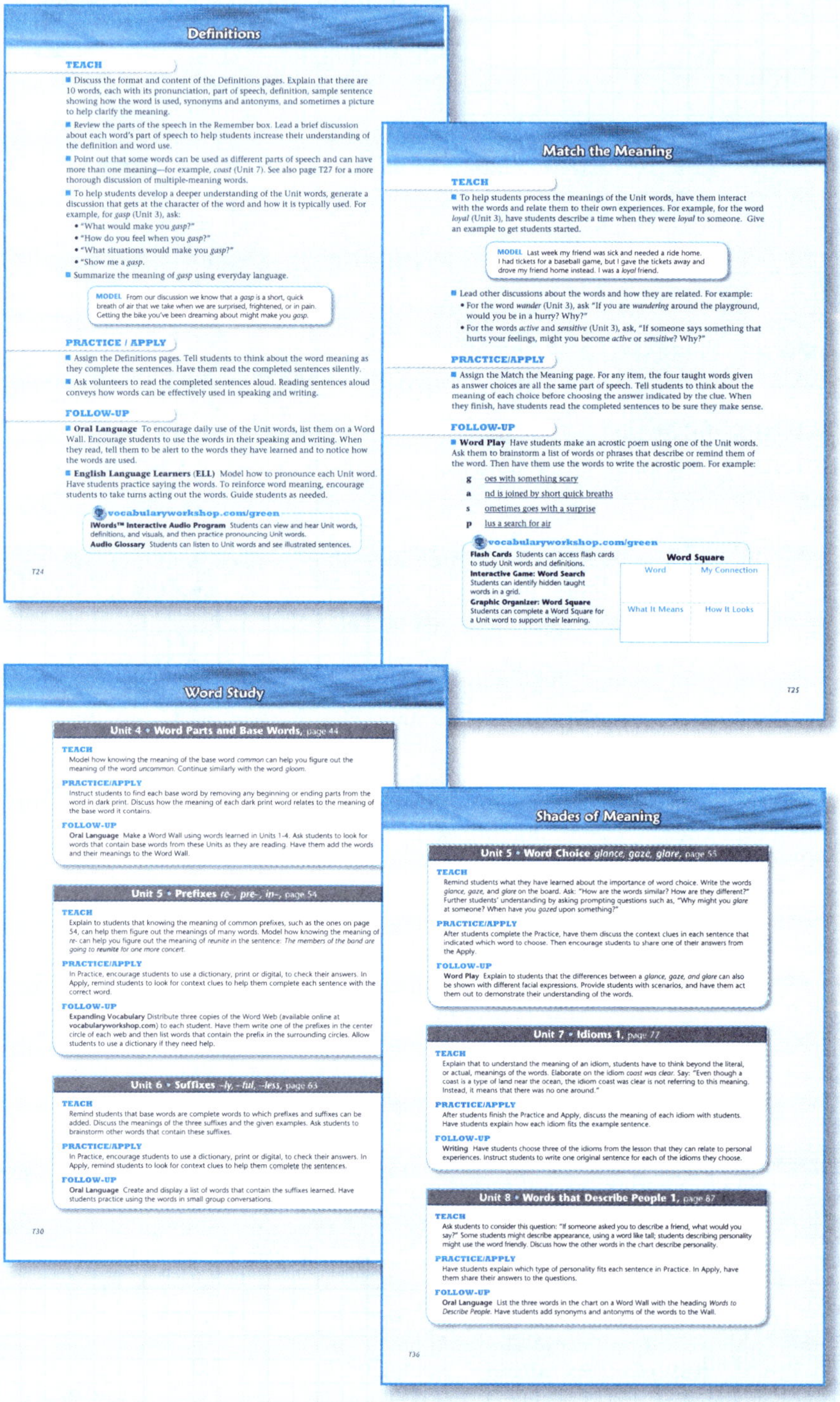

Definitions

TEACH

- Discuss the format and content of the Definitions pages. Explain that there are 10 words, each with its pronunciation, part of speech, definition, sample sentence showing how the word is used, synonyms and antonyms, and sometimes a picture to help clarify the meaning.
- Review the parts of the speech in the Remember box. Lead a brief discussion about each word's part of speech to help students increase their understanding of the definition and word use.
- Point out that some words can be used as different parts of speech and can have more than one meaning—for example, *coast* (Unit 7). See also page T27 for a more thorough discussion of multiple-meaning words.
- To help students develop a deeper understanding of the Unit words, generate a discussion that gets at the character of the word and how it is typically used. For example, for *gasp* (Unit 3), ask:
  - "What would make you *gasp*?"
  - "How do you feel when you *gasp*?"
  - "What situations would make you *gasp*?"
  - "Show me a *gasp*.
- Summarize the meaning of *gasp* using everyday language.

MODEL From our discussion we know that a *gasp* is a short, quick breath of air that we take when we are surprised, frightened, or in pain. Getting the bike you've been dreaming about might make you *gasp*.

PRACTICE / APPLY

- Assign the Definitions pages. Tell students to think about the word meaning as they complete the sentences. Have them read the completed sentences silently.
- Ask volunteers to read the completed sentences aloud. Reading sentences aloud conveys how words can be effectively used in speaking and writing.

FOLLOW-UP

- **Oral Language** To encourage daily use of the Unit words, list them on a Word Wall. Encourage students to use the words in their speaking and writing. When they read, tell them to be alert to the words they have learned and to notice how the words are used.
- **English Language Learners (ELL)** Model how to pronounce each Unit word. Have students practice saying the words. To reinforce word meaning, encourage students to take turns acting out the words. Guide students as needed.

vocabularyworkshop.com/green

iWords™ Interactive Audio Program Students can view and hear Unit words, definitions, and visuals, and then practice pronouncing Unit words.

Audio Glossary Students can listen to Unit words and see illustrated sentences.

T24

Match the Meaning

TEACH

- To help students process the meanings of the Unit words, have them interact with the words and relate them to their own experiences. For example, for the word *loyal* (Unit 3), have students describe a time when they were *loyal* to someone. Give an example to get students started.

MODEL Last week my friend was sick and needed a ride home. I had tickets for a baseball game, but I gave the tickets away and drove my friend home instead. I was a *loyal* friend.

- Lead other discussions about the words and how they are related. For example:
  - For the word *wander* (Unit 3), ask "If you are *wandering* around the playground, would you be in a hurry? Why?"
  - For the words *active* and *sensitive* (Unit 3), ask, "If someone says something that hurts your feelings, might you become *active* or *sensitive*? Why?"

PRACTICE/APPLY

- Assign the Match the Meaning page. For any item, the four taught words given as answer choices are all the same part of speech. Tell students to think about the meaning of each choice before choosing the answer indicated by the clue. When they finish, have students read the completed sentences to be sure they make sense.

FOLLOW-UP

- **Word Play** Have students make an acrostic poem using one of the Unit words. Ask them to brainstorm a list of words or phrases that describe or remind them of the word. Then have them use the words to write the acrostic poem. For example:

g oes with something scary
a nd is joined by short quick breaths
s ometimes goes with a surprise
p lus a search for air

vocabularyworkshop.com/green

Flash Cards Students can access flash cards to study Unit words and definitions.

Interactive Game: Word Search Students can identify hidden taught words in a grid.

Graphic Organizer: Word Square Students can complete a Word Square for a Unit word to support their learning.

Word Square

Word	My Connection
What It Means	How It Looks

T25

Word Study

Unit 4 • Word Parts and Base Words, page 44

TEACH

Model how knowing the meaning of the base word *common* can help you figure out the meaning of the word *uncommon*. Continue similarly with the word *gloom*.

PRACTICE/APPLY

Instruct students to find each base word by removing any beginning or ending parts from the word in dark print. Discuss how the meaning of each dark print word relates to the meaning of the base word it contains.

FOLLOW-UP

Oral Language Make a Word Wall using words learned in Units 1-4. Ask students to look for words that contain base words from these Units as they are reading. Have them add the words and their meanings to the Word Wall.

Unit 5 • Prefixes *re-*, *pre-*, *in-*, page 54

TEACH

Explain to students that knowing the meaning of common prefixes, such as the ones on page 54, can help them figure out the meanings of many words. Model how knowing the meaning of *re-* can help you figure out the meaning of *reunite* in the sentence: *The members of the band are going to* ***reunite*** *for one more concert.*

PRACTICE/APPLY

In Practice, encourage students to use a dictionary, print or digital, to check their answers. In Apply, remind students to look for context clues to help them complete each sentence with the correct word.

FOLLOW-UP

Expanding Vocabulary Distribute three copies of the Word Web (available online at **vocabularyworkshop.com**) to each student. Have them write one of the prefixes in the center circle of each web and then list words that contain the prefix in the surrounding circles. Allow students to use a dictionary if they need help.

Unit 6 • Suffixes *-ly*, *-ful*, *-less*, page 63

TEACH

Remind students that base words are complete words to which prefixes and suffixes can be added. Discuss the meanings of the three suffixes and the given examples. Ask students to brainstorm other words that contain these suffixes.

PRACTICE/APPLY

In Practice, encourage students to use a dictionary, print or digital, to check their answers. In Apply, remind students to look for context clues to help them complete the sentences.

FOLLOW-UP

Oral Language Create and display a list of words that contain the suffixes learned. Have students practice using the words in small group conversations.

T30

Shades of Meaning

Unit 5 • Word Choice *glance, gaze, glare*, page 55

TEACH

Remind students what they have learned about the importance of word choice. Write the words *glance, gaze,* and *glare* on the board. Ask: "How are the words similar? How are they different?" Further students' understanding by asking prompting questions such as, "Why might you *glare* at someone? When have you *gazed* upon something?"

PRACTICE/APPLY

After students complete the Practice, have them discuss the context clues in each sentence that indicated which word to choose. Then encourage students to share one of their answers from the Apply.

FOLLOW-UP

Word Play Explain to students that the differences between a *glance, gaze, and glare* can also be shown with different facial expressions. Provide students with scenarios, and have them act them out to demonstrate their understanding of the words.

Unit 7 • Idioms 1, page 77

TEACH

Explain that to understand the meaning of an idiom, students have to think beyond the literal, or actual, meanings of the words. Elaborate on the idiom *coast was clear*. Say: "Even though a coast is a type of land near the ocean, the idiom coast was clear is not referring to this meaning. Instead, it means that there was no one around."

PRACTICE/APPLY

After students finish the Practice and Apply, discuss the meaning of each idiom with students. Have students explain how each idiom fits the example sentence.

FOLLOW-UP

Writing Have students choose three of the idioms from the lesson that they can relate to personal experiences. Instruct students to write one original sentence for each of the idioms they choose.

Unit 8 • Words that Describe People 1, page 87

TEACH

Ask students to consider this question: "If someone asked you to describe a friend, what would you say?" Some students might describe appearance, using a word like tall; students describing personality might use the word friendly. Discuss how the other words in the chart describe personality.

PRACTICE/APPLY

Have students explain which type of personality fits each sentence in Practice. In Apply, have them share their answers to the questions.

FOLLOW-UP

Oral Language List the three words in the chart on a Word Wall with the heading *Words to Describe People*. Have students add synonyms and antonyms of the words to the Wall.

T36

Teacher Support

- Consistent instructional routines with teacher modeling.
- Follow-up activity choices to support and extend learning.
- iWords Audio Program, available online, includes a recording of each vocabulary word, its definition, and an illustrative sentence.
- Audio Glossary, available online, can be accessed by alphabetical order of words or by Unit.
- Printable Graphic Organizers available online: Concept Circle, Word Square, Word Web.

Curriculum Mapping

As you develop or execute curriculum maps that address Vocabulary Acquisition and use Common Core State Standards, you can integrate the taught words through a variety of activities.

- **Index Card File** Have students keep an ongoing card file of new words with both literal and figurative meanings. Students can use them to analyze word relationships and sort them by prefix, suffix, root words, meaning, and so on.
- **Semantic Word Maps** By using a semantic map, students can conceptually explore a new word. Graphic organizers, available online, may be used to create individual or class webs that develop organically.

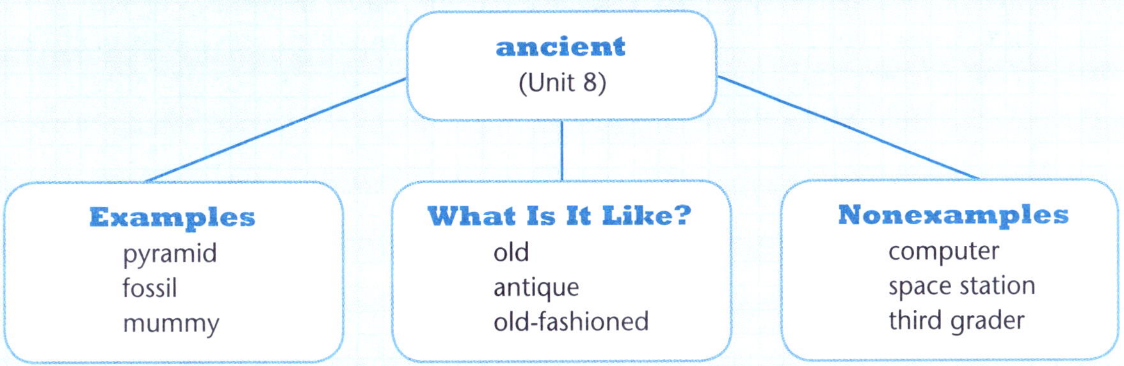

Additional Online Components

Use online components to complement, extend, and enrich instruction in the Student Book. For interactive whiteboard (IWB)-compatible components, see page T9.

vocabularyworkshop.com	
Online Component	**Purpose**
Common Core State Standards, Language Standards K–5	Aligns the Vocabulary Acquisition and Use standards with Vocabulary Workshop.
Planning and Pacing Guide	Details how to implement Level Green over an academic year.
Beginning-of-Year Diagnostic Assessment	Assesses students' vocabulary knowledge of words to be taught.
Graphic Organizers	Provides a visual format for vocabulary development.
Test-Taking Strategies	Provides a printable list of test-taking tips.

Additional Components

*The Web-based **Online Assessment** allows teachers to quickly and easily create secure, interactive Unit practice and assessment pages that are automatically scored and provide students with immediate, prescriptive feedback. With a data base of nearly 2,000 items per level, teachers have the option to individualize tests.

*Optional purchase

Assessment

Vocabulary Workshop Level Green provides several comprehensive ways to assess students' knowledge of words. Multiple assessment tools available for formative and summative assessments can provide insight into students' understanding of the Unit words. Formative assessment tools can inform instruction and provide feedback to students, while summative assessment tools can provide a snapshot of students' understanding of Unit words at a given time. A classroom list of Test-Taking Strategies can be found online at **vocabularyworkshop.com**.

Beginning-of-Year Diagnostic Assessment

Begin the school year with a benchmark assessment of students' vocabulary knowledge of Level Green words to be taught. The printable Beginning-of-Year Diagnostic Assessment is available at **vocabularyworkshop.com**. This assessment can also serve as a before-and-after comparison when combined with the end-of-year Final Mastery Test in the *Test Booklet.

Final Mastery Test

Accompanying the Level Green Student Book is an online, printable version of the Final Mastery Test, which can be found at **vocabularyworkshop.com**. Used upon completion of the 18 Units, this year-end test applies vocabulary learning, gives insight into children's word knowledge to date, and serves to prepare children for vocabulary sections of standardized test.

Interactive Unit Quiz and Practice Worksheet

Interactive Unit Quizzes assess students' knowledge of vocabulary words within a given unit. These quizzes are administered at the end of each Unit. Teachers can send students to appropriate follow-up material for additional experiences with the Unit words. Depending on their needs, students can use any of a number of sources, including the Practice Worksheet for the Unit (see below), interactive games, and the audio components, available online.

Each Interactive Unit Quiz has these additional unique features:

- Standardized-test format
- Automatic scoring and student feedback
- Student self-assessment
- Printable version, which is also available online

An online printable Practice Unit Worksheet can be used after the Interactive Unit Quiz to provide differentiated instruction and practice as well as extension, as needed. These worksheets can be a valuable reteaching tool for English Language Learners.

* Optional purchase

Ongoing Assessment

There are many ways to assess students' knowledge of the words in Level Green. The suggestions below for systematic observation can provide insight into students' understanding. See instructional routines on pages T24–T28.

- **Oral Language** Listen for students' use of taught words in conversations, classroom discussions, and oral reports.
- **Student Writing** Note students' attempts to use taught words in their writing, including keeping a portfolio of their writing.
- **Daily Use** Observe whether students recognize taught words when they hear them or see them in print.
- **Vocabulary Notebook** Check to see how students expand their knowledge of taught words.

Additional Assessment Components

***Test Booklet** Forms A and B provide Unit, Midyear, and Final Mastery Tests. Unit Tests, in standardized-test format, assess each Unit word at least twice. The Answer Key can be found on pages T44–T48 of this Teacher's Edition.

***Online Assessment** The Web-based VOCABULARY WORKSHOP Level Green Online Assessment allows teachers to quickly and easily create secure, interactive Unit practice and assessment pages that are automatically scored and provide students with immediate, prescriptive feedback. With a database of nearly 2,000 items per Level, teachers have the option to individualize tests.

The Online Assessment provides:

- the ability to create and edit question sets and tests,
- the ability to scramble answer choices and/or questions so that multiple versions of the same test can be administered securely,
- a wide assortment of question types: definitions, match the meaning, synonyms, antonyms, sentence completions,
- preformatted Unit tests, ready for immediate use
- a secure portal to assign practice/test pages, with the option to print these pages,
- immediate feedback on each question,
- a detailed end-of-assignment report to help you know exactly how students are progressing
- the ability to track student progress through a comprehensive reporting system,
- a way to create detailed reports on class and individual student results, and
- the option to send practice/test pages and student results to learning management systems.

See page T19 for recommendations on how the Online Assessment may be used in conjunction with the Student Text and other components.

* Optional purchase

Sample Unit

The **Vocabulary Workshop** program is designed to be used with any Reading or Language Arts program. The teaching approach of **Vocabulary Workshop** is one of direct instruction. The program provides multiple exposures to words in a variety of contexts to help deepen meaning. It also provides a blend of print and mixed media to support and meet all students' needs.

Teachers can dedicate two weeks to each Unit. The Planning and Pacing Guide on page T19, or online at **vocabularyworkshop.com**, shows how the entire program can be taught over an academic year.

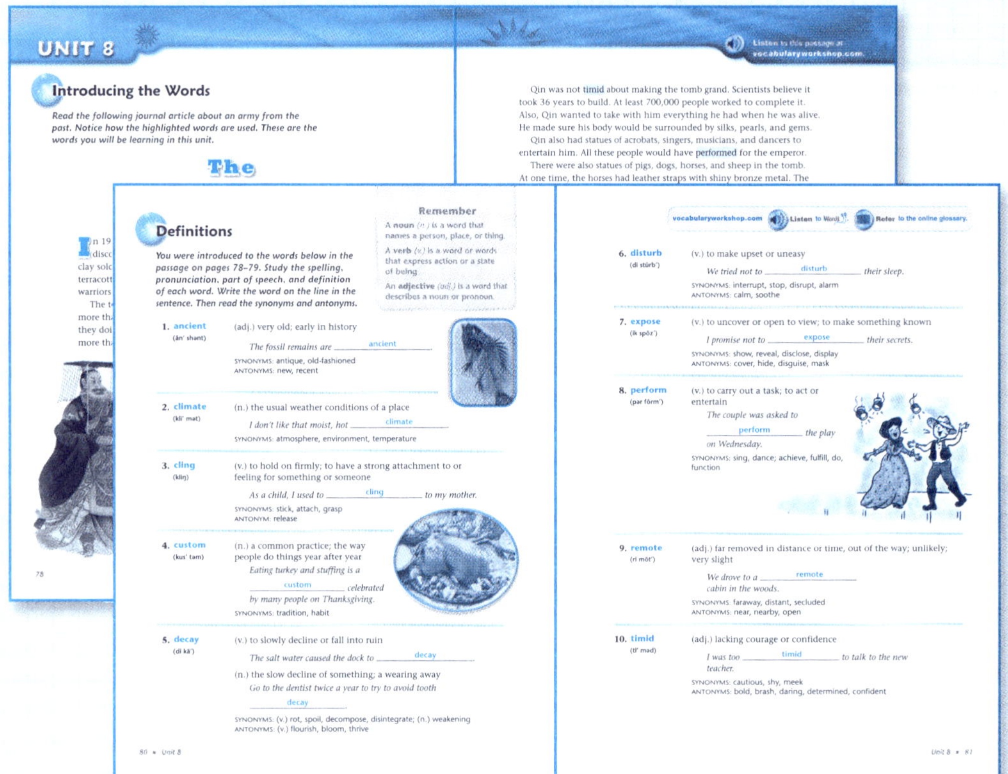

UNIT 8

Introducing the Words

Read the following journal article about an army from the past. Notice how the highlighted words are used. These are the words you will be learning in this unit.

The

Listen to this passage at vocabularyworkshop.com.

Qin was not timid about making the tomb grand. Scientists believe it took 36 years to build. At least 700,000 people worked to complete it. Also, Qin wanted to take with him everything he had when he was alive. He made sure his body would be surrounded by silks, pearls, and gems.

Qin also had statues of acrobats, singers, musicians, and dancers to entertain him. All these people would have performed for the emperor.

There were also statues of pigs, dogs, horses, and sheep in the tomb. At one time, the horses had leather straps with shiny bronze metal. The

Definitions

You were introduced to the words below in the passage on pages 78–79. Study the spelling, pronunciation, part of speech, and definition of each word. Write the word on the line in the sentence. Then read the synonyms and antonyms.

Remember

A **noun** (n.) is a word that names a person, place, or thing.

A **verb** (v.) is a word or words that express action or a state of being.

An **adjective** (adj.) is a word that describes a noun or pronoun.

vocabularyworkshop.com — Listen to Words — Refer to the online glossary.

1. **ancient** (ān' shənt) (adj.) very old; early in history
The fossil remains are ancient.
SYNONYMS: antique, old-fashioned
ANTONYMS: new, recent

2. **climate** (klī' mət) (n.) the usual weather conditions of a place
I don't like that moist, hot climate.
SYNONYMS: atmosphere, environment, temperature

3. **cling** (kliŋ) (v.) to hold on firmly; to have a strong attachment to or feeling for something or someone
As a child, I used to cling *to my mother.*
SYNONYMS: stick, attach, grasp
ANTONYM: release

4. **custom** (kus' təm) (n.) a common practice; the way people do things year after year
Eating turkey and stuffing is a custom *celebrated by many people on Thanksgiving.*
SYNONYMS: tradition, habit

5. **decay** (di kā') (v.) to slowly decline or fall into ruin
The salt water caused the dock to decay.
(n.) the slow decline of something; a wearing away
Go to the dentist twice a year to try to avoid tooth decay.
SYNONYMS: (v.) rot, spoil, decompose, disintegrate; (n.) weakening
ANTONYMS: (v.) flourish, bloom, thrive

6. **disturb** (di stûrb') (v.) to make upset or uneasy
We tried not to disturb *their sleep.*
SYNONYMS: interrupt, stop, disrupt, alarm
ANTONYMS: calm, soothe

7. **expose** (ik spōz') (v.) to uncover or open to view; to make something known
I promise not to expose *their secrets.*
SYNONYMS: show, reveal, disclose, display
ANTONYMS: cover, hide, disguise, mask

8. **perform** (pər fôrm') (v.) to carry out a task; to act or entertain
The couple was asked to perform *the play on Wednesday.*
SYNONYMS: sing, dance, achieve, fulfill, do, function

9. **remote** (ri mōt') (adj.) far removed in distance or time, out of the way; unlikely; very slight
We drove to a remote *cabin in the woods.*
SYNONYMS: faraway, distant, secluded
ANTONYMS: near, nearby, open

10. **timid** (tim' id) (adj.) lacking courage or confidence
I was too timid *to talk to the new teacher.*
SYNONYMS: cautious, shy, meek
ANTONYMS: bold, brash, daring, determined, confident

80 • Unit 8 — Unit 8 • 81

Introducing the Words
- Introduces 10 Unit words in context.
- Presents contextual learning of Unit words.

Definitions
- Provides word meanings and illustrative sentences.

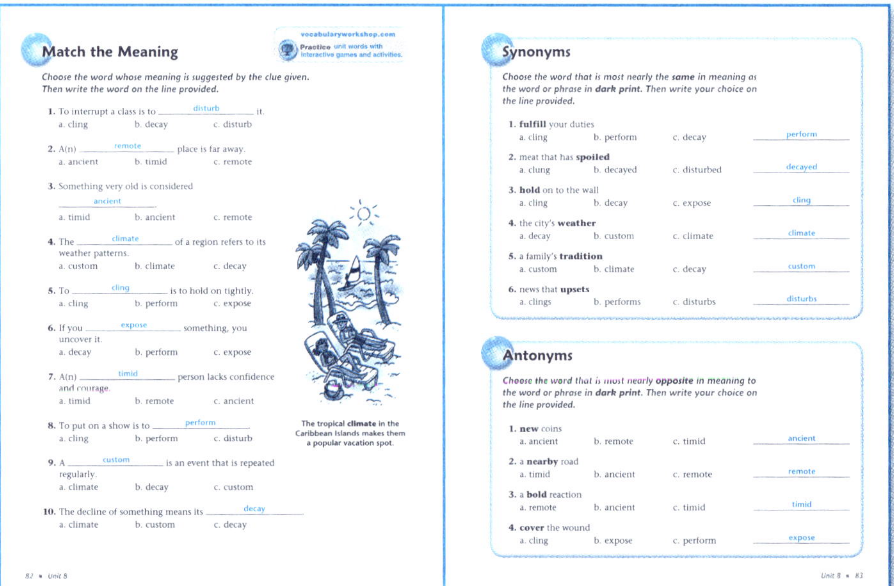

Match the Meaning

vocabularyworkshop.com — Practice unit words with interactive games and activities.

Choose the word whose meaning is suggested by the clue given. Then write the word on the line provided.

1. To interrupt a class is to disturb it.
a. cling b. decay c. disturb
2. A(n) remote place is far away.
a. ancient b. timid c. remote
3. Something very old is considered ancient.
a. timid b. ancient c. remote
4. The climate of a region refers to its weather patterns.
a. custom b. climate c. decay
5. To cling is to hold on tightly.
a. cling b. perform c. expose
6. If you expose something, you uncover it.
a. decay b. perform c. expose
7. A(n) timid person lacks confidence and courage.
a. timid b. remote c. ancient
8. To put on a show is to perform.
a. cling b. perform c. disturb
9. A custom is an event that is repeated regularly.
a. climate b. decay c. custom
10. The decline of something means its decay.
a. climate b. custom c. decay

The tropical **climate** in the Caribbean Islands makes them a popular vacation spot.

Synonyms

*Choose the word that is most nearly the **same** in meaning as the word or phrase in **dark print**. Then write your choice on the line provided.*

1. **fulfill** your duties — a. cling b. perform c. decay — perform
2. meat that has **spoiled** — a. clung b. decayed c. disturbed — decayed
3. **hold** on to the wall — a. cling b. decay c. expose — cling
4. the city's **weather** — a. decay b. custom c. climate — climate
5. a family's **tradition** — a. custom b. climate c. decay — custom
6. news that **upsets** — a. clings b. performs c. disturbs — disturbs

Antonyms

*Choose the word that is most nearly **opposite** in meaning to the word or phrase in **dark print**. Then write your choice on the line provided.*

1. **new** coins — a. ancient b. remote c. timid — ancient
2. a **nearby** road — a. timid b. ancient c. remote — remote
3. a **bold** reaction — a. remote b. ancient c. timid — timid
4. **cover** the wound — a. cling b. expose c. perform — expose

82 • Unit 8 — Unit 8 • 83

Match the Meaning
- Processes and applies word meanings.

Synonyms/Antonyms
- Promote analysis of word relationships.

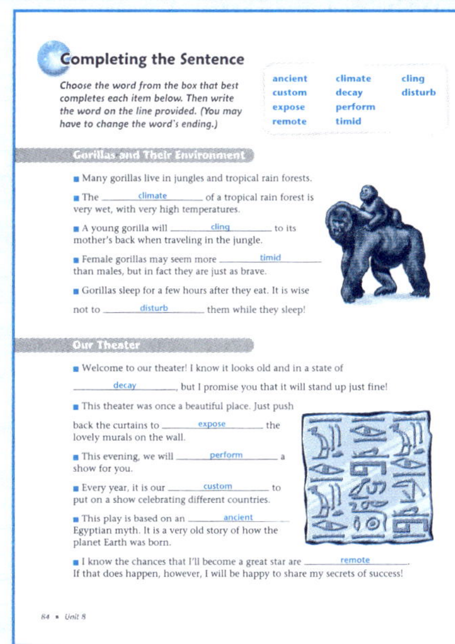

Completing the Sentence

Choose the word from the box that best completes each item below. Then write the word on the line provided. (You may have to change the word's ending.)

ancient	climate	cling
custom	decay	disturb
expose	perform	
remote	timid	

Gorillas and Their Environment

- Many gorillas live in jungles and tropical rain forests.
- The ___climate___ of a tropical rain forest is very wet, with very high temperatures.
- A young gorilla will ___cling___ to its mother's back when traveling in the jungle.
- Female gorillas may seem more ___timid___ than males, but in fact they are just as brave.
- Gorillas sleep for a few hours after they eat. It is wise not to ___disturb___ them while they sleep!

Our Theater

- Welcome to our theater! I know it looks old and in a state of ___decay___, but I promise you that it will stand up just fine!
- This theater was once a beautiful place. Just push back the curtains to ___expose___ the lovely murals on the wall.
- This evening, we will ___perform___ a show for you.
- Every year, it is our ___custom___ to put on a show celebrating different countries.
- This play is based on an ___ancient___ Egyptian myth. It is a very old story of how the planet Earth was born.
- I know the chances that I'll become a great star are ___remote___. If that does happen, however, I will be happy to share my secrets of success!

84 • Unit 8

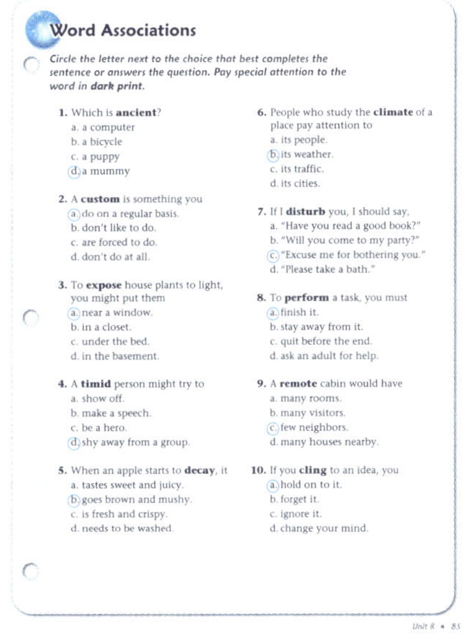

Word Associations

*Circle the letter next to the choice that best completes the sentence or answers the question. Pay special attention to the word in **dark print**.*

1. Which is **ancient**?
   a. a computer
   b. a bicycle
   c. a puppy
   (d.) a mummy
2. A **custom** is something you
   (a.) do on a regular basis.
   b. don't like to do.
   c. are forced to do.
   d. don't do at all.
3. To **expose** house plants to light, you might put them
   (a.) near a window.
   b. in a closet.
   c. under the bed.
   d. in the basement.
4. A **timid** person might try to
   a. show off.
   b. make a speech.
   c. be a hero.
   (d.) shy away from a group.
5. When an apple starts to **decay**, it
   a. tastes sweet and juicy.
   (b.) goes brown and mushy.
   c. is fresh and crispy.
   d. needs to be washed.
6. People who study the **climate** of a place pay attention to
   a. its people.
   (b.) its weather.
   c. its traffic.
   d. its cities.
7. If I **disturb** you, I should say,
   a. "Have you read a good book?"
   b. "Will you come to my party?"
   (c.) "Excuse me for bothering you."
   d. "Please take a bath."
8. To **perform** a task, you must
   (a.) finish it.
   b. stay away from it.
   c. quit before the end.
   d. ask an adult for help.
9. A **remote** cabin would have
   a. many rooms.
   b. many visitors.
   (c.) few neighbors.
   d. many houses nearby.
10. If you **cling** to an idea, you
    (a.) hold on to it.
    b. forget it.
    c. ignore it.
    d. change your mind.

Unit 8 • 85

Completing the Sentence

- Uses context clues to reveal word meanings.

Word Associations

- Promotes interaction with words and word relationships.

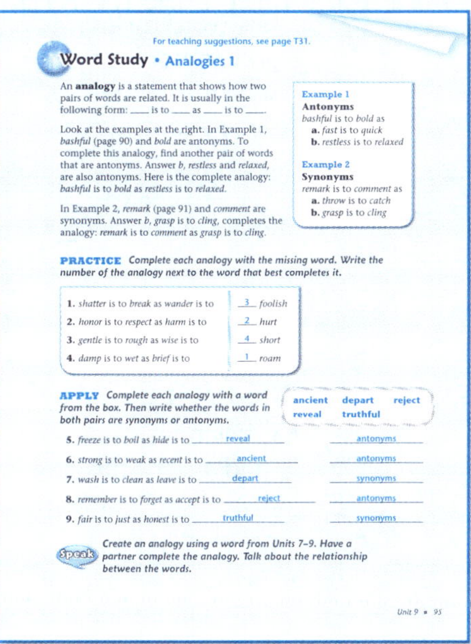

For teaching suggestions, see page T31.

Word Study • Analogies 1

An **analogy** is a statement that shows how two pairs of words are related. It is usually in the following form: ___ is to ___ as ___ is to ___.

Look at the examples at the right. In Example 1, *bashful* (page 90) and *bold* are antonyms. To complete this analogy, find another pair of words that are antonyms. Answer *b, restless* and *relaxed*, are also antonyms. Here is the complete analogy: *bashful* is to *bold* as *restless* is to *relaxed*.

In Example 2, *remark* (page 91) and *comment* are synonyms. Answer *b, grasp* is to *cling*, completes the analogy: *remark* is to *comment* as *grasp* is to *cling*.

Example 1
Antonyms
bashful is to *bold* as
a. *fast* is to *quick*
b. *restless* is to *relaxed*

Example 2
Synonyms
remark is to *comment* as
a. *throw* is to *catch*
b. *grasp* is to *cling*

PRACTICE *Complete each analogy with the missing word. Write the number of the analogy next to the word that best completes it.*

1. *shatter* is to *break* as *wander* is to	_3_ *foolish*
2. *honor* is to *respect* as *harm* is to	_2_ *hurt*
3. *gentle* is to *rough* as *wise* is to	_4_ *short*
4. *damp* is to *wet* as *brief* is to	_1_ *roam*

APPLY *Complete each analogy with a word from the box. Then write whether the words in both pairs are synonyms or antonyms.*

ancient	depart	reject
reveal	truthful	

5. *freeze* is to *boil* as *hide* is to ___reveal___ ___antonyms___
6. *strong* is to *weak* as *recent* is to ___ancient___ ___antonyms___
7. *wash* is to *clean* as *leave* is to ___depart___ ___synonyms___
8. *remember* is to *forget* as *accept* is to ___reject___ ___antonyms___
9. *fair* is to *just* as *honest* is to ___truthful___ ___synonyms___

Speak *Create an analogy using a word from Units 7–9. Have a partner complete the analogy. Talk about the relationship between the words.*

Unit 9 • 95

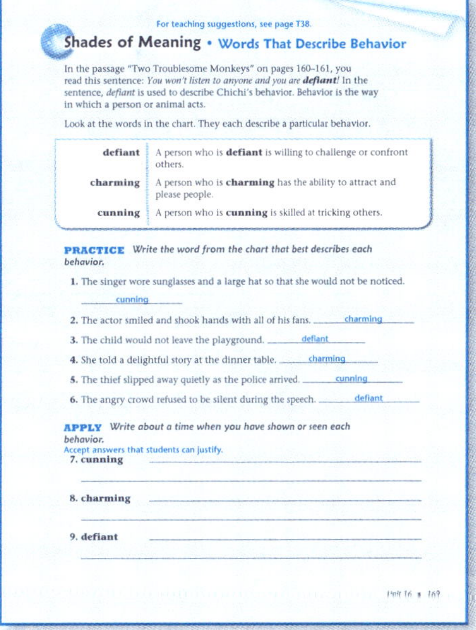

For teaching suggestions, see page T38.

Shades of Meaning • Words That Describe Behavior

In the passage "Two Troublesome Monkeys" on pages 160–161, you read this sentence: *You won't listen to anyone and you are **defiant**!* In the sentence, *defiant* is used to describe Chichi's behavior. Behavior is the way in which a person or animal acts.

Look at the words in the chart. They each describe a particular behavior.

defiant	A person who is **defiant** is willing to challenge or confront others.
charming	A person who is **charming** has the ability to attract and please people.
cunning	A person who is **cunning** is skilled at tricking others.

PRACTICE *Write the word from the chart that best describes each behavior.*

1. The singer wore sunglasses and a large hat so that she would not be noticed. ___cunning___
2. The actor smiled and shook hands with all of his fans. ___charming___
3. The child would not leave the playground. ___defiant___
4. She told a delightful story at the dinner table. ___charming___
5. The thief slipped away quietly as the police arrived. ___cunning___
6. The angry crowd refused to be silent during the speech. ___defiant___

APPLY *Write about a time when you have shown or seen each behavior.*
Accept answers that students can justify.

7. **cunning** ______________________
8. **charming** ______________________
9. **defiant** ______________________

Unit 16 • 16?

Word Study

- Presents topics such as multiple-meaning words, homographs, and analogies to expand students' vocabularies.
- Builds word-study skills, including using affixes and roots as clues to the meaning of a word.
- Teaches how to use context clues to figure out word meaning.
- Instructs how to use references, print and digital, to find or clarify meanings.
- Provides speaking and writing activities to apply word-study skills.

Shades of Meaning

- Teaches students how to distinguish shades of meaning among related words.
- Promotes understanding of literal and nonliteral meanings of words.
- Introduces students to common idioms.
- Develops skills in analyzing figurative language, word relationships, and nuances in word meanings.

Sample Review

Vocabulary Workshop Level Green provides Reviews that apply vocabulary learning and prepare students for vocabulary and writing-related sections of standardized tests.

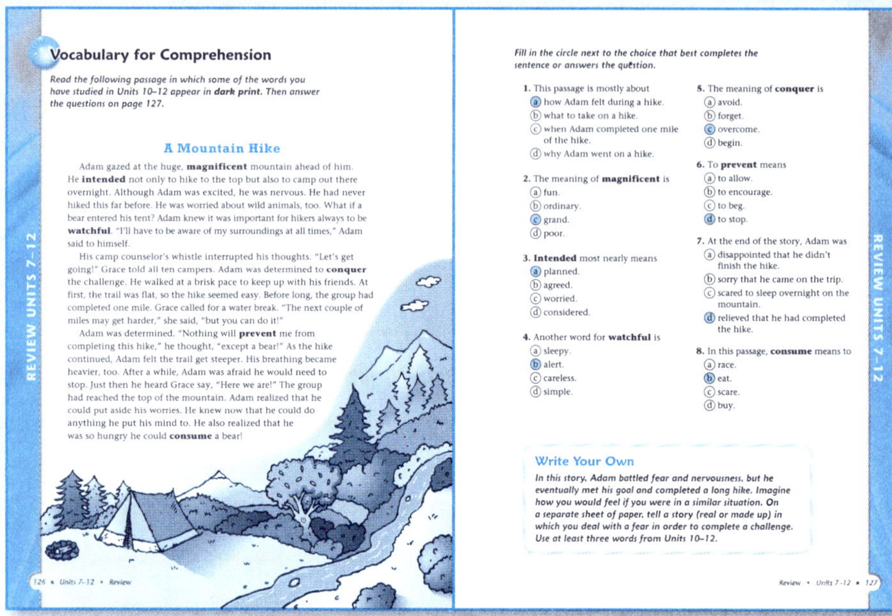
Vocabulary for Comprehension

*Read the following passage in which some of the words you have studied in Units 10–12 appear in **dark print**. Then answer the questions on page 127.*

A Mountain Hike

Adam gazed at the huge, **magnificent** mountain ahead of him. He **intended** not only to hike to the top but also to camp out there overnight. Although Adam was excited, he was nervous. He had never hiked this far before. He was worried about wild animals, too. What if a bear entered his tent? Adam knew it was important for hikers always to be **watchful**. "I'll have to be aware of my surroundings at all times," Adam said to himself.

His camp counselor's whistle interrupted his thoughts. "Let's get going!" Grace told all ten campers. Adam was determined to **conquer** the challenge. He walked at a brisk pace to keep up with his friends. At first, the trail was flat, so the hike seemed easy. Before long, the group had completed one mile. Grace called for a water break. "The next couple of miles may get harder," she said, "but you can do it!"

Adam was determined. "Nothing will **prevent** me from completing this hike," he thought, "except a bear!" As the hike continued, Adam felt the trail get steeper. His breathing became heavier, too. After a while, Adam was afraid he would need to stop. Just then he heard Grace say, "Here we are!" The group had reached the top of the mountain. Adam realized that he could put aside his worries. He knew now that he could do anything he put his mind to. He also realized that he was so hungry he could **consume** a bear!

REVIEW UNITS 7–12

126 • Units 7–12 • Review

Fill in the circle next to the choice that best completes the sentence or answers the question.

1. This passage is mostly about
ⓐ how Adam felt during a hike.
ⓑ what to take on a hike.
ⓒ when Adam completed one mile of the hike.
ⓓ why Adam went on a hike.

2. The meaning of **magnificent** is
ⓐ fun.
ⓑ ordinary.
ⓒ grand.
ⓓ poor.

3. **Intended** most nearly means
ⓐ planned.
ⓑ agreed.
ⓒ worried.
ⓓ considered.

4. Another word for **watchful** is
ⓐ sleepy.
ⓑ alert.
ⓒ careless.
ⓓ simple.

5. The meaning of **conquer** is
ⓐ avoid.
ⓑ forget.
ⓒ overcome.
ⓓ begin.

6. To **prevent** means
ⓐ to allow.
ⓑ to encourage.
ⓒ to beg.
ⓓ to stop.

7. At the end of the story, Adam was
ⓐ disappointed that he didn't finish the hike.
ⓑ sorry that he came on the trip.
ⓒ scared to sleep overnight on the mountain.
ⓓ relieved that he had completed the hike.

8. In this passage, **consume** means to
ⓐ race.
ⓑ eat.
ⓒ scare.
ⓓ buy.

Write Your Own

In this story, Adam battled fear and nervousness, but he eventually met his goal and completed a long hike. Imagine how you would feel if you were in a similar situation. On a separate sheet of paper, tell a story (real or made up) in which you deal with a fear in order to complete a challenge. Use at least three words from Units 10–12.

REVIEW UNITS 7–12

Review • Units 7–12 • 127

Vocabulary for Comprehension

- Reviews words from the previous three units in the context of a passage.
- Provides contextual learning in a variety of genres.
- Presents questions that test word meaning and comprehension, similar in format to standardized tests.

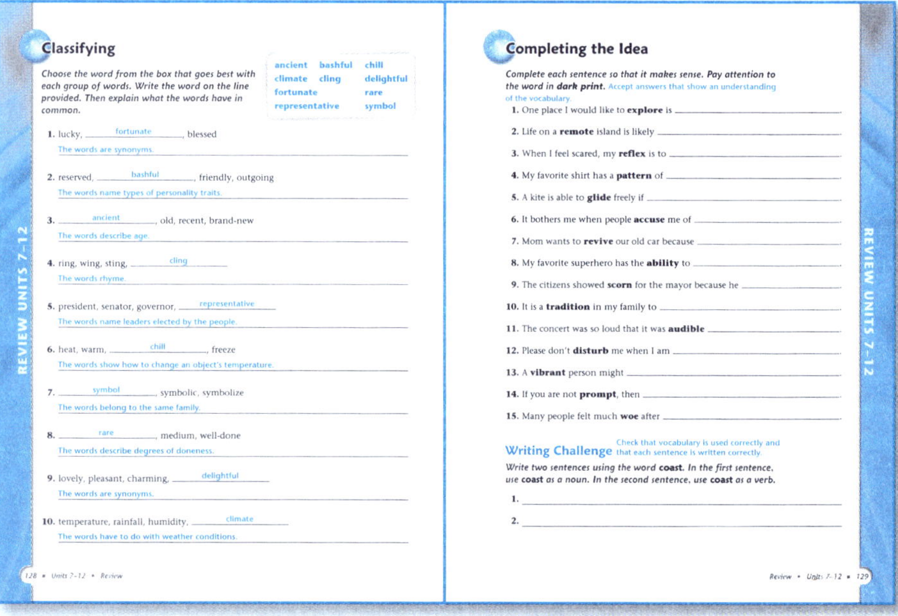
Classifying

Choose the word from the box that goes best with each group of words. Write the word on the line provided. Then explain what the words have in common.

ancient	bashful	chill
climate	cling	delightful
fortunate		rare
representative		symbol

1. lucky, fortunate, blessed
The words are synonyms.
2. reserved, bashful, friendly, outgoing
The words name types of personality traits.
3. ancient, old, recent, brand-new
The words describe age.
4. ring, wing, sting, cling
The words rhyme.
5. president, senator, governor, representative
The words name leaders elected by the people.
6. heat, warm, chill, freeze
The words show how to change an object's temperature.
7. symbol, symbolic, symbolize
The words belong to the same family.
8. rare, medium, well-done
The words describe degrees of doneness.
9. lovely, pleasant, charming, delightful
The words are synonyms.
10. temperature, rainfall, humidity, climate
The words have to do with weather conditions.

REVIEW UNITS 7–12

128 • Units 7–12 • Review

Completing the Idea

*Complete each sentence so that it makes sense. Pay attention to the word in **dark print**.* Accept answers that show an understanding of the vocabulary.

1. One place I would like to **explore** is
2. Life on a **remote** island is likely
3. When I feel scared, my **reflex** is to
4. My favorite shirt has a **pattern** of
5. A kite is able to **glide** freely if
6. It bothers me when people **accuse** me of
7. Mom wants to **revive** our old car because
8. My favorite superhero has the **ability** to
9. The citizens showed **scorn** for the mayor because he
10. It is a **tradition** in my family to
11. The concert was so loud that it was **audible**
12. Please don't **disturb** me when I am
13. A **vibrant** person might
14. If you are not **prompt**, then
15. Many people felt much **woe** after

Writing Challenge Check that vocabulary is used correctly and that each sentence is written correctly.

*Write two sentences using the word **coast**. In the first sentence, use **coast** as a noun. In the second sentence, use **coast** as a verb.*

1.
2.

REVIEW UNITS 7–12

Review • Units 7–12 • 129

Classifying

- Challenges students to identify a missing word from words that are alike in some way.
- Has students explain the relationship among the words in a group.

Completing the Idea

- Asks students to complete sentence stems that contain taught words.
- Has students make connections between vocabulary words and real-life experiences.

Supporting English Language Learners

In many of today's classrooms, students come from diverse backgrounds with varying degrees of English proficiency. **VOCABULARY WORKSHOP** Level Green provides print materials and also an iWords™ Audio Program with visuals, available online, to support all learners. Here are more suggestions that will support English Language Learners in their acquisition of vocabulary.

- **Real-World Connections** Use realia, pictures, gestures, and facial expressions to teach words and clarify meaning.
- **Active Participation** Encourage active participation by repeating directions and modeling how to perform tasks. Remember that because of cultural differences, some students may be reluctant to participate.
- **Integrating Vocabulary Daily** Focus on vocabulary instruction several times during the day, integrating vocabulary development with other lessons. Encourage students to use English as much as possible to gain confidence over time.
- **Modeling Correct Usage** Model proper usage and correct errors judiciously. Use corrections to positively reinforce students' use of English.

vocabularyworkshop.com

- **Audio of Unit Passages** Encourage students to track print as they listen to the Unit passage.
- **iWords™ Audio Program** Guide students as the definition of each Unit vocabulary word comes to life through oral model and oral practice, along with visuals.
- **Visuals of Unit Words** Direct students to the visuals in the iWords™ Audio Program to enable them to see context for the words.
- **Audio Glossary** Have students read and listen to this glossary in order to self-correct pronunciation and clarify meaning.
- **Interactive Unit Quizzes** Give students opportunities to review synonyms and words with multiple meanings.
- **Practice Unit Worksheets** Provide needed additional interaction with Unit words.
- **Interactive Word Map** Help students gain deeper understanding of word meaning as they build vocabulary concept maps for Unit words.

Additional Support

***Online Assessment**
Choose from a bank of items to review words for which students need additional practice.

*Optional purchase

Common Core State Standards

The Common Core Enriched Edition of Vocabulary Workshop Level Green correlates to the Common Core State Standards, Language Standards K–5: Vocabulary Acquisition and Use.

Language Standards K–5: Vocabulary Acquisition and Use

Standards Grade 3	Vocabulary Workshop Level Green
4. Determine or clarify the meaning of unknown and multiple-meaning word and phrases based on *grade 3 reading and content*, choosing flexibly from a range of strategies.	
a. Use sentence-level context as a clue to the meaning of a word or phrase.	Introducing the Words Passages, pp. 6–7, 16–17, 26–27, 36–37, 46–47, 56–57, 68–69, 78–79, 88–89, 98–99, 108–109, 118–119, 130–131, 140–141, 150–151, 160–161, 170–171, 180–181 Definitions, pp. 8–9, 18–19, 28–29, 38–39, 48–49, 58–59, 70–71, 80–81, 90–91, 100–101, 110–111, 120–121, 132–133, 142–143, 152–153, 162–163, 172–173, 182–183 Match the Meanings, pp. 10, 20, 30, 40, 50, 60, 72, 82, 92, 102, 112, 122, 134, 144, 154, 164, 174, 184 Synonyms, Antonyms, pp. 11, 21, 31, 41, 51, 61, 73, 83, 93, 103, 113, 123, 135, 145, 155, 165, 175, 185 Completing the Sentence, pp. 12, 22, 32, 42, 52, 62, 74, 84, 94, 104, 114, 124, 136, 146, 156, 166, 176, 186 Word Associations, pp. 13, 23, 43, 53, 75, 85, 105, 115, 137, 147, 167, 177 Vocabulary for Comprehension, pp. 34–35, 64–65, 96–97, 126–127, 158–159, 188–189 Completing the Idea, pp. 67, 129, 191 Word Study, pp. 24, 86
b. Determine the meaning of the new word formed when a known affix is added to a known word (e.g., *agreeable/disagreeable, comfortable/uncomfortable, care/careless, heat/preheat*).	Word Study, pp. 33, 54, 63, 106, 116, 168, 178
c. Use a known root word as a clue to the meaning of an unknown word with the same root (e.g., *company, companion*).	Word Study, pp. 33, 44, 187
d. Use glossaries or beginning dictionaries, both print and digital, to determine or clarify the precise meaning of key words and phrases.	Word Study, pp. 14, 33, 54, 106, 187
5. Demonstrate understanding of word relationships and nuances in word meanings.	
a. Distinguish the literal and nonliteral meanings of words and phrases in context (e.g., *take steps*).	Shades of Meaning, pp. 25, 77, 107
b. Identify real-life connections between words and their use (e.g., describe people who are *friendly* or *helpful*).	Shades of Meaning, pp. 15, 45, 55, 87, 117, 169, 179 Classifying, pp. 66, 128, 190 Completing the Idea, pp. 67, 129, 190
c. Distinguish shades of meaning among related words that describe states of mind or degrees of certainty (e.g., *knew, believed, suspected, heard, wondered*).	Shades of Meaning, pp. 139, 149
6. Acquire and use accurately grade-appropriate conversational, general academic, and domain-specific words and phrases, including those that signal spatial and temporal relationships (e.g., *After dinner that night we went looking for them*).	Vocabulary for Comprehension, pp. 34–35, 64–65, 96–97, 126–127, 158–159, 188–189 Introducing the Word Passages, See *Introducing the Word Passages* at the top of this column.

Planning and Pacing Guide

The **Vocabulary Workshop** program is designed to be used with any Reading and Language Arts program. Its simple format allows for great flexibility. This chart shows how Level Green might be taught and assessed over an academic year.

Weeks	Student Book	Resources to Enrich, Support, and Assess
1–2	**Unit 1**, pp. 6–15	†**Online Beginning-of-Year Diagnostic Assessment**
3–4	**Unit 2**, pp. 16–25	**Follow-Up Activities**, pp. T22–T38
5–6	**Unit 3**, pp. 26–33 **Review**, pp. 34–35	†**Online Resources** (audio, visual, interactive) Units 1–3 ***Test Booklet** Units 1–3 Tests, pp. 1–6 ***Online Assessment**
7–8	**Unit 4**, pp. 36–45	**Follow-Up Activities**, pp. T22–T38
9–10	**Unit 5**, pp. 46–55	†**Online Resources** (audio, visual, interactive) Units 4–6
11–12	**Unit 6**, pp. 56–63 **Review**, pp. 64–67	***Test Booklet** Units 4–6 Tests, pp. 7–12 ***Online Assessment**
13–14	**Unit 7**, pp. 68–77	**Follow-Up Activities**, pp. T22–T38
15–16	**Unit 8**, pp. 78–87	†**Online Resources** (audio, visual, interactive) Units 7–9
17–18	**Unit 9**, pp. 88–95 **Review**, pp. 96–97	***Test Booklet** Units 7–9 Tests, pp. 13–18 • Midyear Test, pp. 19–22 ***Online Assessment**
19–20	**Unit 10**, pp. 98–107	**Follow-Up Activities**, pp. T22–T38
21–22	**Unit 11**, pp. 108–117	†**Online Resources** (audio, visual, interactive) Units 10–12
23–24	**Unit 12**, pp. 118–125 **Review**, pp. 126–129	***Test Booklet** Units 10–12 Tests, pp. 23–28 ***Online Assessment**
25–26	**Unit 13**, pp. 130–139	**Follow-Up Activities**, pp. T22–T38
27–28	**Unit 14**, pp. 140–149	†**Online Resources** (audio, visual, interactive) Units 13–15
29–30	**Unit 15**, pp. 150–157 **Review**, pp. 158–159	***Test Booklet** Units 13–15 Tests, pp. 29–34 ***Online Assessment**
31–32	**Unit 16**, pp. 160–169	**Follow-Up Activities**, pp. T22–T38
33–34	**Unit 17**, pp. 170–179	†**Online Resources** (audio, visual, interactive) Units 16–18
35–36	**Unit 18**, pp. 180–187 **Review**, pp. 188–191	***Test Booklet** Units 16–18 Tests, pp. 35–40 • Final Mastery Test, pp. 41–44 ***Online Assessment**

*Optional purchase †vocabularyworkshop.com

vocabularyworkshop.com

Choose from this menu of online resources to meet the individual needs of your students.

- Audio of Unit Passages
- iWords Audio Program with Visuals
- Audio Glossary
- Interactive Games
- Interactive Word Map
- Interactive Unit Quizzes
- Practice Unit Worksheets
- Family Games
- Graphic Organizers
- Test-Taking Strategies
- Final Mastery Test

Developing Vocabulary Through Literature

Vocabulary Workshop Level Green can be combined with the grade-level appropriate titles listed below to form a literature-based approach to vocabulary study. Seeing the words encountered in such classic and contemporary literature can reinforce students' appreciation of the value of possessing a strong vocabulary.

Literature to Use with Vocabulary Workshop		
Author	**Title**	**Type**
Ada, Alma Flor	*Under the Royal Palms: A Childhood in Cuba*	Autobiography/Children's Book Author
Atwater, Richard and Florence	*Mr. Popper's Penguins*	Humor/Newbery
Banks, Lynne Reid	*I, Houdini*	Animal/Adventure
Brock, Betty	*No Flying in the House*	Mystery/Fantasy
Brooks, Bruce	*Everywhere*	African American/Family
Bulla, Clyde Robert	*Shoeshine Girl*	Realistic Fiction
Butterworth, Oliver	*The Enormous Egg*	Dinosaurs/Humor
Calmenson, Stephanie	*The Principal's New Clothes*	Humor
Cleary, Beverly	*Ramona Quimby, Age Eight*	Family/Newbery
Coerr, Eleanor	*Sadako and the Thousand Paper Cranes*	Historical Fiction/Hiroshima
Dahl, Roald	*The Minpins*	Adventure/Fantasy
Eager, Edward	*Half Magic*	Adventure/Historical/Middle Ages
Estes, Eleanor	*The Hundred Dresses*	Historical/Newbery
Fritz, Jean	*What's the Big Idea, Ben Franklin?*	Biography
Gardiner, John R.	*Stone Fox*	Adventure
Heide, Florence Parry	*The Shrinking of Treehorn*	Humor
Howe, James and Deborah	*Bunnicula: A Rabbit Tale of Mystery*	Mystery/Animal/Humor
Hurwitz, Johanna	*Aldo Applesauce*	Realistic/Family
Law, Ingrid	*Savvy*	Fantasy/Adventure
Lin, Grace	*Where the Mountain Meets the Moon*	Fantasy/Chinese
*Lindgren, Astrid Ericsson	*Pippi Longstocking*	Adventure/Humor
Lord, Cynthia	*Rules*	Realistic/Family/Disabilities
Lovelace, Maud Hart	*Betsy-Tacy*	Realistic/Friendship
*Mahy, Margaret	*Girl with the Green Ear*	Short Stories/Nature
Paterson, Katherine	*Flip-Flop Girl* *Bridge to Terabithia*	Realistic/Family Realistic/Friendship
*Ryan, Pam Munoz	*Riding Freedom*	Historical Fiction
Sachar, Louis	*Holes*	Mystery/Humor
Selznick, Brian	*The Boy of a Thousand Faces*	Fantasy/Adventure
*Steig, William	*The Real Thief*	Animal/Humor/Fantasy
Walter, Mildred Pitts	*Justin and the Best Biscuits in the World*	African American/Realistic/Cowboy
*White, E. B.	*Stuart Little*	Family/Animal/Adventure
Wilder, Laura Ingalls	*The Adventures of Laura and Jack*	Historical Fiction
Yolen, Jane	*Sleeping Ugly*	Fairy Tale

*Good for read-alouds and read-alongs but difficult for independent reading.

The UNIT

vocabularyworkshop.com

Teacher Center Administer the online Beginning-of-Year Diagnostic Assessment prior to introducing Unit 1. (See Assessment, pages T12–T13).

Each Unit of **Vocabulary Workshop** has a unique structure designed to give maximum coverage to each of the key words within the space available. Units of the Student Edition include the following lessons.

Unit Overview	
Introducing the Words (Unit Passages)	In **Introducing the Words**, students read a passage that incorporates all the words they will be learning in the Unit. A different genre and theme are presented in each passage.
Definitions	In **Definitions**, students are introduced to the ten vocabulary words in the Unit. After learning about the definitions and various elements associated with a word, students complete the sample sentence(s).
Match the Meaning	In **Match the Meaning**, students choose the taught word indicated by the clue. These exercises are designed to reinforce students' understanding and recall of the words' meanings.
Synonyms and Antonyms	In **Synonyms**, students select the taught word that is the synonym for the highlighted word in an illustrative phrase. In **Antonyms**, students choose the antonym for the highlighted word.
Completing the Sentence	In **Completing the Sentence**, students use context clues to choose the word that meaningfully completes each sentence. The sentences are connected by a theme.
Word Associations	In **Word Associations**, students demonstrate understanding by applying word knowledge in a way that calls for a measure of inference, reasoning, perception, and imagination.
Word Study	In **Word Study**, students build vocabulary by applying strategies, such as using context clues and analyzing word parts, including roots and affixes.
Shades of Meaning	In **Shades of Meaning**, students deepen their understanding of word meanings by examining relationships between related words and by analyzing nuances of meaning.

Because each Unit has a similar structure, the teaching notes on pages T22–T28 can be used for any given Unit. More comprehensive teaching notes for Word Study and Shades of Meaning can be found on pages T29–T38. Correlations to the Common Core State Standards for Unit, Word Study, and Shades of Meaning lessons are also identified below the teaching notes on pages T22-T38.

Introducing the Words

Each Unit passage introduces the ten words students will learn in the Unit. When reading a passage, students will want to pay close attention to the context of these highlighted Unit words. This will both improve their comprehension of the passage and help them to begin to figure out the word meanings.

PREPARING TO READ

■ **Access Prior Knowledge** Ask students prompting questions to help them access their prior knowledge about the theme or topic of the passage. In a class discussion, expand on the topic to help students build background knowledge. See page T23.

■ **Presenting the Words** Introduce the ten Unit words to students. Read aloud each word, emphasizing correct pronunciation. Have students repeat each word after you. Provide students with a brief explanation of each word that will prepare them for their encounter with the word within the passage.

DURING READING

As students read the passage, point out its key elements, and ask questions to encourage critical thinking.

■ With students, read the brief introduction. Discuss the genre of the passage, and encourage students to name other stories and books they have read in the genre. Discuss any photographs or illustrations, pointing out how students can use the information in these visuals to help them better appreciate the passage.

■ Depending on the needs of individual students, assign the passage as independent reading, allow them to read it together as a Read Aloud, or have them listen to the audio version of the passage while reading.

■ Guide students' focus and comprehension by having them answer key questions about the story.

■ Remind students to pay attention to context clues that can help them figure out the meanings of the words and develop a better understanding of the passage.

AFTER READING

Invite students to summarize the story. Then review the answers to the questions that were asked while they were reading. Encourage students to ask any questions they may have about the story or the meanings of the words.

■ Return to each of the highlighted words in the passage. Discuss context clues and the meanings of the words as they relate to the story.

■ Remind students that they will be learning more about the words throughout the Unit. Point out that the more connections students make to the words, the easier it will be to remember the words and interact with them in other contexts.

Audio of Unit Passages Students can read along as they listen to the passages.

CCSS Vocabulary: 4.a. (See p. T18.)

Background Information

As students prepare to read each passage, provide background information about the theme or topic they will encounter. Although some themes will be familiar to students, others will be new and pique their curiosity. Encourage students to make connections to any prior knowledge and to further explore these topics.

- **The Fox and the Grapes** Unit 1 pp. 6–7: The storyteller Aesop was born in ancient Greece more than 2,000 years ago. Aesop's fables, including "The Fox and the Grapes" and "The Tortoise and the Hare," are world-famous and enduring. It is commonly believed that the idiom "sour grapes" is derived from "The Fox and the Grapes."

- **Driving on Route 66** Unit 2 pp. 16–17: At its start, Route 66 covered over 2,000 miles across eight states. The first drive-thru restaurant was built along the highway. Route 66 was removed from the highway system in 1985 and was replaced by Interstate highways.

- **Going Green Every Day** Unit 3 pp. 26–27: Each year, Americans produce about 200 million tons of garbage, much of which can be composted, reused, or recycled. Recycling paper creates 74 percent less air pollution than making new paper. Recycling aluminum saves 95 percent of the energy needed to make new aluminum. And glass can be recycled forever.

- **The Handsome Stag** Unit 4 pp. 36–37: Other versions of this classic folktale include *The Vain Stag*, *The Conceited Stag*, *The Foolish Stag*, and *The Stag and His Reflection*.

- **The International Space Station** Unit 5 pp. 46–47: Sixteen countries have contributed to the International Space Station. Currently, crews stay in the station for about six months at a time. A typical workday for astronauts in the station is sixteen hours long.

- **King Tut Then and Now** Unit 6 pp. 56–57: Scientists today continue to make discoveries about King Tut's health and family history using DNA material from his bones.

- **The Liberty Bell** Unit 7 pp. 68–69: The Liberty Bell weighs about 2,000 pounds and is made up of 70 percent copper. Each year, about 1.5 million people visit the bell.

- **The Terracotta Army** Unit 8 pp. 78–79: Shortly after its discovery, Qin Shi Huang's burial site became a historical museum. The Qin Shi Huang Terracotta Warriors and Horses Museum remains one of the most-visited tourist locations in China today.

- **The Talent Show** Unit 9 pp. 88–89: Many fiction stories offer lessons that readers can apply to their own lives. This story shows how overcoming fear can often have positive results.

- **The Princess and the Pea** Unit 10 pp. 98–99: The original version of this tale is attributed to Hans Christian Andersen, who is said to have based it on a Swedish folktale he heard as a child. The story has also been told in the Broadway musical *Once Upon a Mattress*.

- **Treasure Among Diamonds** Unit 11 pp. 108–109: After 500 years, many artifacts from the *Bom Jesus* remained in the same area due to the amount of copper ingots weighing down the wreckage. Rare coins among the artifacts were particularly helpful in tracing the ship's history.

- **The Tiger's Promise** Unit 12 pp. 118–119: Tigers have been symbolic in Korean culture dating back to ancient mythology. Some people refer to Siberian tigers as Korean tigers since many used to live in Korea. The mascot of the 1988 Olympics held in Seoul, Korea, was a tiger.

- **The Winter Olympics** Unit 13 pp. 130–131: At the first Winter Olympics in 1924, 258 athletes competed in 16 events. The games have since greatly expanded. During the 2010 Winter Olympics, over 2,000 athletes competed in more than 85 medal events.

- **Amelia Earhart (1897-1937)** Unit 14 pp. 140–141: Another of Earhart's accomplishments was cofounding and serving as the first president of the Ninety-Nines, the International Organization of Women Pilots. Still in existence, the organization has over 5,000 women pilots as members.

- **The Great Barrier Reef** Unit 15 pp. 150–151: With over 2,800 coral reefs, the Great Barrier Reef is the largest structure in the world built by living things, and the only living thing visible from space.

- **Two Troublesome Monkeys** Unit 16 pp. 160–161: Monkeys are social animals and often communicate using noises, facial expressions, and body movements.

- **The Nile Crocodile** Unit 17 pp. 170–171: The Nile crocodile is often considered to be a man-eater as it is estimated that about 200 people are killed each year by Nile crocodiles.

- **Gold! Gold! Gold!** Unit 18 pp. 180–181: The California Gold Rush began on January 24, 1848, when gold was discovered in Coloma, California. Families from across the United States trekked to California to find gold. Many gold-seekers were called forty-niners after the year of their arrival.

Definitions

TEACH

■ Discuss the format and content of the Definitions pages. Explain that there are ten words. Each one is accompanied by its pronunciation, part of speech, and definition; a sample sentence showing how the word is used; synonyms and antonyms; and sometimes a picture to help clarify the meaning.

■ Review the parts of speech in the Remember box. Lead a brief discussion about each word's part of speech to help students increase their understanding of the definition and word use.

■ Point out that some words can be used as different parts of speech and can have more than one meaning—for example, *coast* (Unit 7). See also page T27 for a more thorough discussion of multiple-meaning words.

■ To help students develop a deeper understanding of the Unit words, generate a discussion that gets at the character of the word and how it is typically used. For example, for *gasp* (Unit 3), ask:

- "How do you feel when you *gasp*?"
- "What situations would make you *gasp*?"
- "Show me a *gasp*."

■ Summarize the meaning of *gasp* using everyday language.

> **MODEL** From our discussion, we know that a *gasp* is a short, quick breath of air that we take when we are surprised, frightened, or in pain. Getting the bike you've been dreaming about might make you *gasp*.

PRACTICE / APPLY

■ Assign the Definitions pages. Tell students to think about each word's meaning as they complete the sentences. Have them read the completed sentences silently.

■ Ask volunteers to read the completed sentences aloud. Reading sentences aloud conveys how words can be effectively used in speaking and writing.

FOLLOW-UP

■ **Oral Language** To encourage daily use of the Unit words, list them on a Word Wall. Encourage students to use the words in their speaking and writing. When they read, tell them to be alert to the words they have learned and to notice how the words are used.

■ **English Language Learners (ELL)** Model how to pronounce each Unit word. Have students practice saying the words. To reinforce word meaning, encourage students to take turns acting out the words. Guide students as needed.

> **vocabularyworkshop.com**
>
> **iWords™ Audio Program** Students can view and hear Unit words, definitions, and visuals, and then practice pronouncing Unit words.
>
> **Audio Glossary** Students can listen to Unit words and see illustrated sentences.

CCSS Vocabulary: 4.a. (See p. T18.)

Match the Meaning

TEACH

■ To help students process the meanings of the Unit words, have them interact with the words and relate them to their own experiences. For example, for the word *loyal* (Unit 3), have students describe a time when they were *loyal* to someone. Give an example to get students started.

> **MODEL** Last week, my friend was sick and needed a ride home. I had tickets for a baseball game, but I gave the tickets away and drove my friend home instead. I was a *loyal* friend.

■ Lead other discussions about the words and how they are related. For example:

- For the word *wander* (Unit 3), ask, "If you are *wandering* around the playground, would you be in a hurry? Why?"
- For the words *active* and *sensitive* (Unit 3), ask, "If someone says something that hurts your feelings, might you become *active* or *sensitive*? Why?"

PRACTICE/APPLY

■ Assign the Match the Meaning page. For any item, the three taught words given as answer choices are all the same part of speech. Tell students to think about the meaning of each choice before choosing the answer indicated by the clue. When they finish, have students read the completed sentences to be sure they make sense.

FOLLOW-UP

■ **Word Play** Have students make an acrostic poem using one of the Unit words. Ask them to brainstorm a list of words or phrases that describe or remind them of the word. Then have them use the words to write the acrostic poem. For example:

g oes with something scary

a nd is joined by short, quick breaths

s ometimes goes with a surprise

p lus a search for air

vocabularyworkshop.com

Flash Cards Students can access flash cards to study Unit words and definitions.

Interactive Game: Word Search Students can identify hidden taught words in a grid.

Graphic Organizer: Word Square Students can complete a Word Square for a Unit word to support their learning.

Word Square

Word	My Connection
What It Means	How It Looks

CCSS Vocabulary: 4.a. (See p. T18.)

Synonyms and Antonyms

TEACH

■ Tell students that learning synonyms and antonyms can help them expand their vocabularies. Explain that synonyms are words that have the same or similar meanings; for example, *change* and *vary* (Unit 3) are synonyms.

> **MODEL** Instead of saying, "The number of students in school *changes* each day," I can say, "The number of students in school *varies* each day." The words *changes* and *varies* are synonyms. They both mean about the same thing.

■ Provide other sentences with *vary*. Ask students to give synonyms that could replace the word. Remind students that the synonym must make sense in the sentence.

■ Explain that antonyms are words with opposite meanings; for example, *active* (Unit 3) and *passive* are antonyms. Elicit from students other words that are the opposite of *active*. Guide them by providing sentences such as "I am an *active* person." Ask students to replace *active* with a word that is opposite in meaning and would make sense in the sentence. *(lazy)*

■ Use other examples of synonyms and antonyms that are related to students' experiences.

■ To help students expand their vocabularies, revisit and discuss the synonyms and antonyms on the Definitions pages. Have students use some of the words in sentences. Encourage students to relate the words to their own experiences.

PRACTICE/APPLY

■ Assign the Synonyms/Antonyms page. Tell students to read each phrase and consider each choice before choosing their answers. Remind them to substitute their choices for the word in dark print to be sure it makes sense.

FOLLOW-UP

■ **Expanding Vocabulary** Have students begin a Vocabulary Notebook in which they write the meanings of the taught words and add to them as they learn more about the words. For example, have them list additional synonyms and antonyms.

■ **Writing** Have students list the Unit words in their Vocabulary Notebooks by part of speech. Also have them list synonyms and antonyms for the Unit words. Students can choose from these lists to make their writing more interesting.

vocabularyworkshop.com

Interactive Word Map or **Graphic Organizer: Word Web** Select a Unit word, and ask questions to elicit responses that are either synonyms or antonyms. Complete the Interactive Word Map with students' responses.

Interactive Game: Concentration Students can test their understanding and memory by matching synonym and antonym pairs.

CCSS Vocabulary: 4.a. (See p. T18.)

Completing the Sentence

TEACH

■ Remind students that some words have more than one meaning. Explain that when a multiple-meaning word is used in a sentence, they can figure out the intended meaning by using the context clues. Point out, however, that they first need to be familiar with the various meanings. Provide cloze sentences with enough context for students to figure out which Unit word correctly completes a sentence.

■ Explain that context clues in sentences can be before or after an unfamiliar word. The context clue is sometimes a single word located within the same sentence.

■ Write the following on the board:

I will ______ the shapes and colors I use to make a more interesting painting.

> **MODEL** To figure out the Unit word that fits in the sentence, I look for clues in the sentence. The words *shapes* and *colors* and *more interesting painting* make me think that *vary* (Unit 3) is the correct word. I know that *vary* can mean "different," and I know that an interesting painting usually has lots of different colors and shapes. When I reread the sentence with the word *vary,* it makes sense.

PRACTICE/APPLY

■ Briefly discuss the topics on the Completing the Sentence page. Explain that each sentence can be completed using one of the Unit words in the box at the top of the page. Each word can be used only once. Point out that as required by the sentence, the missing word may be the plural form of a noun or any tense or form (participle, for example) of a verb.

■ Have students tell the context clues they used to complete the sentences.

FOLLOW-UP

■ **Synonyms** Challenge student pairs to complete the student page again, this time reading aloud the sentences and using synonyms, where possible, in place of Unit words.

■ **Unit Assessment** When Completing the Sentence is the last page before Word Study, assess students' understanding of the taught words. See pages T12 and T13 to select appropriate practice and assessment tools, including online Interactive Unit Quizzes, online Practice Unit Worksheets, and Unit Tests in the Test Booklet.

vocabularyworkshop.com

Interactive Game: What's the Word? Students can use a hint to identify missing letters of a taught word in this timed activity.

Interactive Unit Quiz: Students can assess their understanding of Unit words in standardized-test format.

Practice Unit Worksheet Assign leveled practice based on students' performance on the Interactive Unit Quiz.

CCSS Vocabulary: 4.a. (See p. T18.)

TEACH

- Help students continue to build on the meanings of the Unit words. Ask questions that require them to associate Unit words with known words. For example, ask the following questions using the Unit 3 words *sensitive, loyal,* and *active.*
  - "Which word would you use to describe a rash on your arm, *sensitive* or *loyal*? Why?"
  - "Would you want a pet that is *loyal* or *active*? Why?"
- In another activity, show how you might connect a Unit word to a phrase. For example:

bargain	surprise party
wander	mountain lake
gasp	discount store

MODEL I know that something that is a *bargain* is something that is sold cheaply. A *discount store* is a place that cuts the prices on the things it sells. *Bargain* goes with *discount store.*

- Ask students to relate *wander* and *gasp* to the remaining phrases and then explain the relationships.

PRACTICE/APPLY

- The exercises on the Word Associations page are comprised of sentence completions and questions, each containing a highlighted Unit word.
- Assign the Word Associations page. When students finish, have them explain their choices.

FOLLOW-UP

- **Unit Assessment** When Word Associations is the last page before Word Study, assess students' understanding of the taught words. See pages T12–T13 to select appropriate practice and assessment tools, including online Interactive Unit Quizzes, online Practice Unit Worksheets, and Unit Tests in the Test Booklet.

vocabularyworkshop.com

Interactive Unit Quiz Students can assess their understanding of Unit words in standardized-test format.

Practice Unit Worksheet Assign leveled practice based on students' performance on the Interactive Unit Quiz.

Graphic Organizer: Word Web
To help students expand their vocabularies, have them write a Unit word or a phrase with the word in the center circle and then write other words or phrases they associate with it. They can add as many circles as needed.

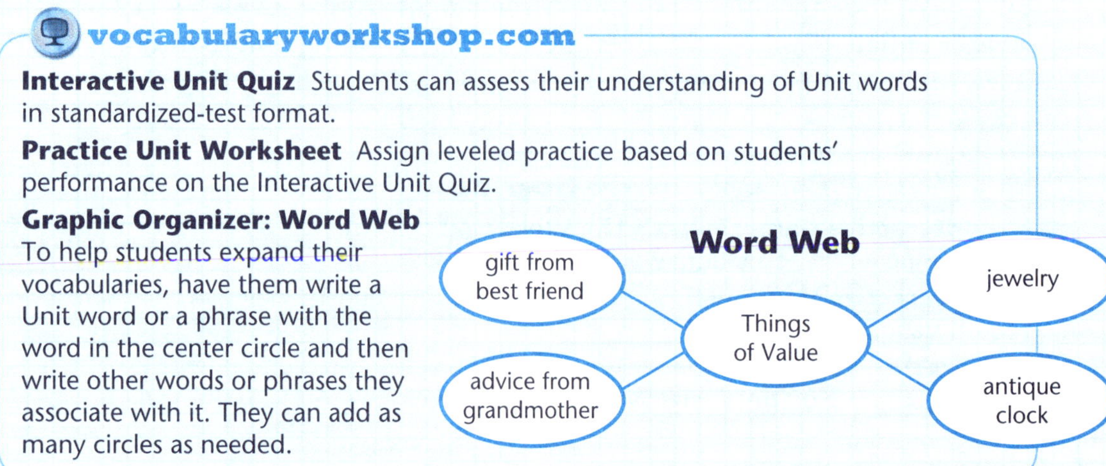

CCSS Vocabulary: 4.a. (See p. T18.)

Unit 1 • Dictionary: Multiple-Meaning Words, page 14

TEACH

Explain that when students look up a word in the dictionary, they will often find more than one meaning for the same word. Discuss which context clues students used to determine the meaning of the word *goal* in the sample sentence.

PRACTICE/APPLY

In Practice, remind students to use context clues to help select the correct word. In Apply, have students tell which meaning of the multiple-meaning words they illustrated.

FOLLOW-UP

Expanding Vocabulary Have students draw pictures to illustrate the multiple meanings of the words in the chart on the page. Students can also write captions.

CCSS Vocabulary: 4.d. (See p. T18.)

Unit 2 • Context Clues 1, page 24

TEACH

Discuss with students the kind of information each type of context clue provides. Provide additional sample sentences, as necessary.

PRACTICE/APPLY

In Practice, have students tell which context clues helped them figure out the meanings of the words in dark print. In Apply, have students volunteer to share one sentence they wrote.

FOLLOW-UP

Writing Instruct students to choose three Unit words. Then have students write one sentence for each word that gives the definition of the word using context clues.

CCSS Vocabulary: 4.a. (See p. T18.)

Unit 3 • Word Families, page 33

TEACH

Explain that the words *loyal, loyalty,* and *loyally* belong to the same word family. Point out how the endings added to *loyal* can change the part of speech and meaning of the word. Demonstrate how knowing the meaning of the word *loyal* can help you figure out the meaning of the related words.

PRACTICE/APPLY

In Practice, have students use what they know about the words in the box, along with context clues, to select the correct word. In Apply, discuss with students how the endings change the parts of speech and the meanings of the words in dark print.

FOLLOW-UP

Informal Assessment Instruct students to create a four-column chart with these headings: *Noun, Adjective, Verb,* and *Adverb*. Have students fill in the chart using the words in the box and the related words from each word's word family.

CCSS Vocabulary: 4.a., 4.b., 4.c., 4.d. (See p. T18.)

Word Study

Unit 4 • Word Parts and Base Words, page 44

TEACH

Model how knowing the meaning of the base word *common* can help you figure out the meaning of the word *uncommon*. Continue similarly with the word *gloom*.

PRACTICE/APPLY

Instruct students to find each base word by removing any beginning or ending parts from the word in dark print. Discuss how the meaning of each dark-print word relates to the meaning of the base word it contains.

FOLLOW-UP

Oral Language Make a Word Wall using words learned in Units 1–4. Ask students to look for words that contain base words from these Units as they are reading. Have them add the words and their meanings to the Word Wall.

 **CCSS** Vocabulary: 4.c. (See p. T18.)

Unit 5 • Prefixes *re-, pre-, in-*, page 54

TEACH

Explain to students that knowing the meaning of common prefixes, such as the ones on page 54, can help them figure out the meanings of many words. Model how knowing the meaning of *re-* can help you figure out the meaning of *reunite* in this sentence: *The members of the band are going to* ***reunite*** *for one more concert.*

PRACTICE/APPLY

In Practice, encourage students to use a dictionary, print or digital, to check their answers. In Apply, remind students to look for context clues to help them complete each sentence with the correct word.

FOLLOW-UP

Expanding Vocabulary Distribute three copies of the Word Web (available online at **vocabularyworkshop.com**) to each student. Have them write one of the prefixes in the center circle of each web and then list words that contain the prefix in the surrounding circles. Allow students to use a dictionary if they need help.

 **CCSS** Vocabulary: 4.b., 4.d. (See p. T18.)

Unit 6 • Suffixes *-ly, -ful, -less*, page 63

TEACH

Remind students that base words are complete words to which prefixes and suffixes can be added. Discuss the meanings of the three suffixes and the given examples. Ask students to brainstorm other words that contain these suffixes.

PRACTICE/APPLY

In Practice, encourage students to use a dictionary, print or digital, to check their answers. In Apply, remind students to look for context clues to help them complete the sentences.

FOLLOW-UP

Oral Language Create and display a list of words that contain the suffixes learned. Have students practice using the words in small-group conversations.

CCSS Vocabulary: 4.b. (See p. T18.)

Unit 7 • Homophones, page 76

TEACH

Introduce the topic by writing the following on the board: "Did you see my plain black coat? I want to wear it on the plane tomorrow." Ask: "How are the words *plain* and *plane* alike and different? What happens if you switch the two words?" Then discuss the chart words.

PRACTICE/APPLY

Remind students to use context clues for the Practice sentences. Have students choose a sentence they wrote in the Apply exercise to share with the class.

FOLLOW-UP

Informal Assessment Create several sentences in which homophones are used correctly or incorrectly—for example, "The injury will take time to heel." Have students write *right* or *wrong* after each sentence to indicate whether the correct homophone was used.

Unit 8 • Context Clues 2, page 86

TEACH

Explain that context clues sometimes give examples of the unknown word. On the board, write the example sentence, "The stove, dishwasher, and microwave are different kitchen appliances." Model how to figure out the meaning of *appliances* in this sentence.

PRACTICE/APPLY

For both Practice and Apply, have students discuss the context clues used in each sentence. Then have students share the sentences they completed in Apply.

FOLLOW-UP

Word Play Have students form two teams. Give both teams a word, such as *transportation*. Instruct the teams to list as many examples of the word as they can. After one minute, have the teams share the words they listed. Whichever team has the most unique examples earns one point. Continue playing until one team has earned five points.

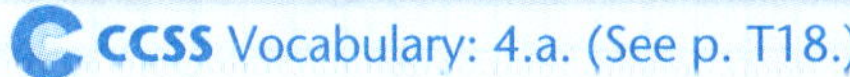
CCSS Vocabulary: 4.a. (See p. T18.)

Unit 9 • Analogies 1, page 95

TEACH

Explain that to complete an analogy, students must first figure out the relationship between the first two words. Model the process with this example: "*short* is to *tall* as *left* is to ___." Continue the discussion with the examples in the chart.

PRACTICE/APPLY

Remind students to think about the relationship between the first pair of words in order to complete the second pair of words in each analogy.

FOLLOW-UP

Writing Have students rewrite each Apply analogy and fill in a new word to complete the analogy. For example, *freeze* is to *boil* as *hide* is to *show*.

Unit 10 • Prefixes *un-, de-, over-,* page 106

TEACH

Have students recall the prefixes they learned on page 54. Model how knowing the meaning of *un-* can help you figure out the meaning of *unable* in: "I am *unable* to attend the party this weekend." Review the other prefix meanings and the example words.

PRACTICE/APPLY

Ask students for an example of each new word. Remind them to use context clues to help them choose the answer for each Apply sentence. After they complete the sentences, ask students to relate the prefix of each inserted word to the context of the sentence.

FOLLOW-UP

Informal Assessment Tell students to write three words that contain a prefix on the front of separate note cards. On the reverse side, students can write any things they associate with the word. For example, for *defrost*, they might list *cold, car setting, melting ice,* and *winter*.

CCSS Vocabulary: 4.b., 4d. (See p. T18.)

Unit 11 • Suffixes *-ness, -er, -or,* page 116

TEACH

Have students recall suffixes. Write the lesson's suffixes on the board. Discuss their meanings and the given examples. Ask prompting questions to further students' understanding, such as "Who is your favorite *actor*?"

PRACTICE/APPLY

Encourage students to use a dictionary, print or digital, to check their answers. Further the discussion by asking for examples of each new word. In Apply, remind students to use context clues to help them choose the correct word.

FOLLOW-UP

Expanding Vocabulary After students add new words to the chart, have students choose one new word for each suffix. Have students complete a Word Square (available online at **vocabularyworkshop.com/green**) for each new word they choose.

CCSS Vocabulary: 4.b. (See p. T18.)

Unit 12 • Homographs 1, page 125

TEACH

Introduce the topic by writing the following on the board: "What kind of friend is she? A friend who is kind and giving." Discuss the meaning of *kind* in each sentence.

PRACTICE/APPLY

Have students use the words from the chart to complete the sentences in Practice and Apply. Remind them to use context clues when deciding which meaning of the word to use.

FOLLOW-UP

Oral Language Have student pairs ask and answer questions using the homographs, such as "Why might someone go to a *bank*?"/"A person may go to a *bank* to deposit a check."

Word Study

Unit 13 • Compound Words, page 138

TEACH

Explain to students that the word *jellyfish* is a compound word, a word made by joining two smaller words. Model how using what you know about *jelly* and *fish* can help you figure out the meaning of the word *jellyfish.* Encourage students to list other compound words they know.

PRACTICE/APPLY

In Practice, tell students to use what they know about the two smaller words to figure out the meaning of the compound words. In Apply, remind them to use context clues to help them choose which words to use.

FOLLOW-UP

Expanding Vocabulary Give students three words that can form compound words with a fourth common word, and have students guess the fourth word. For example: *base, meat, snow*; they can all form compound words with the word *ball.*

Unit 14 • Homographs 2, page 148

TEACH

Have students use a dictionary, print or digital, to look up the word *exhaust.* Discuss how students can use context clues to determine which meaning of *exhaust* is used in this sentence: "The *exhaust* from the car formed a thick, black cloud."

PRACTICE/APPLY

Have students use the words from the chart to complete the sentences in Practice and Apply. Remind students to use context clues when deciding which meaning of the word to use.

FOLLOW-UP

Word Play Have students write alliterative tongue-twister sentences using both words in the homograph pairs. For example: *The broken bridge could not* ***bear*** *the weight of the big, brown* ***bear****.*

Unit 15 • Analogies 2, page 157

TEACH

Ask students to recall what they have learned about analogies. Model how to complete this analogy: "*broom* is to *sweep* as *pencil* is to _______." Further the discussion of object/function analogies using the example in the chart.

PRACTICE/APPLY

In Practice and Apply, have students share their answers and suggest other pairs of words that could complete each analogy.

FOLLOW-UP

Informal Assessment Provide students with incomplete analogies that only give the first pair of words, and have them complete the analogies with a second pair of words that have the same relationship.

Unit 16 • Prefixes *dis-, mis-, im-,* page 168

TEACH

Model how knowing the meaning of *dis-* can help you figure out the meaning of *disagree* in this sentence: "My brother and I often *disagree* on what to eat for dinner." Review the other prefix meanings and the example words.

PRACTICE/APPLY

Further the discussion of new words by asking students for examples of each new word. Remind students to use context clues. After students complete the sentences, ask how the prefix of each inserted word relates to the context of the sentence.

FOLLOW-UP

Writing Have students continue the Practice chart by listing words with the prefixes *dis-, mis-,* and *im-,* and the words' meanings. Allow students to use a dictionary.

 CCSS Vocabulary: 4.b. (See p. T18.)

Unit 17 • Suffixes *-ion, -ment, -able,* page 178

TEACH

Write the lesson's suffixes on the board. Discuss their meanings and the given examples. Ask prompting questions to further students' understanding, such as "What are some things that are *breakable*?"

PRACTICE/APPLY

Encourage students to use a dictionary, print or digital, to check their answers. Further the discussion by asking for examples of each new word. In Apply, remind students to use context clues to help them choose the correct words.

FOLLOW-UP

Writing Instruct students to write an original paragraph that uses all four words from the Practice chart (*connection, enjoyable, agreement,* and *respectable*).

 CCSS Vocabulary: 4.b. (See p. T18.)

Unit 18 • Roots *loc, aud,* page 187

TEACH

Model how knowing the meaning of the root *loc* can help you figure out the meaning of *locate* in the following: "Can you *locate* our school on this map?" Continue similarly with the word *audible.* Then relate the meanings of each root and each chart word.

PRACTICE/APPLY

Begin by asking students to brainstorm examples of each word in the chart. Remind students to use context clues when completing the Practice sentences. Have students explain how their responses to the Apply sentences relate to the meanings of each root.

FOLLOW-UP

Word Play Have students work in small groups. One at a time, students can give a clue, and the rest of the group can guess the word that matches the clue. For example, a student may give this clue: "You may go to this place to see a play: _______" (*auditorium*)

CCSS Vocabulary: 4.c., 4.d. (See p. T18.)

Shades of Meaning

Unit 1 • Words That Describe How Things Taste, page 15

TEACH

Write the words *lemon* and *strawberry* on the board. Ask: "How would you describe the taste of these fruits?" Tell students that there are many words that can be used to describe taste. Have students name examples of foods that have the types of tastes listed in the chart. Encourage students to list other words that describe how things taste.

PRACTICE/APPLY

Discuss the Practice exercise with students. Then have students choose one of their responses to the Apply sentences to share with the class.

FOLLOW-UP

Writing Have students think of three of their favorite foods. Then tell them to write a descriptive sentence for each type of food, using words that describe taste.

Unit 2 • Literal and Nonliteral Meanings, page 25

TEACH

Write the phrase *drive home* on the board. Ask: "What does this phrase typically mean?" Then ask, "What does it mean to *drive home* a point?" Further clarify the two meanings by discussing the example sentences.

PRACTICE/APPLY

Remind students to use context clues to help them choose which meaning of the phrase is used in each Practice sentence. In Apply, have students choose one sentence they wrote to share with the class.

FOLLOW-UP

Oral Language Have student pairs share the rest of the sentences they wrote for the Apply exercise. As one partner reads their sentences, the other partner can state which meaning of the phrase is used in each sentence.

Unit 4 • Word Choice *capture, snatch, trap,* page 45

TEACH

Explain that writers choose words carefully to get across specific thoughts. On the board, write: "Hunters wanted to capture the stag." Ask: "How would the meaning of the sentence change if the writer had used the word *snatch* instead?" Continue to discuss the differences between the words *capture, snatch,* and *trap.*

PRACTICE/APPLY

After students complete Practice and Apply, have them discuss the context clues in each sentence that indicated which word to choose.

FOLLOW-UP

Expanding Vocabulary Distribute three copies of the Word Square (available online at **vocabularyworkshop.com**) to each student. Have students complete a Word Square page for each word in the chart.

CCSS Vocabulary: 5.b. (See p. T18.)

Unit 5 • Word Choice *glance, gaze, glare,* page 55

TEACH

Remind students what they have learned about the importance of word choice. Write the words *glance, gaze,* and *glare* on the board. Ask: "How are the words similar? How are they different?" Further students' understanding by asking prompting questions such as, "Why might you *glare* at someone? When have you *gazed* upon something?"

PRACTICE/APPLY

After students complete the Practice, have them discuss the context clues in each sentence that indicated which word to choose. Then encourage students to share one of their answers from Apply.

FOLLOW-UP

Word Play Explain to students that the differences between a *glance, gaze,* and *glare* can also be shown with different facial expressions. Provide students with scenarios, and have them act them out to demonstrate their understanding of the words.

 **CCSS** Vocabulary: 5.b. (See p. T18.)

Unit 7 • Idioms 1, page 77

TEACH

Explain that to understand the meaning of an idiom, students have to think beyond the literal, or actual, meanings of the words. Elaborate on the idiom *coast was clear.* Say: "Even though a coast is a type of land near the ocean, the idiom *coast was clear* is not referring to this meaning. Instead, it means that there was no one around."

PRACTICE/APPLY

After students finish the Practice and Apply, discuss the meaning of each idiom with students. Have students explain how each idiom fits the example sentence.

FOLLOW-UP

Writing Have students choose three of the idioms from the lesson that they can relate to personal experiences. Instruct students to write one original sentence for each of the idioms they choose.

 **CCSS** Vocabulary: 5.a. (See p. T18.)

Unit 8 • Words That Describe People 1, page 87

TEACH

Ask students to consider this question: "If someone asked you to describe a friend, what would you say?" Some students might describe appearance, using a word like *tall*; students describing personality might use the word *friendly*. Discuss how the other words in the chart describe personality.

PRACTICE/APPLY

Have students explain which type of personality fits each sentence in Practice. In Apply, have them share their answers to the questions.

FOLLOW-UP

Oral Language List the three words in the chart on a Word Wall with the heading *Words to Describe People*. Have students add synonyms and antonyms of the words to the Wall.

 **CCSS** Vocabulary: 5.b. (See p. T18.)

Shades of Meaning

Unit 10 • Idioms 2, page 107

TEACH

Ask students to recall what they know about idioms. Explain that many idioms refer to how people feel. Write the example, "So many answers on the test looked right that the girl was <u>at her wit's end</u>." Remind students that the meaning of an idiom is different from the actual meanings of the words in the saying. Discuss what the idiom actually means.

PRACTICE/APPLY

After students complete the exercises, discuss the meaning of each idiom. Have students explain how each idiom fits the sentence.

FOLLOW-UP

Word Play Tell students to write an idiom on the front of a note card, and on the reverse side, any thoughts, feelings, and things they associate with the idiom. For example, for *fish out of water,* they might list *uncomfortable, worried, new student in school.* Ask volunteers to read their clues aloud, and have the rest of the class guess the idiom.

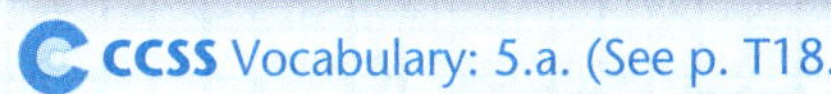
CCSS Vocabulary: 5.a. (See p. T18.)

Unit 11 • Words That Describe People 2, page 117

TEACH

Have students recall words that describe people. Write on the board: "In those days, ship travel was not for the meek or easily frightened sailor." Ask: "Which words in this sentence describe people?" Continue the discussion with the other words in the chart.

PRACTICE/APPLY

Have students explain which type of personality fits each sentence in Practice. In Apply, have them share a sentence about someone they know.

FOLLOW-UP

Informal Assessment Provide Concept Circles (available online at **vocabularyworkshop.com/green**) that contain three adjectives—two that can be used to describe people and one that cannot. (For example, *brief, clever, patient*) Have students identify the misplaced adjective and replace it with a third adjective that can be used to describe people.

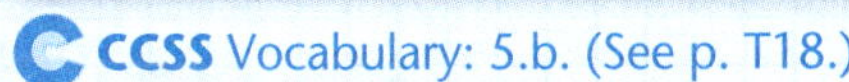
CCSS Vocabulary: 5.b. (See p. T18.)

Unit 13 • Word Choice *declare, mutter, admit,* page 139

TEACH

Have students recall what they have learned about word choice. Write the words *declare, mutter,* and *admit* on the board. Ask: "How are the words similar? How are they different?" Then read these two sentences: "I *declared* that I was the one who broke the vase," and "I *admitted* that I was the one who broke the vase." Ask: "What is the difference between these two ideas?"

PRACTICE/APPLY

After students complete Practice and Apply, have them discuss the context clues in each sentence that indicated which word to choose.

FOLLOW-UP

Writing Tell students that writers often use the words *declare, mutter,* and *admit* in dialogue to describe how characters are speaking. Have student pairs write a brief dialogue between two people that uses the words *declare, mutter,* and *admit.*

CCSS Vocabulary: 5.c. (See p. T18.)

Unit 14 • Word Choice *predict, suspect, wonder,* page 149

TEACH

Write the words *predict, suspect,* and *wonder* on the board. Ask: "How are the words similar? How are they different?" Then read these two sentences: "I *suspect* that my sister ate the last cookie," and "I *wonder* if my sister ate the last cookie." Ask students: "What is the difference between these two ideas?"

PRACTICE/APPLY

In Practice, have students identify the context clues in each sentence that indicated which word to choose. Then discuss the Apply questions as a class.

FOLLOW-UP

Informal Assessment Distribute three copies of the Word Web (available online at **vocabularyworkshop.com**) to each student. Have them write one of the words in the center circle of each web and then list related concepts in the surrounding circles.

CCSS Vocabulary: 5.c. (See p. T18.)

Unit 16 • Words That Describe Behavior, page 169

TEACH

Discuss the word *defiant* as it is found in the passage—that is, to describe Chichi's behavior. Continue the discussion with the words *charming* and *cunning* by asking questions such as "Why do you think a fairy-tale prince is often called *charming*?" and "Why might the Big Bad Wolf in the story *The Three Little Pigs* be called *cunning*?"

PRACTICE/APPLY

Ask students to explain how each word fits the behavior described in Practice. After they complete Apply, have them describe how somebody might react to each behavior.

FOLLOW-UP

Oral Vocabulary List the three words in the chart on a Word Wall with the heading *Words That Describe Behavior*. As students read in class and at home, have them find other behavior words and add them to the wall.

CCSS Vocabulary: 5.b. (See p. T18.)

Unit 17 • Words That Describe Appearance, page 179

TEACH

Write this example sentence on the board: "Its elegant neck reaches down to the water." Discuss how the word *elegant* can be used to describe appearance. As you discuss the other words in the chart, have students name examples of things that may look *shabby* or *tidy*. Encourage students to name other words that can be used to describe appearance.

PRACTICE/APPLY

In Practice, have students discuss the context clues in each sentence that indicated which word to choose. Have students choose a description from the Apply exercise to share with the class.

FOLLOW-UP

Expanding Vocabulary Have students draw and label pictures to depict the words *elegant, shabby* and *tidy*.

CCSS Vocabulary: 5.b. (See p. T18.)

The REVIEW

Each sequence of three Units of **Vocabulary Workshop** is followed by a review in the form of Vocabulary for Comprehension, which contains words from those three Units. Each sequence of six Units additionally includes Classifying and Completing the Idea as part of the review. These pages review words from the previous six Units. The Reviews are designed to provide additional exposure to the taught words and to allow students to apply and expand their word knowledge.

Overview of the Review	
Vocabulary for Comprehension	In **Vocabulary for Comprehension**, students read a passage that incorporates six of the taught words from the three Units. After reading, students answer questions based on the passage. Each Vocabulary for Comprehension concludes with **Write Your Own**. This writing prompt gives students the opportunity to demonstrate an understanding of the taught words as part of their writing vocabularies. The prompt may ask students to interact with the reading and vocabulary in a variety of ways, including expanding on the theme of the passage, expressing feelings about the subject, and relating the passage to personal experience.
Classifying	In **Classifying**, students look for a relationship among a group of words and choose the word that may be considered a member of the group. Students then explain the relationship.
Completing the Idea	In **Completing the Idea**, students apply their knowledge of word meanings by completing a writing activity. They relate their prior knowledge or a personal experience to a sentence starter that contains a taught word, and then they complete the thought. Each Completing the Idea concludes with a **Writing Challenge.** This writing exercise provides students with the opportunity to demonstrate an understanding of multiple-meaning words. For each Writing Challenge, students write sentences that provide context clues for different meanings and parts of speech of a given taught word.

All six Reviews include Vocabulary for Comprehension. Because of their similar structure, the teaching notes on pages T40–T41 can be applied to all Reviews. Teaching notes on pages T42–T43 can be applied to Classifying and Completing the Idea pages. Correlations to the Common Core State Standards for the Review lessons are also identified below the teaching notes on pages T40-T43.

Vocabulary for Comprehension

TEACH

- Tell students that to understand what they are reading, they must know the meanings of key words or be able to figure out the meanings. They must also use comprehension skills to help them grasp the meaning of the passage.
- Present the paragraph and questions below.

On April 14, 1912, the *Titanic*, a magnificent ocean liner, hit an iceberg about 400 miles off Newfoundland, Canada. Nobody knew at first how bad the damage was. People were very calm. But soon, it was clear that the ship was doomed. Shortly after midnight on the 15th, the *Titanic* split into two pieces and sank.

1. What is the main idea of the paragraph?
2. What details tell about the main idea?
3. What is the meaning of *doomed*?
4. What do you think happened to the people on board the ship?

- Discuss the reading skills below. Model how to use them to answer the questions.
- **Identify Main Idea/Details** The main idea of a passage is what the passage is about. It is the most important point that the author makes about a topic or subject. The main idea is often stated at the beginning of the passage. The rest of the passage usually gives details that help explain or support the main idea.

> **MODEL** To answer the first two questions about the *Titanic*, I use the information in the paragraph. The main idea tells me what the paragraph is about. From reading the paragraph, I know that it is mainly about the sinking of the *Titanic*. The details tell me when the *Titanic* sank (April 15, 1912), where it sank (about 400 miles off Newfoundland, Canada), and why it sank (hit an iceberg).

- **Vocabulary in Context** Sometimes using context clues can help a reader figure out the meaning of a word. The clues can be in the surrounding sentences, or they can be other words in the sentence.

> **MODEL** To figure out the meaning of *doomed*, I look at the other words in the sentence and at the sentences that come before it. In the sentence with *doomed*, the word *but* tells me that the situation was not hopeful. This, together with the other clues, makes me think that *doomed* means "certain to fail or be destroyed."

- **Make Inferences** Authors do not always state directly everything that happens. Instead, they provide details that allow readers to figure out things for themselves. Making inferences is using clues or details in the passage and the readers' prior knowledge to make logical decisions about events and actions that are not stated.

> **MODEL** To answer the last question, I put together everything that I know that happened. I know that the *Titanic* hit an iceberg, and I know that the ship was doomed. The last sentence tells me that the *Titanic* split in two and sank. All this makes me think that the people on board drowned.

Using the paragraph, model how to monitor comprehension. Show how you would stop and reread to understand important details or what you might do to clarify confusing parts.

MODEL The *Titanic* hit an iceberg about 400 miles off the coast of Newfoundland. It's hard to imagine what a distance of 400 miles is like. To help me better understand the situation, I will ask the librarian to help me find a map of the North Atlantic that shows the coast of Newfoundland. Then I will ask for help in pinpointing a distance that is about 400 miles off the coast.

PRACTICE/APPLY

- Assign the Vocabulary for Comprehension pages. Tell students that they will use their word knowledge and reading skills by reading a passage and answering questions based on the passage. Point out that the passage and questions are similar to those on standardized tests. Tell students to read carefully and to be sure to base their answer choices on what they read. Point out that there may be answer choices that make sense but that are not based on the passage.
- In **Write Your Own**, students have the opportunity to write on a topic related to the passage. The sentences or paragraph(s) may expand on the passage, or they may tell how students feel about what they read. Remind students to use some of the taught words in their writing.

FOLLOW-UP

- **Oral Language** Create a Word Wall of interesting words. Have students contribute new words encountered in their reading, in conversations, on TV, and in their daily experiences. Before you add a word, encourage students to tell where they found it and describe the situation in which it was used.

Interactive Game: Crosswords Students can complete a crossword puzzle given the definition of taught words.

CCSS Vocabulary: 4.a., 6 (See p. T18.)

Classifying

TEACH

■ Explain that words can be classified, or grouped together, according to the way in which they are alike. For example, *shoes*, *socks*, and *slippers* are all things that are worn on the feet. *Bushes*, *trees*, and *flowers* are all things that are planted. Tell students that classifying words can help them see the connection between words. It can help them build their vocabularies.

■ Write the following words on the board: *fragile*, *dainty*, and *frail*. Discuss which word, *clever*, *delicate*, or *active* belongs with the group of words.

> **MODEL** To figure out the answer, I look to see what the words *fragile*, *dainty*, and *frail* have in common. I see that they all describe someone or something that requires careful handling or things that could be easily broken. Of the three words, *delicate* goes best with these words.

PRACTICE/APPLY

■ Assign the Classifying page. Have students familiarize themselves with the words in the word box before completing the page.

FOLLOW-UP

■ **Word Play** Have students make up questions such as the following for a partner to answer. Partners should be prepared to explain their answers.

- Which words are related to a trip, *journey*, *depart*, *passage*, or *swift*?
- Which words might you use to talk about a lake, *shallow*, *resource*, *plunge*, or *swift*?

vocabularyworkshop.com

Graphic Organizer: Concept Circle For informal assessment or additional practice, provide Concept Circles that incorporate some of the words students have learned so far. Have students replace the word that does not belong with a taught word that does. Then have them write a phrase that tells how the words in the circle are related.

Words That Describe How I Feel

restless

vibrant

~~avoid~~

fortunate

CCSS Vocabulary: 5.b. (See p. T18.)

Completing the Idea

TEACH

■ To help make the taught words a permanent part of students' vocabularies, give students many opportunities to use and think about the words. Have students discuss and answer questions such as the following:

- Can something or someone be both *brilliant* and *harsh*? Explain.
- How is a *talent* like a *treasure*? How is it different?
- Can a *resource* be a *bargain*? Why?

Tell students that any answer they can adequately support is acceptable. Model how you might answer the first question. Encourage students to offer other answers.

> **MODEL** The sun is *brilliant* on a bright, sunny day. And the heat that the sun produces can be *harsh*, making it uncomfortable to stay outdoors. The sun is an example of something that is both *brilliant* and *harsh*.

■ Remind students that some words have more than one meaning. Explain that when a multiple-meaning word is used in a sentence, they can figure out the intended meaning by using the context clues. Point out, however, that first they need to be familiar with the various meanings.

PRACTICE/APPLY

■ Assign the **Completing the Idea** page. Point out that the taught words in the sentence stem are in boldface. Tell students to think about the definition of each taught word and how to complete the idea meaningfully before they begin to write. Remind them that there is more than one correct way to complete an idea.

■ In **Writing Challenge**, students are provided with a multiple-meaning word from the reviewed Units. They must provide a sentence for two different meanings of the word. Remind students to use the parts of speech indicated in the directions. For example, one sentence should use the Unit word as a verb, and the other as an adjective.

FOLLOW-UP

■ **Expanding Vocabulary** Have students keep track of unfamiliar words that they encounter in their reading. For each word, have them consult a dictionary and use prior knowledge to explain its meaning. Have them also include examples and nonexamples, as well as synonyms and antonyms, if appropriate.

■ **ELL** Dictate sentences that include the taught words so students can hear them in context. Ask students to touch each word in the sentence with their pencils as you repeat it. You might also tell students how many words are in the sentence and allow them time to count. Provide at least three opportunities for students to hear a sentence before moving on to the next one.

CCSS Vocabulary: 4.a., 5.b. (See p. T18.)

Answer Key to Level Green Test Booklet
Form A

UNIT 1
1. **b** prefer
2. **c** allow
3. **a** goal
4. **b** faint
5. **c** bitter
6. patient
7. firm
8. force
9. trace
10. common
11. **c** let
12. **c** track
13. **c** calm
14. **b** aim
15. **b** rather
16. **a** unusual
17. **c** refuse
18. **c** sweet
19. **b** weakness
20. **c** happy

UNIT 2
1. **b** mild
2. **b** ruin
3. **c** aim
4. **c** refuse
5. **a** defeat
6. solid
7. route
8. aware
9. drift
10. pause
11. **a** reject
12. **c** float
13. **b** point
14. **b** path
15. **a** firm
16. **c** win
17. **b** clueless
18. **c** spicy
19. **a** go on
20. **a** fix

UNIT 3
1. **b** loyal
2. **c** struggle
3. **a** wander
4. **a** value
5. **b** resource
6. gasp
7. vary
8. sensitive
9. bargain
10. active
11. **b** stray
12. **a** deal
13. **a** strive
14. **c** supply
15. **c** alter
16. **b** sigh
17. **a** treacherous
18. **c** reject
19. **a** uncaring
20. **c** lazy

UNIT 4
1. **a** gloomy
2. **a** talent
3. **c** insist
4. **b** shallow
5. **a** passage
6. restless
7. exclaim
8. capture
9. coward
10. shatter
11. **b** require
12. **a** smash
13. **c** knack
14. **b** weakling
15. **a** tunnel
16. **c** murmur
17. **c** deep
18. **a** peaceful
19. **b** bright
20. **b** release

UNIT 5
1. **b** glance
2. **c** precious
3. **a** convince
4. **b** harsh
5. **b** atmosphere
6. brilliant
7. endure
8. swift
9. unite
10. plunge
11. **c** environment
12. **c** withstand
13. **b** drop
14. **b** rapid
15. **a** persuade
16. **b** dull
17. **a** stare
18. **c** worthless
19. **c** split
20. **b** pleasant

UNIT 6
1. **b** clasp
2. **c** wisdom
3. **a** certain
4. **c** observe
5. **c** journey
6. treasure
7. depart
8. border
9. fierce
10. superb
11. **c** outing
12. **a** abide by
13. **b** boundary
14. **c** understanding
15. **b** wealth
16. **a** indefinite
17. **b** mild
18. **b** detach
19. **c** inferior
20. **a** stay

UNIT 7
1. **a** pierce
2. **c** coast
3. **a** clever
4. **b** symbol
5. **b** rare
6. accuse
7. delicate
8. triumph
9. explore
10. imitate
11. **a** glide
12. **c** search
13. **c** perforate
14. **c** mark
15. **c** copy
16. **b** praise
17. **a** coarse
18. **b** defeated by
19. **a** frequent
20. **b** unintelligent

UNIT 8
1. **c** timid
2. **b** decay
3. **c** cling
4. **a** ancient
5. **b** perform
6. climate
7. remote
8. exposed
9. custom
10. disturb
11. **c** environment
12. **a** disrupt
13. **a** play
14. **c** habit
15. **b** stick
16. **a** confident
17. **b** cover
18. **c** new
19. **c** nearby
20. **b** bloom

UNIT 9
1. **c** honor
2. **b** remark
3. **c** bashful
4. **a** compete
5. **b** reflex
6. ability
7. delightful
8. brief
9. avoid
10. consider
11. **b** comment
12. **a** elude
13. **a** response
14. **b** contend
15. **b** aptitude
16. **c** joyless
17. **c** disgrace
18. **a** brash
19. **b** decline
20. **b** long

Midyear Test (UNITS 1–9)
1. refuse
2. active
3. allow
4. explore
5. convince
6. decay
7. accuse
8. resource
9. coward
10. border
11. consider
12. reflex
13. expose
14. wisdom
15. delicate
16. depart
17. triumph
18. gasp
19. no change: pause
20. trace
21. shallow
22. no change: loyal
23. gloomy
24. brilliant
25. compete
26. **a**
27. **c**
28. **b**
29. **b**
30. **d**
31. **b**
32. **a**
33. **a**
34. **d**
35. **b**
36. solid
37. aware
38. avoid
39. sensitive
40. symbol

Form A continued

41. disturb
42. capture
43. rare
44. timid
45. bargain
46. brief
47. firm
48. bitter
49. treasure
50. superb

UNIT 10

1. **a** conquer
2. **c** vibrant
3. **c** brink
4. **a** intend
5. **b** pattern
6. actual
7. wit
8. chill
9. fury
10. fortunate
11. **b** control
12. **b** verge
13. **b** expect
14. **a** rage
15. **c** sequence
16. **a** unlucky
17. **c** unreal
18. **b** warmth
19. **c** stupidity
20. **b** unremarkable

UNIT 11

1. **a** revive
2. **b** meek
3. **c** wreckage
4. **b** watchful
5. **a** approach
6. tradition
7. approve
8. prompt
9. glory
10. magnificent
11. **b** splendor
12. **b** ritual
13. **c** destruction
14. **b** endorse
15. **c** quiet
16. **b** avoid
17. **a** ordinary
18. **c** kill
19. **a** sleepy
20. **a** discourage

UNIT 12

1. **b** punctuate
2. **c** glide
3. **c** woe
4. **a** stout
5. **b** prevent
6. audible
7. origin
8. scorn
9. representative
10. consume
11. **a** cruise
12. **c** deplete
13. **a** root
14. **a** interrupt
15. **b** clear
16. **c** allow
17. **a** happiness
18. **b** timid
19. **b** embrace
20. **a** atypical

UNIT 13

1. **b** clarify
2. **a** Authentic
3. **b** yearn
4. **c** opponent
5. **c** arch
6. declare
7. valid
8. grant
9. modest
10. grave
11. **c** wish
12. **b** curvature
13. **c** sound
14. **b** proclaim
15. **a** challenger
16. **a** obscure
17. **b** lighthearted
18. **a** proud
19. **c** false
20. **b** refuse

UNIT 14

1. **c** devotion
2. **b** predict
3. **c** automatic
4. **c** distant
5. **b** stunt
6. admirable
7. dreary
8. separation
9. kindle
10. exhaust
11. **a** deplete
12. **b** foretell
13. **a** first-rate
14. **c** performance
15. **b** rift
16. **a** deliberate
17. **c** stifle
18. **c** faithlessness
19. **b** lively
20. **b** neighboring

UNIT 15

1. **a** slumber
2. **b** formal
3. **c** predator
4. **b** conceive
5. **b** picturesque
6. abundant
7. privilege
8. barrier
9. inquire
10. penalize
11. **c** develop
12. **a** bandit
13. **b** discipline
14. **c** advantage
15. **c** copious
16. **a** awareness
17. **c** drab
18. **b** passageway
19. **a** unofficial
20. **c** respond

UNIT 16

1. **c** merit
2. **a** wretched
3. **c** revoke
4. **a** fearsome
5. **b** ambition
6. advantage
7. purify
8. negotiate
9. imply
10. defiant
11. **b** goal
12. **b** discuss
13. **c** warrant
14. **a** remove
15. **c** benefit
16. **a** submissive
17. **a** pollute
18. **b** happy
19. **c** announce
20. **b** reassuring

UNIT 17

1. **b** tiresome
2. **a** inspect
3. **b** channel
4. **c** absorb
5. **c** elegant
6. amateur
7. grace
8. tranquil
9. suspend
10. lame
11. **c** plow
12. **b** check
13. **c** beginner
14. **a** serene
15. **b** adorn
16. **c** unfashionable
17. **a** resume
18. **b** strong
19. **c** secrete
20. **c** stimulating

UNIT 18

1. **c** invest
2. **c** eloquent
3. **a** boast
4. **b** ripple
5. **c** sufficient
6. glisten
7. uproar
8. locate
9. infectious
10. ideal
11. **a** undulate
12. **a** transmittable
13. **b** find
14. **c** contribute to
15. **a** gleam
16. **b** calmness
17. **b** belittle
18. **a** inadequate
19. **c** tongue-tied
20. **c** real

Final Mastery Test

1. actual
2. vibrant
3. valid
4. inquire
5. devotion
6. sufficient
7. boast
8. glory
9. penalize
10. consume
11. origin
12. elegant
13. revive
14. amateur
15. infectious
16. prompt
17. woe
18. absorb
19. invest
20. no change: predict
21. slumber
22. no change: negotiate
23. dreary
24. no change: chill
25. picturesque
26. **a**
27. **d**
28. **b**
29. **b**

Form A continued

30. **c**
31. **b**
32. **a**
33. **b**
34. **b**
35. **b**
36. wit
37. tradition
38. watchful
39. glide
40. punctuate
41. modest
42. grant
43. admirable
44. meek
45. tranquil
46. tiresome
47. formal
48. eloquent
49. imply
50. privilege

Answer Key to Level Green Test Booklet
Form B

UNIT 1
1. **b** firm
2. **c** faint
3. **a** patient
4. **a** trace
5. **c** force
6. bitter
7. trace
8. common
9. allow
10. goal
11. **b** company
12. **c** push
13. **a** outline
14. **b** plan
15. **c** permit
16. **a** dark
17. **c** dislike
18. **a** rare
19. **b** anxious
20. **c** sweet

UNIT 2
1. **a** drift
2. **c** aware
3. **a** Pause
4. **c** route
5. **b** solid
6. defeat
7. aim
8. mild
9. ruin
10. refuse
11. **b** float
12. **c** stop
13. **a** way
14. **c** goal
15. **a** informed
16. **a** victory
17. **a** agree
18. **b** weak
19. **c** fix
20. **b** cold

UNIT 3
1. **a** vary
2. **b** bargain
3. **a** sensitive
4. **c** Active
5. **c** gasp
6. wander
7. loyal
8. value
9. resource
10. struggle
11. **a** haggle
12. **b** delicate
13. **c** supply
14. **b** effort
15. **a** change
16. **c** remain
17. **a** unfaithful
18. **b** passive
19. **b** scorn
20. **c** sigh

UNIT 4
1. **a** restless
2. **b** exclaim
3. **c** capture
4. **b** shatter
5. **c** coward
6. talent
7. gloomy
8. passage
9. insist
10. shallow
11. **b** smash
12. **b** gift
13. **c** section
14. **c** require
15. **a** sullen
16. **a** hero
17. **c** lose
18. **b** whisper
19. **c** patient
20. **b** deep

UNIT 5
1. **c** brilliant
2. **b** harsh
3. **a** unite
4. **a** plunge
5. **c** endure
6. glance
7. atmosphere
8. swift
9. convince
10. precious
11. **a** mood
12. **c** bear
13. **b** dive
14. **b** peek
15. **b** persuade
16. **a** dull
17. **a** slow
18. **c** ordinary
19. **a** pleasant
20. **b** divide

UNIT 6
1. **b** treasure
2. **a** depart
3. **c** border
4. **a** fierce
5. **b** superb
6. observe
7. certain
8. wisdom
9. clasp
10. journey
11. **c** leave
12. **a** edge
13. **c** obey
14. **a** travel
15. **b** grasp
16. **c** unsure
17. **b** neglect
18. **a** ignorance
19. **b** ordinary
20. **c** easygoing

UNIT 7
1. **a** delicate
2. **c** imitate
3. **c** explore
4. **a** accuse
5. **b** triumph
6. pierce
7. coast
8. clever
9. symbol
10. rare
11. **a** examine
12. **c** glide
13. **b** resemble
14. **c** sign
15. **a** penetrate
16. **b** coarse
17. **c** slow
18. **a** absolve
19. **c** usual
20. **b** lose

UNIT 8
1. **b** climate
2. **b** remote
3. **c** expose
4. **a** custom
5. **c** disturb
6. timid
7. decay
8. cling
9. ancient
10. perform
11. **b** weather
12. **c** decompose
13. **b** secluded
14. **a** fulfill
15. **c** tradition
16. **b** release
17. **a** soothe
18. **a** recent
19. **c** mask
20. **c** daring

Form B continued

UNIT 9

1. **c** consider
2. **a** ability
3. **c** avoid
4. **b** brief
5. **b** delightful
6. honor
7. remark
8. bashful
9. compete
10. reflex
11. **a** strive
12. **b** statement
13. **c** esteem
14. **a** ponder
15. **b** response
16. **c** seek
17. **a** lengthy
18. **b** bold
19. **c** unpleasant
20. **a** powerlessness

Midyear Test (UNITS 1–9)

1. patient
2. harsh
3. vary
4. delightful
5. shatter
6. triumph
7. drift
8. custom
9. capture
10. avoid
11. loyal
12. prefer
13. imitate
14. precious
15. border
16. no change: consider
17. passage
18. climate
19. perform
20. no change: remark
21. clever
22. clasp
23. talent
24. no change: value
25. atmosphere
26. **c**
27. **b**
28. **a**
29. **a**
30. **c**
31. **d**
32. **b**
33. **a**
34. **b**
35. **c**
36. restless
37. sensitive
38. coward
39. fierce
40. active
41. shallow
42. convince
43. exclaim
44. accuse
45. coast
46. brief
47. ability
48. allow
49. mild
50. common

UNIT 10

1. **a** actual
2. **c** chill
3. **b** fury
4. **c** wit
5. **a** fortunate
6. conquer
7. vibrant
8. brink
9. intend
10. pattern
11. **b** edge
12. **c** system
13. **c** mean
14. **b** overcome
15. **a** anger
16. **a** defrost
17. **c** stupidity
18. **b** lifeless
19. **b** nonexistent
20. **a** unlucky

UNIT 11

1. **a** tradition
2. **c** approve
3. **b** prompt
4. **c** glory
5. **b** magnificent
6. meek
7. wreckage
8. approach
9. watchful
10. revive
11. **a** ruins
12. **c** practice
13. **b** renew
14. **a** impressive
15. **c** attitude
16. **b** reject
17. **c** disgrace
18. **b** outspoken
19. **a** delayed
20. **c** unaware

UNIT 12

1. **c** prevent
2. **a** scorn
3. **c** audible
4. **b** representative
5. **b** consume
6. origin
7. woe
8. glide
9. stout
10. punctuate
11. **a** coast
12. **c** emphasize
13. **a** disrespect
14. **b** devour
15. **c** delegate
16. **b** weak
17. **a** joy
18. **b** end
19. **c** indistinct
20. **a** permit

UNIT 13

1. **a** valid
2. **b** grant
3. **c** declare
4. **b** grave
5. **a** modest
6. clarify
7. opponent
8. arch
9. yearn
10. authentic
11. **c** simplify
12. **b** allow
13. **a** pine
14. **b** humble
15. **c** solemn
16. **b** lesser
17. **c** teammate
18. **a** false
19. **b** counterfeit
20. **c** deny

UNIT 14

1. **b** dreary
2. **c** kindle
3. **a** admirable
4. **a** separation
5. **b** exhaust
6. distant
7. stunt
8. automatic
9. predict
10. devotion
11. **c** loyalty
12. **b** expect
13. **c** excite
14. **a** mechanical
15. **b** bleak
16. **a** enliven
17. **c** connection
18. **b** stimulate
19. **b** mediocre
20. **c** warm

UNIT 15

1. **b** barrier
2. **a** abundant
3. **b** penalize
4. **c** inquire
5. **a** privilege
6. slumber
7. formal
8. predator
9. conceive
10. picturesque
11. **a** ask
12. **c** imagine
13. **b** scenic
14. **b** honor
15. **a** thief
16. **b** entrance
17. **c** casual
18. **c** reward
19. **a** meager
20. **b** stir

UNIT 16

1. **c** defiant
2. **a** advantage
3. **c** purify
4. **b** negotiate
5. **b** imply
6. fearsome
7. merit
8. wretched
9. ambition
10. revoke
11. **a** hint
12. **c** terrifying
13. **a** goal
14. **b** rebellious
15. **c** discuss
16. **b** fault
17. **a** drawback
18. **a** provide
19. **c** pleased
20. **b** dirty

Form B continued

UNIT 17

1. **b** amateur
2. **c** lame
3. **a** tranquil
4. **c** suspend
5. **b** grace
6. tiresome
7. absorb
8. elegant
9. inspect
10. channel
11. **a** engage
12. **b** examine
13. **c** waterway
14. **b** stop
15. **a** feeble
16. **b** coarse
17. **c** exciting
18. **b** noisy
19. **a** master
20. **c** inelegance

UNIT 18

1. **a** locate
2. **c** Infectious
3. **a** uproar
4. **b** ideal
5. **c** glisten
6. eloquent
7. sufficient
8. invest
9. boast
10. ripple
11. **b** sparkle
12. **b** wave
13. **c** spend
14. **c** contagious
15. **a** pinpoint
16. **a** sparse
17. **b** deprecate
18. **c** calmness
19. **a** awkward
20. **b** real

Final Mastery Test

1. chill
2. reflex
3. locate
4. barrier
5. tranquil
6. imply
7. meek
8. distant
9. tiresome
10. prevent
11. declare
12. uproar
13. purify
14. fortunate
15. opponent
16. exhaust
17. no change: wretched
18. arch
19. eloquent
20. no change: glisten
21. privilege
22. approach
23. clarify
24. stunt
25. suspend
26. **a**
27. **b**
28. **b**
29. **b**
30. **a**
31. **d**
32. **a**
33. **b**
34. **a**
35. **d**
36. fury
37. infectious
38. revoke
39. modest
40. yearn
41. prompt
42. picturesque
43. consume
44. woe
45. devotion
46. watchful
47. distant
48. conceive
49. amateur
50. lame

Vocabulary Workshop®

Level Green

Enriched Edition with iWords™ Audio Program

Jerry L. Johns, Ph.D.
Senior Reading Consultant

Distinguished Teaching Professor Emeritus
Department of Literacy Education
Northern Illinois University

Consultants

Joseph Czarnecki, Ph.D.
Faculty Associate, School of Education
Johns Hopkins University
Baltimore, MD

Christine Gialamas-Antonucci
Reading Specialist
Chicago Public Schools
Chicago, IL

Lucy Lugones
Technology Consultant
St. Luke's School
New York, NY

Helen Wood Turner, Ed.D.
Reading Specialist
Turning Point Academy
Lanham, MD

Sadlier

Vocabulary Workshop®

Enriched Edition with iWords™ Audio Program

Advisers

The publisher wishes to thank the following teachers and administrators, who read portions of the series prior to publication, for their comments and suggestions.

Khawla Asmar
Assistant Principal
Milwaukee, WI

Ann Jennings
English Specialist
Rustburg, VA

Megan Mayfield
Teacher
Woodstock, GA

Carolyn Branch
Lead Charter Administrator
Kansas City, MO

Amy Cristina
Teacher
Panama City, FL

Cora M. Kirby
Reading Specialist
Washington, DC

Julie Cambonga
Assistant Principal/Teacher
Sierra Madre, CA

Tara M. Gaiss
Literacy Specialist
Kings Park, NY

Lisa Mayer
Teacher
Houston, TX

Nancy Wahl
Elementary School Teacher
New York, NY

Photo Credits: Cover: pencil: Used under license from Shutterstock.com/Pedro Nogueria; wood grain on pencil: Used under license from Shutterstock.com/Christophe Testi. Interior: age fotostock/J.D. Dallet: 56 *background*. Alamy/Avico Ltd: 80 *top*; bobo: 96 *right*; Catchlight Visual Services/Denise Hager: 18 *bottom*; Cultura RM/yellowdog: 58; Geoff A. Howard: 79 *background*; imageBROKER: 110 *top*; Mooch Images Ltd: 79 *bottom right*; nobleIMAGES/David Noble: 153 *top*; Alex Segre: 18 *top*; VStock: 120. Artville: 171. Bridgeman Images/Victoria & Albert Museum, London: 99 *top*. ChinaStock/Liu Liqun/Dennis Cox: 78 *bottom left*. Dreamstime.com/Icefields: 130; Ivo13: 183; Kingjon: 68. Fotosearch/Iconotec: 142. Getty Images: 17 *right*, 133 *bottom*; AFP: 182; Asia Images Group: 8; Pallava Bagla: 110 *bottom*; Bettmann: 140, 141, 153 *bottom*; Brand X Pictures/Jupiterimages: 27 *top*; Digital Vision/Chris Windsor: 91; Kevin Fleming: 49; Stephen Frink: 151 *inset*; Todd Gipstein: 26; Hulton Archive: 163; John E. Kelly: 80 *bottom*; Layne Kennedy: 100; Bob Krist: 69 *bottom*; Library of Congress: 143; Library of Congress/T.E. Marr: 69 *top*; LOOK/Florian Werner: 121; LOOK-foto/Don Fuchs: 150 *background*, 151 *inset*; Kaz Mori: 29 *top*; Owaki-Kulla: 16 *left*; Photodisc/Jules Frazier: 64 *left*; Scott Quinn Photography: 16 *center left*; Cameron Spencer: 131 *top*; Jean-Marc Truchet: 71; The Christian Science Monitor/Melanie Stetson Freeman: 34. iStockphoto.com/45RPM: 78 *bottom right*, 79 *bottom left*; craigrobinsonphoto: 9; HultonArchive: 180 *right*; jonpic: 171 *background*; magicinfoto: 26 *background*; protocolmedia: 88 *left*; Stuartb: 118; vasiliki: 131 *bottom*; zts: 119. Levi Strauss & Co. Archives: 96 *left*. Mary Evans Picture Library/Classic Stock/C.P. Cushing: 181 *right*. Minden Pictures/NPL/Stephen Dalton: 29 *bottom*. NASA: 46-47. National Geographic Stock: 109; Jon Foster: 108 *bottom*; Amy Toesing: 108 *bottom right*. National Historic Route 66 Federation: 17 *left*. North Wind Picture Archives: 180 *left*. Photodisc: 181. Photolibrary/Blend Images/Karin Dreyer: 27 *bottom right*; Imagebroker/Christian Heinrich: 170 *bottom*; Rubberball: 162. Punchstock/Blend Images: 70; Brand X Pictures: 101; photosindia: 89 *bottom*; Rubberball: 39 *bottom*. Science Source/Jerry Schad: 48. Used under license from Shutterstock.com/Blinka: 27 *center right*; Dr_Flash: 16 *background*; J. Helgason: 181 *left*; DG Jervis: 58 *bottom*; JinYoung Lee: 118 *background*; pirita: 173; Ronald Sumners: 88 *right*, 89 *top*; Magdalena Szachowska: 39 *top*; Christophe Testi: 88 *bottom*; Tihis: 99 *bottom*. Superstock/Robert Harding Picture Library: 57. The Granger Collection, NY: 64 *right*; Rue des Archives: 182. The Image Works/Suzanne Dunn: 172; David Lassman: 90; Lee Snider: 133 *top*. Visuals Unlimited/Brandon Cole: 158.

Illustrators: Scott Angle: 160–161. Janet Broxon: 36–37. Mike Gordon: 6–7. Tim Haggerty: 9, 10, 38, 40, 90, 92, 143,144. Martin Lemelman: 19, 20, 42, 49, 50, 74, 101, 102 124, 126, 156, 163, 188. Bob Ostrom: 22, 59, 60, 111, 112, 183, 184. Zina Saunders: 32, 52, 71, 72, 84 *top*, 94, 120, 122, 136, 152, 154, 164. Daryl Stevens: 62, 104, 114, 136, 146, 166, 176, 186. Chris Vallo: 12, 28, 30, 81, 82, 132, 134, 173, 174.

For additional online resources, go to **vocabularyworkshop.com** and enter the Student Access Code VWL11S9FBQT4.

Address inquiries to Permissions Department, William H. Sadlier, Inc., 25 Broadway, New York, NY 10004-1010.

Printed in the United States of America.
ISBN: 978-0-8215-8003-5
11 12 13 14 15 BRR 24 23 22 21 20

Note to the Student

Most of the vocabulary words in **Level Green** will be new to you. Some words you may recognize. Others you may not know at all. The words have been chosen because they are words you will come across often. You will see them in schoolbooks and on tests. You will see them in books and magazines, as well as on the Internet. You will also hear them spoken by teachers and others in a variety of professions.

In each of the 18 units, you will read a passage that contains the 10 unit words. You will see and hear how the words are used in the passage. Then you will learn more about them, including their definitions, pronunciations, parts of speech, and how they are used in sentences. You will also find synonyms and antonyms for the words. As you complete the pages in the unit, not only will you practice using the words, but you will also show what you know about them.

Each unit also helps you build vocabulary beyond the unit words. For example, in **Word Study**, you will learn how to use word parts (prefixes, suffixes, roots) to figure out the meanings of unfamiliar words. In **Shades of Meaning**, you will learn some phrases that have special meanings. You will also learn some idioms.

When you have finished this book, your vocabulary will have grown. All the words you have learned will be part of your personal vocabulary, helping you to become a better reader, writer, and speaker.

Interactive Online Activities

Don't forget to look at the online activities that extend and enrich the instruction and practice contained in **Level Green**. Access to these free activities and more is available at vocabularyworkshop.com.

Contents

UNIT 1

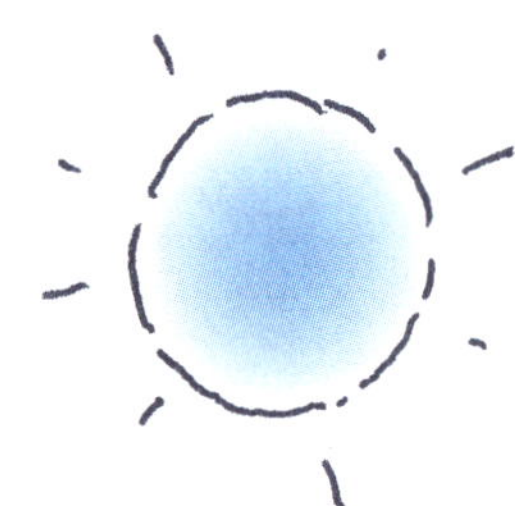

Introducing the Words

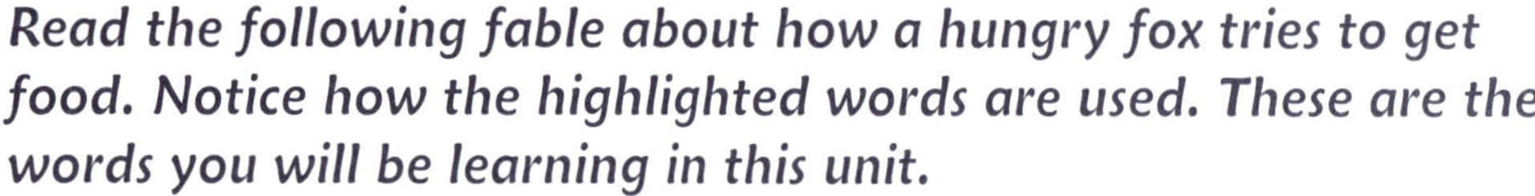

Read the following fable about how a hungry fox tries to get food. Notice how the highlighted words are used. These are the words you will be learning in this unit.

The Fox and the Grapes

(an Aesop Fable)

On a hot summer afternoon, a fox became quite hungry and thirsty. Eagerly, he began to search for his next meal. He looked up and spotted a vine of grapes hanging from a tall tree. As he stared at the juicy fruit, his mouth watered. These grapes were not the common, small green grapes he usually found. Each one was as big as a red plum.

"Ah!" he said. "Red grapes! I truly prefer the red grapes to the green ones! The red grapes are so much sweeter."

He stood up on his back legs and sniffed the grapes. Then he tried to pull them down. Unfortunately, that didn't work. The fox scratched his head and wondered what he should do next. Climbing the tree was out of the question. Still, the grapes were too high to allow him to reach them. He would have to use his strong legs to leap up and snatch a bunch.

He walked back several yards and then ran toward the grapes. He pumped his legs and jumped up with all the force he could gather, but he missed the vine. Instead, he tumbled into a nearby mud puddle.

Now the fox was hungrier than ever. His stomach rumbled like a freight train. He said, "I must try again!"

He walked back twenty yards this time. Then he ran faster toward his goal—the bunch of ripe, juicy grapes. Alas, his second try was no better than the first. He hit his head on the firm ground and then rolled head over heels. He sat on a tree stump and rubbed his head. Hitting the ground like that had given him a horrible headache.

This particular fox had never been a patient creature, and now his hunger was making him anxious and grumpy. He had to get those grapes.

The fox stood up once more, but his legs were unsteady. He wobbled backward and felt a little faint. He sat on the ground until he felt stronger. Finally, there was only a trace of a headache left.

He walked back fifty yards this time. Then he ran full speed ahead. He jumped up, but he missed the grapes and fell into a patch of thorny bushes.

"Ouch!" the fox yelled.

He pulled himself out of the patch. Twigs with thorns tore at his fur, and he howled with each step he took. Then he shook his fist at the grapes.

He yelled, "What a dumb bunch of grapes! Let someone else eat you. I bet you're bitter anyway!"

And with that, he walked away in a huff.

Moral: *It is easier to pretend you do not want what you cannot get.*

Definitions

You were introduced to the words below in the passage on pages 6–7. Study the spelling, pronunciation, part of speech, and definition of each word. Write the word on the line in the sentence. Then read the synonyms and antonyms.

Remember

A **noun** *(n.)* is a word that names a person, place, or thing.

A **verb** *(v.)* is a word or words that express action or a state of being.

An **adjective** *(adj.)* is a word that describes a noun or pronoun.

1. allow (ə lau̇′)

(v.) to let do or happen; to agree

My parents allow *me to ride my bike in good weather.*

SYNONYM: permit
ANTONYMS: forbid, prevent

2. bitter (bit′ ər)

(adj.) sharp and unpleasant; angry or hurt

The unripe fruit tasted bitter.

SYNONYM: harsh
ANTONYMS: sweet, mild

3. common (käm′ ən)

(adj.) found often; average

A cat is a common *pet.*

SYNONYMS: familiar, ordinary
ANTONYMS: unusual, odd

4. faint (fānt)

(v.) to pass out

The hot sun made the dancer faint *on stage.*

(adj.) not clear; weak

The writing was so faint *that I had trouble reading it.*

SYNONYMS: (adj.) unclear, slight, faded
ANTONYMS: (adj.) clear, strong

5. firm (fûrm)

(adj.) solid; steady or strong

The climber kept a firm *grip on the rope.*

(n.) a business or small company

My mother works at a law firm.

SYNONYM: (adj.) hard
ANTONYMS: (adj.) soft; weak

6. force (fôrs)

(n.) strength; power

The ____**force**____ *of the wind knocked over the tree.*

(v.) to cause to do something by using strength or power

Firefighters must sometimes ____**force**____ *their way into a burning building.*

SYNONYMS: (n.) might; (v.) make, push
ANTONYM: (n.) weakness

7. goal (gōl)

(n.) something a person wants and works for; the area into which players must move a ball or puck in order to score in some sports

My ____**goal**____ *in life is to become a scientist.*

SYNONYMS: (n.) target, aim, plan

8. patient (pā′ shənt)

(n.) a person getting medical care

The ____**patient**____ *had to stay in the hospital.*

(adj.) able to stay calm when faced with pain, trouble, or a long wait

My teacher was ____**patient**____ *as I learned the new song.*

ANTONYMS: (adj.) impatient, anxious

9. prefer (pri fûr′)

(v.) to like better than others; to tend to choose

I ____**prefer**____ *summer to winter.*

10. trace (trās)

(n.) a small amount left behind showing that something was there

The air had only a ____**trace**____ *of smoke after the fire.*

(v.) to copy by following over the lines of something as seen through a sheet of paper

If you want to copy a design, you can ____**trace**____ *it.*

SYNONYMS: (n.) mark, sign, track; (v.) outline

Match the Meaning

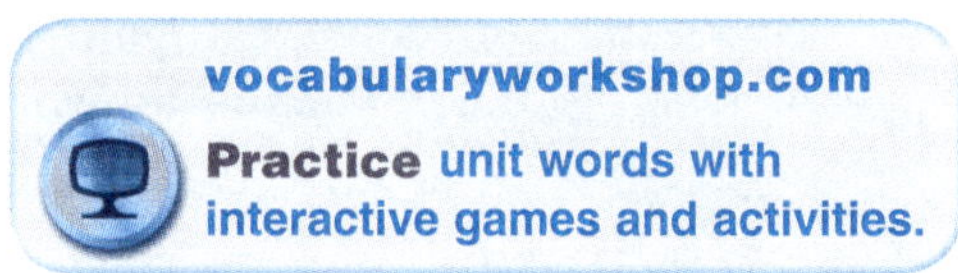

Choose the word whose meaning is suggested by the clue given. Then write the word on the line provided.

1. If you ____prefer____ tacos to pizza, you like tacos better.
a. force b. prefer c. trace

2. A soccer field has a ____goal____ on each end.
a. goal b. trace c. patient

3. When many people have the same name, the name is ____common____.
a. common b. faint c. firm

4. If your parents ____allow____ you to stay up late, they give you permission to do so.
a. trace b. force c. allow

5. A ____bitter____ person may feel angry because of a bad experience.
a. firm b. bitter c. common

6. To be ____patient____ is to be calm and understanding.
a. bitter b. faint c. patient

7. ____Faint____ pencil marks are light and difficult to see.
a. Faint b. Patient c. Firm

8. If you ____force____ open a box, you use your strength to get inside it.
a. force b. faint c. trace

9. About twenty-five people work at the ____firm____.
a. firm b. goal c. patient

10. When you ____trace____ a design, you draw over its lines on another sheet of paper.
a. allow b. trace c. prefer

The soccer player kicked the ball into the **goal**.

Synonyms

*Choose the word that is most nearly the **same** in meaning as the word or phrase in **dark print**. Then write your choice on the line provided.*

1. the **strength** of the wind
a. force b. goal c. patient ____force____

2. like dogs **more than** cats
a. allow b. prefer c. force ____prefer____

3. outline a shape
a. allow b. force c. trace ____trace____

4. a **dim** light
a. bitter b. common c. faint ____faint____

5. a coach who is **understanding**
a. patient b. firm c. bitter ____patient____

6. with a **plan** of finishing early
a. trace b. firm c. goal ____goal____

Antonyms

*Choose the word that is most nearly **opposite** in meaning to the word or phrase in **dark print**. Then write your choice on the line provided.*

1. a **weak** handshake
a. patient b. firm c. faint ____firm____

2. forbid a change in plans
a. trace b. prefer c. allow ____allow____

3. an **unusual** insect
a. common b. faint c. firm ____common____

4. a **sweet** fruit
a. bitter b. patient c. common ____bitter____

Completing the Sentence

Choose the word from the box that best completes each item below. Then write the word on the line provided. (You may have to change the word's ending.)

allow	**bitter**	**common**
faint	**firm**	**force**
goal	**patient**	
prefer	**trace**	

The Broken Arm

- It was a great day for a soccer game. I took my position in the ____goal____.
- A player ran toward me with great ____force____.
- I did not want to ____allow____ anyone to score.
- She gave the ball a ____firm____ kick with her right foot.
- I stopped the ball, but I heard a cracking sound in my arm. The pain was so bad that I thought I was going to ____faint____.
- Soon I was at the hospital. I went from being a player to being a ____patient____.

Spinach Power

- Many people think spinach is too ____bitter____, but I think it is delicious!
- Some people ____prefer____ to eat spinach raw in a salad. Others like cooked spinach.
- It is ____common____ to cook spinach with eggs.
- I like spinach steamed with a ____trace____ of garlic.

Word Associations

Circle the letter next to the choice that best completes the sentence or answers the question. Pay special attention to the word in dark print.

1. What can make you **bitter**?
- a. winning a prize
- b. riding a bike
- c. visiting a friend
- d. losing a race

2. If you **prefer** milk to water, you
- a. would rather drink water.
- b. would rather drink milk.
- c. think milk tastes bad.
- d. don't like milk.

3. A **faint** light is
- a. strong.
- b. very bright.
- c. easy to see.
- d. hard to see.

4. If you **trace** your hand, you
- a. outline it.
- b. color on it.
- c. shake it.
- d. slap it.

5. What may your parents say if they **allow** you to do something?
- a. "It's okay with us."
- b. "You're not old enough."
- c. "We don't think that's a good idea."
- d. "Maybe some other time."

6. Which of these has a strong **force**?
- a. a breeze
- b. a feather
- c. a hurricane
- d. a snow flurry

7. A **patient** person probably
- a. yells a lot.
- b. never feels calm.
- c. doesn't complain too much.
- d. can't sit still.

8. Which of these is **firm**?
- a. a flower
- b. water
- c. mud
- d. frozen ground

9. A **common** mistake is a mistake that
- a. few people make.
- b. is very dangerous.
- c. many people have made before.
- d. has been made for the first time.

10. If your sister met her **goal**, she might say,
- a. "I did it!"
- b. "I can't read these two books by tomorrow."
- c. "I think I can do it."
- d. "I wish I hadn't done that."

For teaching suggestions, see page T29.

Word Study • Dictionary: Multiple-Meaning Words

A **multiple-meaning word** is a word with more than one meaning. One example from this unit is *goal* (page 9). If you look up *goal* in a dictionary, you will find an entry with numbers showing the word's different meanings.

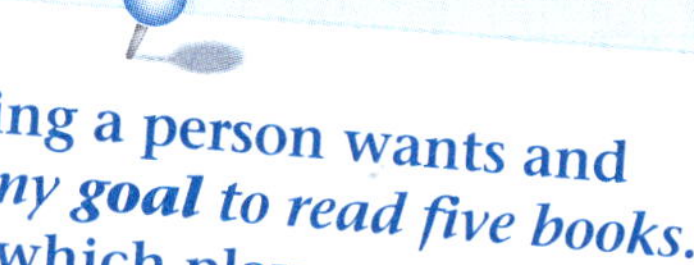

goal 1. something a person wants and works for: *It is my **goal** to read five books.* **2.** the area into which players must move a ball or puck in order to score in some sports: *A hockey **goal** is four feet high.*

Read this sentence: *I ran toward the soccer **goal.*** You can tell from the dictionary entries for *goal* that this sentence uses meaning 2 of *goal*.

Look at the chart to find other examples of multiple-meaning words.

bound	1. to leap; spring 2. held together by ties
store	1. a place where things are sold 2. to gather and keep for future use
tire	1. to use up strength or energy 2. a rubber covering that fits around a wheel

PRACTICE *Write the word from the chart above that best completes each sentence. Then write the number of the meaning.*

__2__ **1.** The robber was __bound__ by his hands.

__1__ **2.** I took a nap so I wouldn't __tire__ easily.

__2__ **3.** A cactus plant can __store__ water in its stem.

__1__ **4.** We watched the deer __bound__ across the lawn.

APPLY *Write a sentence for each word below. Be sure the sentence shows one of the meanings in the chart.*

Accept reasonable answers that demonstrate the meanings.

5. bound ______________________________

6. store ______________________________

7. tire ______________________________

Think of two meanings for each word below. Then use one of the words in a sentence. Ask your partner to tell what the word means.

bat **fly**

For teaching suggestions, see page T35.

Shades of Meaning • Words That Describe How Things Taste

In the passage "The Fox and the Grapes" on pages 6–7, you read this sentence: *I bet you're* ***bitter*** *anyway!* In the sentence, the fox is describing how he thinks the grapes taste. *Bitter* means the opposite of *sweet.* Both *bitter* and *sweet* describe how things taste.

Look at the words in the chart. Learning the words will help you choose the right word to use when you describe how things taste.

bitter	Foods that taste **bitter** have a sharp or unpleasant taste.
bland	Foods that are **bland** are mild and without a strong flavor.
spicy	**Spicy** foods have a strong flavor because they are made with spices, such as hot pepper.

PRACTICE *Write the name of each food under the word that best describes it.*

bread **chili** **cranberry** **grapefruit** **lime**
potato **salsa** **sausage** **white rice**

bitter	bland	spicy
1. lime	4. potato	7. sausage
2. cranberry	5. white rice	8. chili
3. grapefruit	6. bread	9. salsa

APPLY *Use* ***bitter***, ***bland***, *or* ***spicy*** *to complete each sentence so that it makes sense.*

Accept reasonable answers. Possible answers are given.

10. I had to drink lots of water after I ate a spicy taco.

11. I knew it was a grapefruit because it tasted bitter.

12. When I felt sick, I could only eat bland foods like white toast.

Introducing the Words

Read the following magazine article about a famous American highway. Notice how the highlighted words are used. These are the words you will be learning in this unit.

Driving on Route 66

(Magazine Article)

Most likely, the street you live on is smooth and paved, not rough and dusty. But are you aware that paved roads were not always so common? About a hundred years ago, if you wanted to travel, your horse and buggy would use a dirt road. Sometimes, these roads were little more than trails. Their paths drifted this way and that.

In 1908, the Model T Ford was introduced to Americans. This was the first car that people could afford to buy. However, roads that were made for horses weren't good enough for cars. A car had a solid body, and it weighed a lot. It could get stuck when it was driven on a muddy road. An entire trip could be ruined.

In 1916, Congress set aside money to build roads. Later, a paved route that started in chilly Chicago was mapped out. It would go through Oklahoma and end in warm, sunny Los Angeles. The road was named Route 66. In 1938, the last section of the road was paved.

Route 66 was a popular highway. Many people were tired of long, cold winters. Their aim was to move to a place with mild weather. They used Route 66 to travel west. Truckers carrying goods used Route 66, too. Motels and restaurants popped up along the highway.

Over the next thirty years, many people used Route 66. It was nicknamed "Main Street of America." There was even a popular television show called *Route 66*.

Then came much bigger highways that crossed the country. People were buying newer and faster cars. They wanted better roads and more lanes. By the 1980s, these big highways were in place. That was the beginning of the end for Route 66.

Today, Route 66 is no longer a main route westward, but it refuses to disappear. Drivers traveling west on other roads might take a side trip and travel along Route 66. Once there, they might pause at the stores and motels that are still open. There won't be many, though, because many towns have disappeared. Many buildings are empty, and people have moved away.

Route 66 is a story of both success and defeat. It was an important road for many years, but then its importance faded. Many people still seek out Route 66 to discover what life on the highway once was like.

In the early days, people often traveled together.

Definitions

You were introduced to the words below in the passage on pages 16–17. Study the spelling, pronunciation, part of speech, and definition of each word. Write the word on the line in the sentence. Then read the synonyms and antonyms.

Remember

A **noun** *(n.)* is a word that names a person, place, or thing.

A **verb** *(v.)* is a word or words that express action or a state of being.

An **adjective** *(adj.)* is a word that describes a noun or pronoun.

1. aim (ām)

(v.) to point or direct at a target

In archery, you should ____aim____ *for the center of the target.*

(n.) a purpose or goal

My ____aim____ *was to win the state spelling bee.*

SYNONYMS: (v. & n.) plan, target

2. aware (ə wâr′)

(adj.) knowing or realizing

We were ____aware____ *that it was getting late.*

SYNONYM: knowledgeable

3. defeat (di fēt′)

(v.) to beat in a game or battle

The Tigers hoped to ____defeat____ *the Bears in the last game.*

(n.) loss; failure

The ____defeat____ *was difficult for the player because she had worked so hard.*

SYNONYMS: (v.) conquer, overcome; (n.) downfall
ANTONYM: (n.) win

4. drift (drift)

(v.) to be carried away by water or air

The balloon began to ____drift____ *away from the child.*

SYNONYMS: float; wander, stray

5. mild (mīld)

(adj.) gentle, not harsh

The doctor spoke to the young child in a ___mild___ *tone of voice.*

SYNONYMS: calm; warm; ANTONYM: strong

6. pause (pôz)

(v.) to stop for a short time

Let's ___pause___ *to think about what happened.*

(n.) a short stop

There was a ___pause___ *between two scenes in the play.*

SYNONYMS: (v.) halt; (n.) break
ANTONYMS: (v.) continue, proceed

7. refuse (ri fyüz')

(v.) to not accept or agree to something

I ___refuse___ *to admit that I was wrong.*

SYNONYMS: deny, reject
ANTONYMS: accept, agree

8. route (rüt) or (raůt)

(n.) a road or way of travel between two places

My bus takes the quickest ___route___ *to school.*

SYNONYMS: path, course

9. ruin (rü' in)

(v.) to destroy or damage something

Big waves will ___ruin___ *my sand castle.*

SYNONYMS: break, wreck, spoil
ANTONYMS: save, fix, restore

10. solid (sä' lid)

(adj.) having shape and hardness; not liquid or gas; very strong and reliable

After the boat ride, I was happy to be back on ___solid___ *ground.*

SYNONYMS: hard, firm; ANTONYMS: weak, flimsy

Match the Meaning

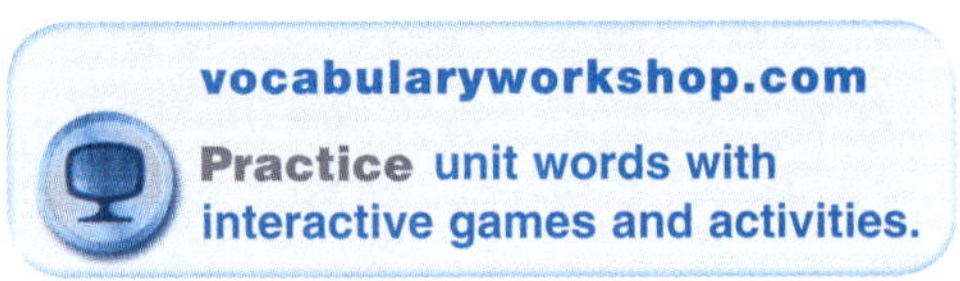

Choose the word whose meaning is suggested by the clue given. Then write the word on the line provided.

1. To ___ruin___ a house is to destroy it.
a. ruin b. aim c. drift

2. A ___route___ is a path from one place to another.
a. pause b. defeat c. route

3. When you ___pause___ a video, you stop it for a little while.
a. aim b. ruin c. pause

4. To ___drift___ is to float away.
a. pause b. drift c. defeat

5. ___Mild___ weather is warm and pleasant.
a. Aware b. Solid c. Mild

6. When you shoot a basketball, you should ___aim___ for the hoop.
a. refuse b. aim c. pause

7. Ice is the ___solid___ form of water.
a. solid b. aware c. mild

8. If you are ___aware___ of the danger, you know about it.
a. mild b. solid c. aware

9. When you ___defeat___ someone in checkers, you win the game.
a. aim b. defeat c. refuse

10. If you ___refuse___ to answer a question, you do not answer it.
a. refuse b. defeat c. pause

The artist carved a toy from a **solid** block of wood.

Synonyms

*Choose the word that is most nearly the **same** in meaning as the word or phrase in **dark print**. Then write your choice on the line provided.*

1. **beat** the other team
   a. refuse b. defeat c. drift defeat

2. **point** at the target
   a. drift b. aim c. refuse aim

3. take a new **way**
   a. route b. pause c. defeat route

4. a **strong and thick** door
   a. solid b. mild c. aware solid

5. **wander** away from the group
   a. drift b. ruin c. defeat drift

Antonyms

*Choose the word that is most nearly **opposite** in meaning to the word or phrase in **dark print**. Then write your choice on the line provided.*

1. **accept** the invitation
   a. aim b. defeat c. refuse refuse

2. **fix** a drawing
   a. pause b. ruin c. aim ruin

3. a **cold** winter
   a. mild b. solid c. aware mild

4. **continue** the game
   a. pause b. aim c. defeat pause

5. **not know** that Dad was waiting
   a. solid b. aware c. mild aware

Completing the Sentence

Choose the word from the box that best completes each item below. Then write the word on the line provided. (You may have to change the word's ending.)

aim	aware	defeat
drift	mild	pause
refuse	route	
ruin	solid	

Body Boarding

- During ____mild____ weather at the beach, you might try body boarding.
- Body boards look like small surfboards. They are usually made out of ____solid____ foam.
- Make sure the body board will not ____drift____ away if you fall off.
- Wade out into the water until it reaches your waist. When a good wave comes, ____aim____ your board toward the shore and jump on.
- Be ____aware____ of other people around you, so you don't crash into them.

The Rainy Parade

- If there's one thing that can ____ruin____ a parade, it's rain.
- Last summer, we ____refused____ to let the weather stop us from going to the Fourth of July parade.
- We grabbed our raincoats and umbrellas and found a great spot along the parade ____route____.
- As we watched, there were a few ____pauses____ in the rainfall.
- We cheered for the soaking wet musicians and performers marching by. We were so glad we didn't let the rain ____defeat____ us!

Word Associations

Circle the letter next to the choice that best completes the sentence or answers the question. Pay special attention to the word in dark print.

1. If you **refuse** to do something, you might say,
a. "It would be my pleasure."
b. "Can you help me with this?"
c. "I'll never do that!"
d. "I guess I could do it."

2. Which of these is **solid**?
a. a bubble
b. a rock
c. a raindrop
d. a cloud

3. If you **defeat** someone in a race, you might
a. cheer.
b. frown.
c. be upset.
d. complain.

4. To find a **route** to your friend's house, you can look
a. in a dictionary.
b. at a compass.
c. at a map.
d. in a science book.

5. If a team wants to **pause** a game, they might ask,
a. "May we take a time-out?"
b. "Which player scored?"
c. "What's the score?"
d. "How can we win?"

6. If your **aim** is to play in the band, you should
a. practice your instrument.
b. give up your instrument.
c. watch TV all day.
d. skip your music lessons.

7. What might **ruin** a good day?
a. getting an A on a test
b. scoring a goal in a game
c. winning an art prize
d. falling in a mud puddle

8. A dog with a **mild** manner might
a. nip at you.
b. sleep on your lap.
c. bark all day.
d. snap at the mail carrier.

9. If scientists are **aware** that a storm is coming, they
a. don't know about it
b. can stop it from happening.
c. have no information about it.
d. can warn people about it.

10. A boat in the lake may **drift** because
a. it's near a lot of boats.
b. it's not tied to the pier.
c. it's late in the day.
d. it's a calm day.

For teaching suggestions, see page T29.

Word Study • Context Clues 1

When you read, you may come across words that you do not know. When this happens, look for **context clues** in the sentence to help you figure out the word's meaning. Sometimes, a sentence will give the definition of the word you do not know. Look at the example below.

Definition	*The short, sharp points on the stem of a rose are called* ***thorns****.* The words ***short****,* ***sharp points*** tell what ***thorns*** means.

PRACTICE *Read each sentence. Write the meaning of the word in* ***dark print*** *on the line.*

1. A **gust** is a sudden blast of wind. a sudden blast of wind
2. She didn't want to **rumple**, or wrinkle, her new skirt. wrinkle
3. He is a **pirate**, a person who robs people on ships. a person who robs people on ships
4. A boat sails on the **surface**, or top part, of the ocean. top part
5. The children sat on the **stoop**, a small staircase that leads to the entrance of a house. a small staircase that leads to the entrance of a house

APPLY *Read each sentence. Underline the words that help you figure out the meaning of the word in* ***dark print****. Then write a new sentence for the word to show that you understand its meaning.*
Accept answers that use the word correctly in context.

6. The four campers floated down the river on a wooden **raft**, a kind of flat boat.

   ____

7. We could hear the **lark**, a song bird, chirping in the early morning.

   ____

8. The **tutor**, a person who gives private lessons, helped me with my writing project.

   ____

Choose a word from the dictionary. Make up a sentence using that word. Make sure your sentence provides good context clues. Ask your partner to figure out the meaning of the word.

For teaching suggestions, see page T35.

Shades of Meaning • Literal and Nonliteral Meanings

In the passage "Driving on Route 66" on pages 16–17, you read that Route 66 was a popular highway for many years. Then faster cars were built, and drivers needed wider lanes for driving. These events helped to **drive home** the need for bigger highways. In this sentence, the phrase *drive home* has a special meaning. It means "to make a strong point."

Now read this sentence: *Yesterday, we had to* ***drive home*** *in the heavy rain.* In this sentence, the words *drive* and *home* have their dictionary meanings. Here, *drive home* has nothing to do with making a point about something.

Look at the words in the first column of the chart below. The words can be thought of as individual words or as phrases. The meanings, when used as words or as phrases, are given in the second column.

take steps	**1.** to move by foot **2.** to take action in order to make something happen or to stop something
turned the corner	**1.** to change the direction you are moving by going around the place where two roads or walls meet **2.** to get better after a difficult time
set aside	**1.** to place out of the way **2.** to save for some reason

PRACTICE *Read each sentence. Look at the words in* ***dark print.*** *Decide which meaning from the chart above is shown. Write the number of the meaning on the line.*

__2__ **1.** We **took steps** to protect our house from storm damage.

__1__ **2.** We **set aside** our homework to set the table for dinner.

__1__ **3.** She **took steps** slowly along the balance beam.

__2__ **4.** I knew I had **turned the corner** when my fever went down.

__2__ **5.** Each week, I **set aside** some of my allowance to help pay for camp.

__1__ **6.** The runner **turned the corner** and raced to the finish line.

APPLY *Write a sentence to show one meaning of the words in* ***dark print.*** *Use those words in your sentence.*
Accept reasonable answers.

7. take steps ____________________________________

8. turned the corner ____________________________________

Introducing the Words

Read the following magazine article about ways to help save natural resources. Notice how the highlighted words are used. These are the words you will be learning in this unit.

Going Green Every Day

(Magazine Article)

Do you want to help save the earth? You can, and it doesn't have to be a struggle. Doing little things every day can really help.

Do you recycle? Recycling helps save Earth's resources. Setting aside paper takes only a few moments, but it can save many trees. Many bottles and cans are returnable for money. You can get five cents or more when you return them to the store. Check the label of these containers to find their return value. Once recycled, paper, bottles, and cans can be used again.

Do you reuse items you already have? Can you bring your lunch in a paper bag? Every bag you use a second time doesn't cost you an extra penny. Now that's a bargain! Think of other items that you can reuse. Tell your family members about them. Listen to them gasp at your ideas.

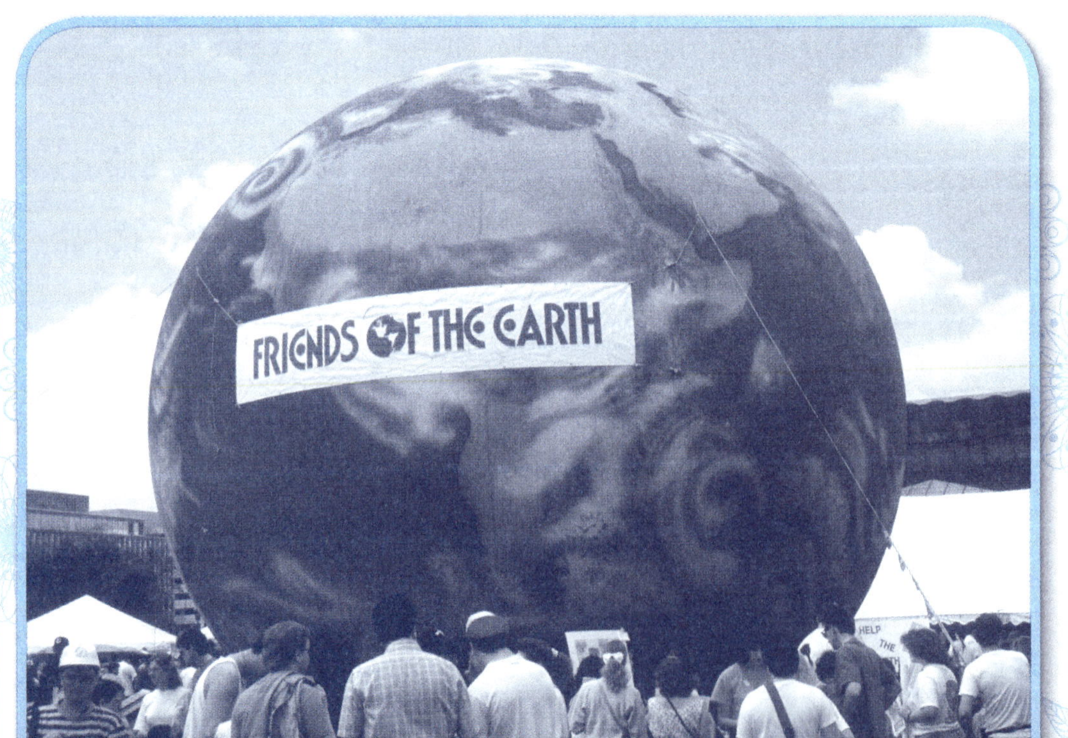

Did you know that you can clean most of the things in your house with water, vinegar, and baking soda? Many people are sensitive to chemical cleaners. These products can cause allergies or skin problems. Baking soda and vinegar are not harmful, yet they can clean sinks, floors, and other big surfaces. These simple, natural cleaners cost less, too.

Water is a natural resource. When you brush your teeth, don't wander away and leave the water running. Turn it off. Reduce the amount of water you use. You will save two gallons or more. You can also reduce the amount of electricity you use by turning off the lights when you leave a room.

Be loyal to your local farmers' markets. Many fruits and vegetables are grown far away. They travel on ships and trucks to get to where you live. Farmers who sell their goods at the local farmers' market don't have to travel as far to bring you your food. Buying from them saves a lot of gas and oil.

Cleaning up your town on Earth Day is a great way to become active in your community. Most towns clear litter from parks, roads, and the banks of rivers on Earth Day. Next April, see what you can do to help!

Going green is as easy as taking a walk and enjoying the outdoors. Vary your walks to see something new each time. Watch a small animal and see where it goes. Nature is a never-ending show, and watching it requires no electricity!

Definitions

Remember

A **noun** *(n.)* is a word that names a person, place, or thing.

A **verb** *(v.)* is a word or words that express action or a state of being.

An **adjective** *(adj.)* is a word that describes a noun or pronoun.

You were introduced to the words below in the passage on pages 26–27. Study the spelling, pronunciation, part of speech, and definition of each word. Write the word on the line in the sentence. Then read the synonyms and antonyms.

1. active (ak′ tiv)

(adj.) taking action; full of movement

To be healthy, it is important to stay active.

SYNONYMS: lively, busy, energetic
ANTONYMS: slow, lazy, passive

2. bargain (bär′ gən)

(n.) an agreement between two people or groups; something sold cheaply; a good deal

The baseball cards were a bargain *at $1 a pack.*

(v.) to ask for a lower price; to agree to sell something for less

Not many store owners like to bargain *with customers.*

SYNONYMS: (n.) "steal"; (v.) haggle

3. gasp (gasp)

(v.) to breathe in quickly or have trouble breathing because of fear or shock; to catch one's breath

I'm sure you're going to gasp *when you see the scary part of the movie.*

(n.) the act of gasping or panting

We heard the sound of a gasp *as the runner crossed the finish line.*

SYNONYM: (v.) pant

4. loyal (loi′ əl)

(adj.) faithful to one's country, a person, or an idea

The loyal *soldier was proud to serve her country.*

ANTONYMS: unfaithful, treacherous

5. resource (rē′ sôrs)

(n.) a source of useful supplies, materials, or information

An encyclopedia is a valuable resource.

SYNONYM: supply

6. sensitive
(sen′ sə tiv)

(adj.) reacting to something quickly; easily hurt or bothered

My teeth are ___sensitive___ *to cold drinks.*

SYNONYMS: touchy, delicate
ANTONYMS: insensitive, uncaring

7. struggle
(strug′ əl)

(n.) an enormous effort or attempt; a battle

It was a ___struggle___ *to climb the mountain.*

(v.) to try hard; to make a great effort; to fight

The father had to ___struggle___ *to win the tug-of-war.*

SYNONYMS: (v.) strive, wrestle

8. value
(val′ yü)

(n.) something important; the worth of something; an amount

I did not know the ___value___ *of the painting.*

(v.) to estimate the worth of; to think highly of

I ___value___ *your opinion because you are so wise.*

SYNONYMS: (n.) importance; (v.) assess, price; treasure
ANTONYMS: (v.) scorn, reject

9. vary
(vâr′ ē)

(v.) to do in a new way; to make different; to change

To make lunch interesting, ___vary___ *your choice of vegetables.*

SYNONYM: alter

10. wander
(wän′ dər)

(v.) to move around without a plan or goal; to get lost

Did you see the deer ___wander___ *into our backyard?*

SYNONYMS: roam, ramble, stray
ANTONYMS: stay, remain

Match the Meaning

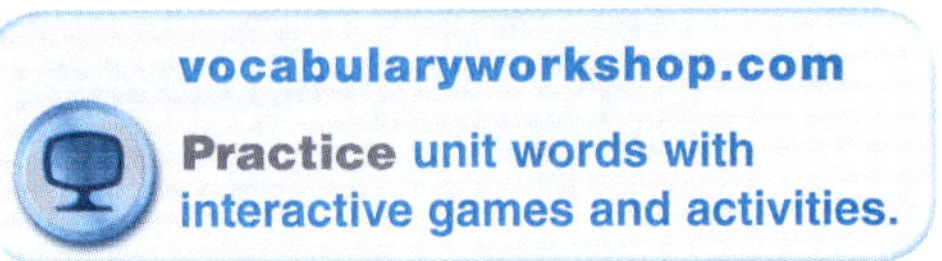

Choose the word whose meaning is suggested by the clue given. Then write the word on the line provided.

1. To be ______loyal______ to your country is to be faithful to it.
a. active b. loyal c. sensitive

2. When you ______vary______ your tasks, you change them.
a. gasp b. wander c. vary

3. A source of useful materials is a ______resource______.
a. resource b. gasp c. bargain

4. If you ______wander______ off without thinking, you can get lost.
a. gasp b. struggle c. wander

5. To ______gasp______ is to take in a deep breath.
a. bargain b. gasp c. vary

6. Soccer is a(n) ______active______ sport because the players run a lot.
a. loyal b. sensitive c. active

7. The worth of a car will tell you its ______value______.
a. struggle b. resource c. value

8. ______Sensitive______ people can get their feelings hurt easily.
a. Sensitive b. Active c. Loyal

9. When you ______bargain______ for something, you often end up paying a lower price.
a. vary b. bargain c. wander

10. To work at a new and difficult job can be a ______struggle______.
a. gasp b. value c. struggle

The noise of the fireworks display caused the girl to **gasp**.

Synonyms

*Choose the word that is most nearly the **same** in meaning as the word or phrase in **dark print**. Then write your choice on the line provided.*

1. hear the jogger **pant**
a. bargain b. wander c. gasp ___gasp___

2. an **effort** to walk
a. resource b. value c. struggle ___struggle___

3. a valuable **supply**
a. bargain b. value c. resource ___resource___

4. **roam** into the woods
a. vary b. bargain c. wander ___wander___

5. **change** your direction
a. vary b. struggle c. bargain ___vary___

6. **haggle** for a better price
a. gasp b. wander c. bargain ___bargain___

Antonyms

*Choose the word that is most nearly **opposite** in meaning to the word or phrase in **dark print**. Then write your choice on the line provided.*

1. an **unfaithful** friend
a. loyal b. active c. sensitive ___loyal___

2. a **slow** morning
a. sensitive b. active c. loyal ___active___

3. an **uncaring** companion
a. sensitive b. loyal c. active ___sensitive___

4. **reject** their advice
a. bargain b. vary c. value ___value___

Completing the Sentence

Choose the word from the box that best completes each item below. Then write the word on the line provided. (You may have to change the word's ending.)

active	**bargain**	**gasp**
loyal	**resource**	**sensitive**
struggle	**value**	
vary	**wander**	

Tools

■ Our neighbor is a carpenter. If you ___wander___ into her garage, you will find many tools.

■ She knows the ___value___ of tools. She takes care of them so that they will last a long time.

■ Our neighbor often buys paint. She is ___loyal___ to her favorite brand of paint and won't buy any other kind. She is happy to find out that the price of paint in the new hardware store is a ___bargain___. She used to pay much more for the same paint in other stores.

■ Carpenters are physically ___active___. They move around a lot while they work.

Seasons

■ In the summer, the weather in the mountains can ___vary___. It might be hot in the morning, rainy in the early afternoon, and cool in the evening.

■ People with ___sensitive___ skin can get bad sunburns in the summer if they don't wear sunscreen.

■ Flowers bloom in the spring and summer. They need water, a natural ___resource___, in order to grow.

■ It can be a ___struggle___ getting to school when there is a snowstorm. It's hard to walk or to drive.

■ Your first breath of the icy air can make you ___gasp___.

For teaching suggestions, see page T29.

Word Study • Word Families

A **word family** is a group of related words that share a basic word part but that have different endings. The words *loyal* (page 28), *loyalty*, and *loyally* all belong to the same word family.

loyal	faithful to one's country, a person, or an idea
loyalty	the quality of being loyal
loyally	doing something in a loyal way

The words in a family share some meaning. If you know one word in a family, you can figure out the meanings of the other words.

PRACTICE *Read each sentence. Each word in* ***dark print*** *is related to a word in the box. Underline the related word that best completes each sentence.*

act	care
collect	company
loyal	

1. I wear a red cap to baseball games to show (**action/loyalty**) to the team.
2. Please walk (**carefully/loyally**) across the wet floor.
3. My favorite (**collection/actor**) is in a new movie.
4. My dog is my best (**companion/loyalty**) on walks through the park.
5. I started (**collecting/acting**) stamps when I was six years old.
6. The (**active/careful**) child would not sit quietly in her chair.

APPLY *Add the ending in parentheses ( ) to form a related word. Then write a sentence with the new word. The first one has been done for you.*

Accept sentences that demonstrate the correct meaning.

7. **teach** (**er**) = teacher

Mr. Smith is a math teacher at the high school.

8. **friend** (**ly**) = friendly

____

9. **select** (**ed**) = selected

____

Choose two words from Units 1–3. Create a word family for each. Write the unit word. Then write all the related words you can think of. Use a dictionary to check spellings and meanings.

Example: drift, drifts, drifted, drifting, drifter

Vocabulary for Comprehension

Read the following passage in which some of the words you have studied in Units 1–3 appear in dark print. Then answer the questions on page 35.

Monkey Business

The saying *monkey business* usually means "acting silly." However, there are some real-life monkeys that are in business. They are in the business of helping people. Helping Hands is the name of the group that offers this service. At Helping Hands, the **goal** is to teach monkeys how to aid people who cannot move parts of their bodies.

Helping Hands trains capuchin (ka pü′ shin) monkeys. Capuchins have great hand skills. This makes them a perfect fit for people who need help. Also, capuchins are very **active**. They enjoy having jobs to do.

When the monkeys are young, they are sent to live in a foster home. Here, they learn what it is like to live with people. After five to ten years, the monkeys go to Monkey College. At Monkey College, the monkeys learn how to do things that disabled people need help with. They learn how to turn on lights and get food from the refrigerator. They even learn how to work a DVD player. The monkeys can put in a disc, play it, and **pause** it. They can take out the disc when it is done. It can take three to four years for a monkey to learn all the skills. The trainers must be **patient**. They must show the monkeys what to do over and over.

Capuchin monkeys are trained to develop special skills to help people.

During the classes at Monkey College, trainers pay attention to what a monkey is good at. The **aim** is to place each monkey with a person whose needs best match the monkey's skills. Once a monkey is placed in a home, it will be a **loyal** friend and helper. That's no monkey business!

Fill in the circle next to the choice that best completes the sentence or answers the question.

1. What would make another good title for this passage?
   - (a) How to Train a Monkey
   - (b) Silly Monkeys
   - (c) Monkeys Who Lend a Hand
   - (d) People Helping Monkeys

2. In this passage, a **goal** is
   - (a) a habit.
   - (b) a plan.
   - (c) an action.
   - (d) a strength.

3. Another word for **active** is
   - (a) lively.
   - (b) lazy.
   - (c) loud.
   - (d) lovely.

4. The meaning of **pause** is
   - (a) start to play.
   - (b) press hard.
   - (c) pull up.
   - (d) stop for a short time.

5. In this passage, **patient** means
   - (a) a person getting medical treatment.
   - (b) nervous.
   - (c) understanding.
   - (d) a person who needs help.

6. Another word for **aim** is
   - (a) challenge.
   - (b) business.
   - (c) goal.
   - (d) need.

7. Based on the passage, you could say that capuchin monkeys are
   - (a) smart.
   - (b) difficult.
   - (c) strong.
   - (d) messy.

8. The meaning of **loyal** is
   - (a) faithful.
   - (b) little.
   - (c) skilled.
   - (d) famous.

Write Your Own

Think about how animals help people in different ways. On a separate sheet of paper, write to tell about another animal and how it helps people. Use at least three words from Units 1–3.

UNIT 4

Introducing the Words

Read the following folktale about a forest animal that learns a lesson. Notice how the highlighted words are used. These are the words you will be learning in this unit.

The Handsome Stag

(Folktale)

There was once a young stag that liked to use a shallow pool of water as a mirror. Every day, he would look down into it to notice how handsome he was. His antlers towered above his head. He moved them this way and that in order to get a better look.

One day, he carried on a silly conversation with himself.

"Ah, what beautiful antlers you have."

"They are nice. Look at your glorious back and neck, though. It's hard to say which part is the most beautiful."

"Don't be ridiculous. I insist that your antlers are the best part."

As the stag moved to get a better view of himself, he caught sight of his legs. Immediately, he felt gloomy. His legs were long and skinny. He wondered how they were able to hold up his large body and giant antlers. Then he sighed and went back to admiring his antlers until he became restless and bored. At last, he moved on to the field to eat grass.

Suddenly, the quiet of the afternoon was ended by the sounds of a hunter's horn and a loud bang. The dry branch of a tree was shattered by the gunshot. The stag raised his head in fear as the pieces of the branch fell to the ground. The stag was no coward. He knew, however, that even a hunter with little shooting talent could cause him harm. He began running. His long, slender legs carried him fast and far.

The stag spotted a passage inside a dark, thick part of the woods. He knew this path would take him to a stream. The hounds would lose his scent there. Then he could escape the hunting party. Faster and faster, he moved, his strong legs pushing him off the ground.

Then, just as the stag entered the thickest part of the forest, some low branches caught his antlers. He struggled and struggled. He pulled this way and that way. He had to avoid capture by the hunters.

The stag tried to free himself for a good five minutes. The branches poked his body, and his skin was scratched and sore. Finally, he pulled his antlers out and ran upstream.

When he was safe, the stag walked to a pool to drink some water and calm down. Before he put his head down to drink, he spotted the image of his body in the pool. All of a sudden, his antlers seemed heavy and useless.

Then he exclaimed, "Long have I admired my antlers and heavy body, but it was my slender, strong legs that saved me today."

Definitions

You were introduced to the words below in the passage on pages 36–37. Study the spelling, pronunciation, part of speech, and definition of each word. Write the word on the line in the sentence. Then read the synonyms and antonyms.

Remember

A **noun** *(n.)* is a word that names a person, place, or thing.

A **verb** *(v.)* is a word or words that express action or a state of being.

An **adjective** *(adj.)* is a word that describes a noun or pronoun.

1. capture (kap′ chər)

(n.) the act of catching or gaining control by force or skill

After the capture *of the ship, the pirates divided its gold and silver.*

(v.) to grab and hold onto; to hold the attention of

I will not read a book that does not capture *my interest.*

SYNONYMS: (v.) catch, seize, clutch, grasp
ANTONYMS: (v.) lose, release

2. coward (kau̇′ ərd)

(n.) one who has no courage or gets scared easily

I behaved like a coward *during the thunderstorm.*

SYNONYMS: weakling, wimp
ANTONYM: hero

3. exclaim (eks klām′)

(v.) to speak with strong feelings or emotions; to cry out

When the phone rings, I always exclaim, *"I'll get it!"*

SYNONYMS: yell, shout
ANTONYMS: whisper, murmur

4. gloomy (glü′ mē)

(adj.) partly or completely dark; wearing a frown

The twins were both gloomy *when they did not get their way.*

SYNONYMS: unhappy, miserable
ANTONYMS: bright; happy, cheerful

5. insist (in sist′)

(v.) to state something or make a demand firmly

I continued to ___insist___ *that I did my homework even though I didn't have it with me.*

SYNONYMS: declare, maintain, stress, require

6. passage (pas′ ij)

(n.) the act of moving from one place to another; a trip by sea or by air; a way in or out; a part of a written work or piece of music

The ___passage___ *from England to India took many days by boat.*

SYNONYMS: tunnel, entrance, exit, opening; paragraph, section

7. restless (rest′ lis)

(adj.) unable to rest, relax, or be still; without rest or sleep

The baby was ___restless___ *all night.*

SYNONYMS: nervous, uneasy, impatient
ANTONYMS: relaxed, peaceful, patient

8. shallow (shal′ ō)

(adj.) not deep; not showing much thought

The lake is ___shallow___*, so it is safe.*

SYNONYMS: empty, simple
ANTONYM: deep

9. shatter (shat′ ər)

(v.) to break into many pieces; to cause much damage

Why did the mirror ___shatter___*?*

SYNONYMS: smash, ruin

10. talent (tal′ ənt)

(n.) an ability to do something well; a skill or gift

You have a natural ___talent___ *for singing.*

SYNONYM: knack

Match the Meaning

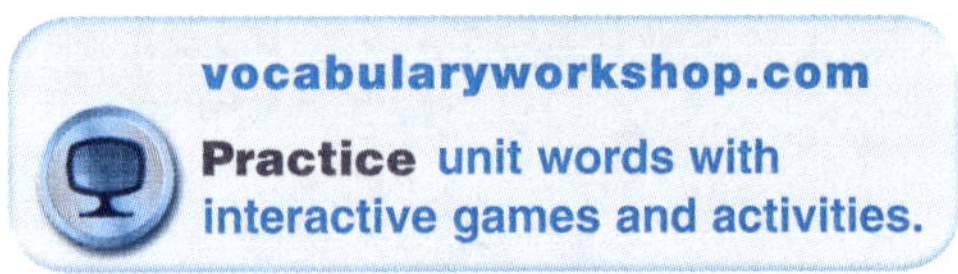

Choose the word whose meaning is suggested by the clue given. Then write the word on the line provided.

1. Someone who ____exclaims____ speaks in an excited way.
a. captures b. shatters c. exclaims

2. A ____shallow____ sink is not very deep.
a. gloomy b. restless c. shallow

3. To ____capture____ an object is to grab and hold on to it.
a. exclaim b. insist c. capture

4. A ____coward____ is a person who is afraid or fearful.
a. talent b. passage c. coward

5. A tunnel is a kind of ____passage____.
a. passage b. capture c. talent

6. If you have a skill, you have a ____talent____.
a. coward b. talent c. passage

7. When you can't sit still, you are ____restless____.
a. shallow b. gloomy c. restless

8. When a glass falls to the floor, it will probably ____shatter____.
a. insist b. capture c. shatter

9. A clown can make both happy and ____gloomy____ faces.
a. restless b. gloomy c. shallow

10. When I ____insist____ on something, I do not give up.
a. capture b. insist c. exclaim

Because of all the rain, it was a **gloomy** day.

Synonyms

*Choose the word that is most nearly the **same** in meaning as the word or phrase in **dark print**. Then write your choice on the line provided.*

1. a **knack** for baking
   a. passage b. coward c. talent ___talent___

2. a **paragraph** about birds
   a. capture b. passage c. coward ___passage___

3. **maintain** their rights
   a. capture b. shatter c. insist on ___insist on___

4. **break** into a hundred pieces
   a. capture b. insist c. shatter ___shatter___

5. **uneasy** with worry
   a. gloomy b. restless c. shallow ___restless___

Antonyms

*Choose the word that is most nearly **opposite** in meaning to the word or phrase in **dark print**. Then write your choice on the line provided.*

1. painted in **cheerful** colors
   a. gloomy b. shallow c. restless ___gloomy___

2. **lose** the chess piece
   a. insist on b. capture c. shatter ___capture___

3. **whisper** your answer
   a. capture b. insist c. exclaim ___exclaim___

4. played a **hero** on stage
   a. talent b. passage c. coward ___coward___

5. a **deep** swimming pool
   a. restless b. gloomy c. shallow ___shallow___

Completing the Sentence

Choose the word from the box that best completes each item below. Then write the word on the line provided. (You may have to change the word's ending.)

capture	**coward**	**exclaim**
gloomy	**insist**	**passage**
restless	**shallow**	
shatter	**talent**	

Games

■ I like to play games with my brothers and sisters. We enjoy swimming in the neighborhood pool. We always stay in the ____shallow____ end to make sure that we are safe.

■ We play baseball in our backyard. We know that if we hit the ball too hard, it might hit the house and ____shatter____ a window. Then our dad would ____exclaim____, "Hey, you broke the window!"

■ Jumping rope is fun. I ____insist____ on being the first one to start jumping rope! That is because I get very ____restless____ when I have to wait.

■ When I'm feeling ____gloomy____, playing games can put me in a much better mood!

The Underground Railroad

■ In the years before the Civil War, many brave men and women risked their lives to free the slaves. It was very dangerous work and not a job for a ____coward____.

■ One way that slaves escaped to freedom was by using a ____passage____ known as the Underground Railroad.

■ Harriet Tubman showed a ____talent____ for not getting caught by going back and forth on the Underground Railroad and helping many slaves escape.

■ It was wonderful how many slaves escaped and managed to avoid ____capture____.

Word Associations

Circle the letter next to the choice that best completes the sentence or answers the question. Pay special attention to the word in dark print.

1. To **shatter** a vase is to
a. break it into pieces.
b. put flowers in it.
c. wash it carefully.
d. replace it.

2. **Shallow** water comes up to my
a. shoulders.
b. ears.
c. ankles.
d. neck.

3. If you read a **passage** from a story, you
a. read the whole story.
b. read a part of the story.
c. read none of the story.
d. understand the whole story.

4. It is best to **capture** a moth
a. with a fan
b. with a hook.
c. with a net.
d. with a pet.

5. Which shows that you **insist**?
a. "May I come in?"
b. "Will you join me?"
c. "It has to be my way."
d. "Whatever you think is okay."

6. A **coward** gets easily
a. cold.
b. scared.
c. bored.
d. thirsty.

7. Someone with **talent** might
a. win a prize.
b. go to sleep.
c. go to the doctor.
d. come in last.

8. Which words might you **exclaim**?
a. "Where is the nearest store?"
b. "My dog ran away!"
c. "What kind of soup is that?"
d. "What day is it?"

9. A person who is **gloomy** doesn't
a. frown.
b. swim.
c. sigh.
d. smile.

10. When I'm **restless**, I can't
a. remember the words.
b. keep still.
c. stop yawning.
d. get warm.

For teaching suggestions, see page T30.

Word Study • Word Parts and Base Words

A **base word** is a complete word. You can add **word parts** to the beginning or end of a base word to make new words. The word *uncommon* is made of the base word *common* (page 8) and the beginning part *un-*. The word *gloomy* (page 38) is made up of the base word *gloom* and the ending part *-y*.

When you see a new word, look for a base word that you might know. This can help you figure out the meaning of the new word.

PRACTICE *Find the base word in each word. Write it on the line.*

1. strongest strong

2. misuse use

3. helpful help

4. freezing freeze

5. rebuild build

6. prettier pretty

7. incorrectly correct

8. unhappiness happy

APPLY *Complete each sentence so that it makes sense. Pay attention to the word in **dark print**. Use what you know about the meaning of its base word.*

Accept answers that demonstrate the correct meaning. Possible answers are given.

9. Because the weed was **firmly** rooted, I had a hard time pulling it out.

10. She will **rewrite** her science report because she found newer information.

11. I was **gasping** for air after I dove under the big wave.

12. I chose the **mildest** soap because I have sensitive skin.

13. Stay at the **shallower** end of the pool if you are not a strong swimmer.

Work with a partner. Search through magazines or newspapers to find words that contain base words and other word parts. Make a list of the words you find. Underline the base words.

For teaching suggestions, see page T35.

Shades of Meaning • Word Choice *capture, snatch, trap*

In the passage "The Handsome Stag" on pages 36–37, you read this sentence: *He had to avoid **capture** by the hunters.* Here, *capture* means "the act of catching and gaining control by force."

Capture has some synonyms, or words with almost the same meaning. But the words do not mean exactly the same thing as *capture*. Look at the chart below. Notice how the meanings of the synonyms are alike and different.

capture	When you **capture** something, you use force to catch it.
snatch	To **snatch** something is take or grab it in a hurry. It is often done in a rude or eager way.
trap	When you **trap** a person, you fool the person in order to catch him or her. When you trap an animal, you catch it in a cage or other box.

PRACTICE ***Write the word from the chart that best completes each sentence.***

1. A thief may try to ___snatch___ a bike when the owner isn't looking.
2. I tried to ___trap___ my brother into telling me about my gift.
3. I hope I can ___snatch___ the last piece of cake.
4. The pirates wanted to ___capture___ the ship and sail it out of the port.

APPLY ***Answer each question. Use the word (or one of the words) in dark print in your answer. Be sure to write complete sentences.***
Accept answers that students can justify.

5. How might you **trap** an insect?

____

6. Why might a parent **snatch** something out of a child's hands?

____

7. Would soldiers **trap** or **capture** an enemy fort? Why?

____

8. Would a park ranger try to **snatch** or **trap** a wild bear? Why?

____

UNIT 5

Introducing the Words

Read the following journal article about a place to live and work while in space. Notice how the highlighted words are used. These are the words you will be learning in this unit.

The International Space Station

(Journal Article)

In a brilliant flash of light, the space shuttle blasts off from a launching pad. It is heading towards the International Space Station, or ISS. The shuttle carries food, equipment, and supplies to this place where astronauts live and work.

The ISS circles Earth more than 150 miles above our planet's atmosphere. If you looked down on the ISS, you would see something that looks like a giant bird. The bird's wings are actually solar panels. These capture energy for the station. The body of the bird contains labs and a place to eat, sleep, and relax.

The International Space Station circles Earth every 90 minutes.

Both Russia and the United States had plans for a space station. They knew that building a station together would be cheaper. Once the two countries were convinced that the project could be successful, they united their plans and worked together. Then other countries plunged into the project. These countries included Japan, Canada, France, and Italy.

Since the year 2000, humans have lived on the space station. Their days are very busy. Some astronauts complete experiments. Others work as mechanics, using robot arms to fix machines. Some workers grow plants.

All astronauts are highly trained. Their actions must be swift and sure when problems arise. Working in space is a dangerous job.

Sometimes, an astronaut must work outside. To do so, he or she puts on a space suit and takes a space walk outside the station. Conditions in space are harsh. It is very cold outside the space station, and there is no air there. A human cannot endure these conditions without the special suit.

Moving around in space is not easy either. Gravity doesn't hold the body in one place. There is always the danger of floating away! Astronauts must tie themselves down when sleeping, cooking, or exercising. On the plus side, heavy things seem light in space. Astronauts can lift and move huge pieces of equipment in space.

Astronaut taking a walk outside

The space station is as big as a football field. Keeping it clean is on the to-do list. Astronauts must cook for themselves, too. They must exercise two hours a day to stay strong. Free time is precious. It is often spent taking photographs, reading, writing e-mails home, or just glancing out the window at Earth below.

The International Space Station is a remarkable workplace in space. Exciting discoveries come from research being done there. Most important, countries are joining together to explore the ultimate frontier: space.

Definitions

You were introduced to the words below in the passage on pages 46–47. Study the spelling, pronunciation, part of speech, and definition of each word. Write the word on the line in the sentence. Then read the synonyms and antonyms.

Remember

A **noun** *(n.)* is a word that names a person, place, or thing.

A **verb** *(v.)* is a word or words that express action or a state of being.

An **adjective** *(adj.)* is a word that describes a noun or pronoun.

1. atmosphere (at′ mə sfir) (n.) the air that surrounds Earth; the feeling or mood in a room or place

Earth's atmosphere *is made up of invisible gases.*

SYNONYM: environment

2. brilliant (bril′ yənt) (adj.) sparkling or full of light; striking and shiny; very smart

Many stars in the universe are brilliant.

SYNONYMS: bright, shining, vivid; clever
ANTONYMS: dull, lifeless

3. convince (kən vins′) (v.) to get someone to believe something or to do something; to win over

It is easy to convince *me to eat two pieces of carrot cake.*

SYNONYMS: persuade, urge, coax
ANTONYM: dissuade

4. endure (en důr′) (v.) to put up with; to continue in the same way for a long time

I cannot endure *your silly jokes!*

SYNONYMS: suffer, bear; withstand, last

5. glance (glans) (v.) to look quickly; to bounce off a surface and fly off to one side

I will glance *at my watch from time to time to make sure my speech isn't too long.*

(n.) a quick look

One glance *told me we would be close friends.*

SYNONYMS: (v. & n.) glimpse, peek
ANTONYM: (v. & n.) stare

6. harsh
(härsh)

(adj.) rough or unpleasant to the senses; unkind in voice or behavior

Try not to speak in a ___harsh___ *tone, even when you are angry.*

SYNONYMS: crude; cruel, severe, demanding
ANTONYMS: smooth; pleasant, kind

7. plunge
(plunj)

(v.) to fall quickly; to quickly throw oneself down or into something

People looking for fun and thrills ___plunge___ *downhill in a roller coaster.*

(n.) the act of jumping in

Enjoy taking a ___plunge___ *into the pool!*

SYNONYMS: (v.) dive, drop; (n.) dive, swim

8. precious
(pre′ shəs)

(adj.) very high-priced; loved and adored

Sapphires and rubies are ___precious___ *jewels.*

SYNONYMS: valuable, special
ANTONYMS: worthless, valueless, ordinary

9. swift
(swift)

(adj.) able to move at a quick speed; quick to respond

The current was ___swift___ *as the canoe reached the rapids.*

SYNONYMS: fast, rapid, speedy; ready
ANTONYMS: slow, gradual

10. unite
(yü nīt′)

(v.) to bring two or more parts together to make a whole

The team's players need to ___unite___ *during a game.*

SYNONYMS: join, combine
ANTONYMS: break, split, undo, divide

Match the Meaning

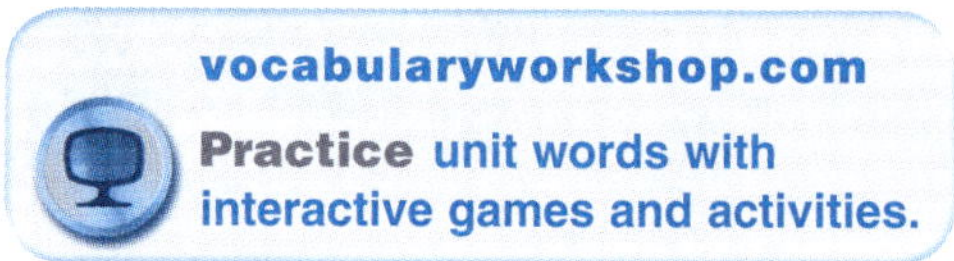

Choose the word whose meaning is suggested by the clue given. Then write the word on the line provided.

1. A very bright moon might be described as ___brilliant___.
   a. brilliant b. harsh c. swift

2. To ___endure___ something is to suffer through it.
   a. convince b. plunge c. endure

3. Sandpaper can feel ___harsh___ against your skin.
   a. harsh b. brilliant c. precious

4. A toy that is loved and adored is said to be ___precious___.
   a. harsh b. swift c. precious

5. To ___unite___ all the parts is to make a whole of them.
   a. convince b. unite c. endure

6. As soon as you walk into a room, you can feel its ___atmosphere___.
   a. atmosphere b. glance c. plunge

7. A person who is able to respond quickly might be described as ___swift___.
   a. precious b. harsh c. swift

8. To ___plunge___ into a task is to jump into it and get it done.
   a. convince b. endure c. plunge

9. If you ___glance___ at something, you give it a quick look.
   a. glance b. convince c. plunge

10. It is not always easy to ___convince___ people to do something difficult.
    a. endure b. plunge c. convince

Only a few brave people went out in the **harsh** weather.

Synonyms

*Choose the word that is most nearly the **same** in meaning as the word or phrase in **dark print**. Then write your choice on the line provided.*

1. **dive** into the sea
   a. unite   b. convince   c. plunge   plunge
2. a winter coat that will **last**
   a. endure   b. glance   c. unite   endure
3. **persuade** me to take dance lessons
   a. convince   b. endure   c. unite   convince
4. a smelly **environment**
   a. plunge   b. glance   c. atmosphere   atmosphere
5. gave the newspaper a **glimpse**
   a. glance   b. convince   c. unite   glance
6. a **valuable** gift
   a. harsh   b. precious   c. swift   precious

Antonyms

*Choose the word that is most nearly **opposite** in meaning to the word or phrase in **dark print**. Then write your choice on the line provided.*

1. **divide** the group
   a. endure   b. convince   c. unite   unite
2. a **lifeless** performance
   a. brilliant   b. swift   c. harsh   brilliant
3. a **gradual** movement
   a. brilliant   b. harsh   c. swift   swift
4. a **kind** comment
   a. harsh   b. precious   c. swift   harsh

Completing the Sentence

Choose the word from the box that best completes each item below. Then write the word on the line provided. (You may have to change the word's ending.)

atmosphere	**brilliant**	**convince**
endure	**glance**	**harsh**
plunge	**precious**	
swift	**unite**	

Vacation

- My sister and I would love to take a ____plunge____ into the cool ocean water.
- This year, we hope to ____convince____ our parents to take the family to a theme park in Florida.
- We like the fun ____atmosphere____ in Florida. Everyone always seems to have such a good time!
- Also, after such a cold and ____harsh____ winter, we thought it would be nice to go someplace warm.
- My parents do not agree. They think it is too hot in Florida. It is hard for them to ____endure____ the heat.
- I know that wherever we go on vacation, we'll have many ____precious____ memories!

Math

- You can add and subtract using pencil and paper. You can also use mental math. Mental math is a ____swift____ way to find sums and differences.
- In our class, there are some ____brilliant____ math students. They can find sums and differences mentally with just a ____glance____ at the numbers.
- In a math contest, the team members will ____unite____ to solve challenging problems.

Word Associations

Circle the letter next to the choice that best completes the sentence or answers the question. Pay special attention to the word in dark print.

1. After a **brilliant** play, fans might
a. yawn.
b. boo.
c. cheer.
d. leave.

2. To **glance** at a magazine is to
a. look at it slowly.
b. look at it quickly.
c. look at it carefully.
d. throw it away.

3. Which animal is the most **swift**?
a. deer
b. snail
c. turtle
d. cow

4. Which is most likely to **endure**?
a. paper
b. brick
c. fruit
d. flowers

5. A **precious** gift is one that I will
a. return for another.
b. give to my dog.
c. hope never to get.
d. value forever.

6. Which are **harsh** words?
a. "We love you."
b. "You are clever."
c. "I hate you."
d. "This cheers me up."

7. Earth's **atmosphere** includes
a. people and houses.
b. animals and plants.
c. oceans and mountains.
d. air and gases.

8. You're most likely to **plunge**
a. into the deep end of a pool.
b. into a glass of juice.
c. into a bucket of sand.
d. into a cake mix.

9. Students would **unite** to sing
a. off-key.
b. softly.
c. together.
d. apart.

10. You need to **convince** me if you know that I
a. already like your idea.
b. do not agree with you.
c. believe in you.
d. will do whatever you say.

For teaching suggestions, see page T30.

Word Study • Prefixes *re-*, *pre-*, *in-*

A **prefix** is a word part that is added to the beginning of a base word. A **base word** is a complete word. It makes sense as a word on its own. Adding a prefix can change the meaning of the word. It can also make a new word.

Prefix		Base Word		New Word		Meaning
re	+	unite	=	**re**unite	→	unite again
pre	+	heat	=	**pre**heat	→	heat before
in	+	direct	=	**in**direct	→	not direct

Look at the prefixes and base words in the chart above. The prefix *re-* means "again." You can add *re-* to *unite* (page 49) to make the word *reunite*. *Reunite* means "unite again."

The prefix *pre-* means "before." The prefix *in-* sometimes means "not." Look at the chart for examples of words with the prefixes *pre-* and *in-*.

PRACTICE *Write the missing prefix. Then write the meaning of the new word.*

Prefix		Base Word		New Word		Meaning
1. pre	+	mix	=	premix	→	mix before
2. re	+	fill	=	refill	→	fill again
3. in	+	complete	=	incomplete	→	not complete
4. re	+	read	=	reread	→	read again

APPLY *Complete each sentence with a word that contains the prefix* re-, pre-, *or* in-. *Choose from the words in the boxes above.*

5. Can you refill my glass of lemonade?
6. I wanted to get an A, but my homework was incomplete.
7. My sister will preheat the oven before baking the muffins.
8. When I didn't understand the story, my teacher said to reread it.

Write *Add the prefix* re-, pre-, *or* in- *to each word below to make a new word. Then write a sentence for each new word. You may use a dictionary if you need help.*

new **correct** **dawn**

For teaching suggestions, see page T36.

Shades of Meaning • Word Choice *glance, gaze, glare*

In the passage "The International Space Station" on pages 46–47, you read this sentence about free time on the space station: *It is often spent taking photographs, reading, writing e-mails home, or just* ***glancing*** *out the window at Earth below.* Here, *glancing* is a form of the verb *glance. Glance* means "to look quickly."

Words may have similar meanings, but no two words have exactly the same meaning. Look at the words in the chart below. They all involve looking at someone or something. Read the words and their meanings. Notice how the words differ in meaning.

glance	When you **glance** at something, you look at it for just a moment.
gaze	When you **gaze**, you look at someone or something for a long time with amazement.
glare	When you **glare**, you look at someone or something in anger.

PRACTICE *Write the word from the chart that best replaces* ***look*** *in each sentence.*

1. I saw my sister **look** harshly at me after I ripped her bag. glare
2. I always **look** around the park to see if any friends are there. glance
3. Could you just take a quick **look** at my math homework? glance
4. Mom would **look** into my eyes for hours when I was a baby. gaze
5. I saw players on the losing team **look** at me when I scored my third goal.
glare

APPLY *Answer each question. Use the word in* ***dark print*** *in your answer. Be sure to write complete sentences.*
Accept answers that students can justify.

6. When might you **glance** at a clock?

7. What might cause you to **gaze** at the sky?

8. How can you tell whether someone is **glaring** at you?

UNIT 6

Introducing the Words

Read the following passage about a king who lived long ago. Notice how the highlighted words are used. These are the words you will be learning in this unit.

King Tut Then and Now

(Historical Nonfiction)

He was only nine years old when he became king. When his father died, he became the ruler, or pharaoh (fâr′ ō). King Tut (short for Tutankhamun) ruled for only ten years. Yet he is one of Egypt's most famous kings.

King Tut isn't known for the wars he won. His fame isn't based on his wisdom or on the cities he built. Instead, he is known for the treasures he left behind.

King Tut ruled more than three thousand years ago. Little is known about his life. What we do know is based on what was found in his tomb.

When a pharaoh died, he was buried with things he might need on a journey. He would carry jewelry, perfume, and clothing. He would need a golden throne. A departing ruler would want to sail away in a ship. The tombs of pharaohs were filled with unbelievable riches.

Many Egyptian pharaohs were buried in the Valley of the Kings.

Listen to this passage at vocabularyworkshop.com.

The Egyptian pharaohs were buried in the Valley of the Kings. In early Egyptian times, this area was guarded to prevent robberies. Still, robbers roamed the valley. They broke through the pharaohs' tombs and stole everything they could.

King Tut's tomb had been basically untouched. Grave robbers had broken in once, but they had not emptied the tomb. That is why the discovery in 1922 was so exciting. No one else had entered King Tut's tomb until an Englishman named Howard Carter discovered it. When he shone a light inside the closed space, he was speechless. He just stared at the superb treasures inside.

For months, Carter explored and studied the tomb. He found the pharaoh inside a solid gold casket. A gold mask covered his face. The room was brightly painted and bordered in gold.

Since then, many people have wondered how King Tut died. Some thought he was poisoned. Others thought he had fallen from a chariot during a race. He might have been killed while hunting lions or other fierce animals, as pharaohs were expected to do. These ideas made good stories, but the truth remained a mystery.

This gold mask is one of the treasures found in King Tut's tomb.

Modern science changed that. Scientists observed and tested King Tut's body. His body told a story about his short life.

Scientists are certain that Tutankhamun was not healthy. He probably couldn't ride a chariot. He definitely couldn't walk very far. King Tut had a bone disease that put him in constant pain. Pictures of the king show him clasping a cane. Many walking canes were found near him in his tomb.

To make matters worse, King Tut caught malaria more than once. Malaria is a disease that is carried by mosquitoes. In early Egyptian times, there was no cure for the disease. Most scientists think that malaria killed King Tut.

Definitions

You were introduced to the words below in the passage on pages 56–57. Study the spelling, pronunciation, part of speech, and definition of each word. Write the word on the line in the sentence. Then read the synonyms and antonyms.

Remember

A **noun** *(n.)* is a word that names a person, place, or thing.

A **verb** *(v.)* is a word or words that express action or a state of being.

An **adjective** *(adj.)* is a word that describes a noun or pronoun.

1. border (bôr′ dər)

(n.) the outer edge of an object; the line where two parts meet

We crossed the border *into Canada.*

(v.) to be next to or near something; to touch at the edge

One city can border *a number of small towns.*

SYNONYM: (n.) boundary

2. certain (sûr′ tən)

(adj.) having no doubt; sure

I am certain *I locked the door.*

SYNONYMS: positive, confident, definite, fixed, settled, agreed
ANTONYMS: uncertain, unsure, indefinite

3. clasp (klasp)

(n.) a device that holds parts together; a strong hold

I lost the clasp *to my watch.*

(v.) to hook something up; to hold tightly

My younger sister likes to clasp *my hand.*

SYNONYMS: (n.) buckle; grasp; (v.) fasten; grasp, seize
ANTONYMS: (v.) undo, loosen, unfasten

4. depart (di pärt′)

(v.) to go away

I will depart *for Miami soon.*

SYNONYM: leave
ANTONYMS: stay, remain

5. fierce (fērs)

(adj.) violent; wild or savage

The tiger that attacked the zookeeper was fierce.

SYNONYMS: cruel, ferocious
ANTONYMS: mild, easygoing

6. journey (jûr′ nē)

(n.) a long trip; a passage from one place to another

Where did you go on your ______journey______*?*

(v.) to go on a trip; to travel

We plan to ______journey______ *to Egypt.*

SYNONYMS: (n.) expedition, tour, voyage, outing; (v.) tour, trek, go

7. observe (əb zûrv′)

(v.) to see; to watch with close attention; to stick to or obey

To understand how the bird gets its food, the boy must ______observe______ *its movements.*

SYNONYMS: notice; abide

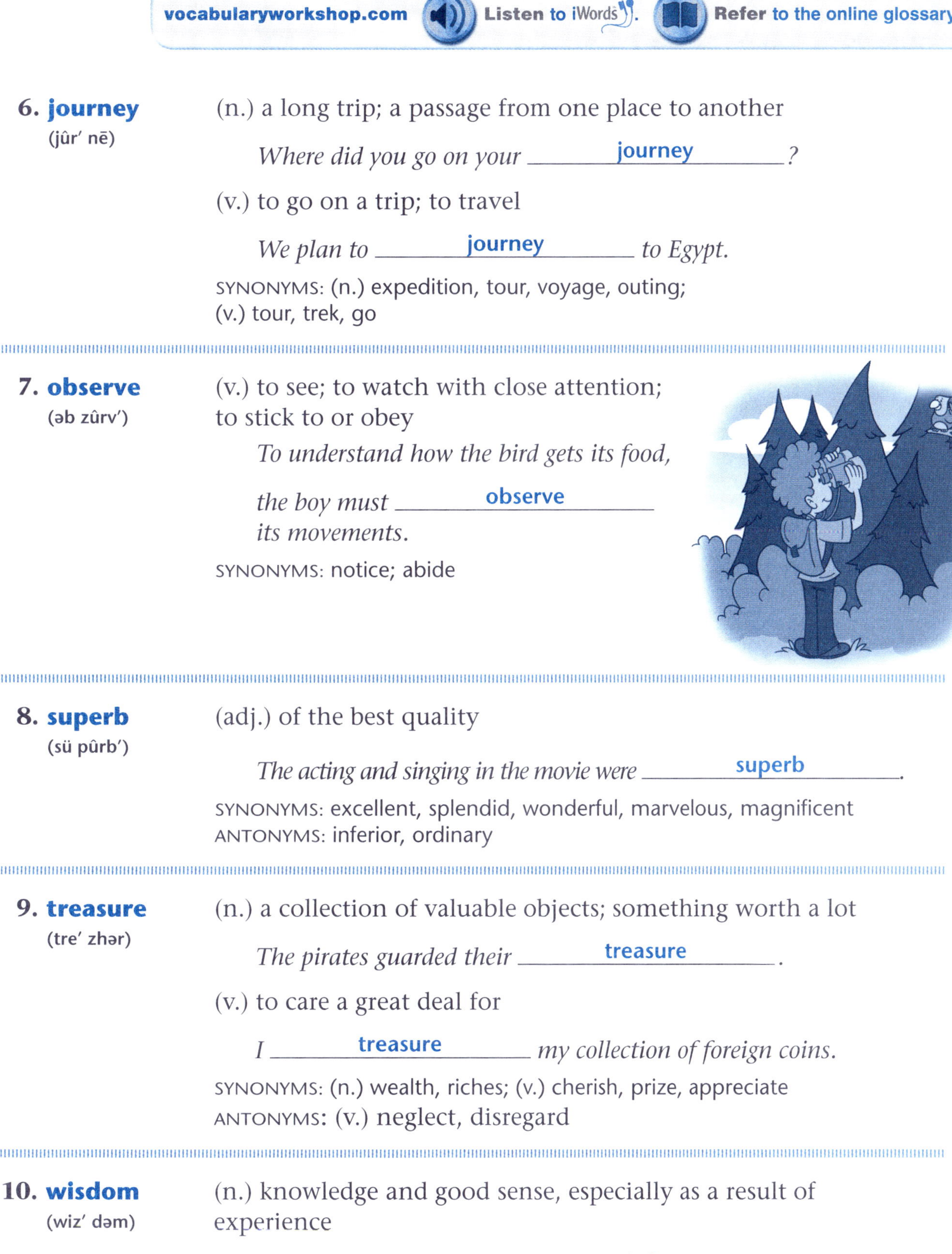

8. superb (sü pûrb′)

(adj.) of the best quality

The acting and singing in the movie were ______superb______.

SYNONYMS: excellent, splendid, wonderful, marvelous, magnificent
ANTONYMS: inferior, ordinary

9. treasure (tre′ zhər)

(n.) a collection of valuable objects; something worth a lot

The pirates guarded their ______treasure______.

(v.) to care a great deal for

I ______treasure______ *my collection of foreign coins.*

SYNONYMS: (n.) wealth, riches; (v.) cherish, prize, appreciate
ANTONYMS: (v.) neglect, disregard

10. wisdom (wiz′ dəm)

(n.) knowledge and good sense, especially as a result of experience

Grandparents have much ______wisdom______ *about life.*

SYNONYMS: judgment, understanding, intelligence
ANTONYM: ignorance

Match the Meaning

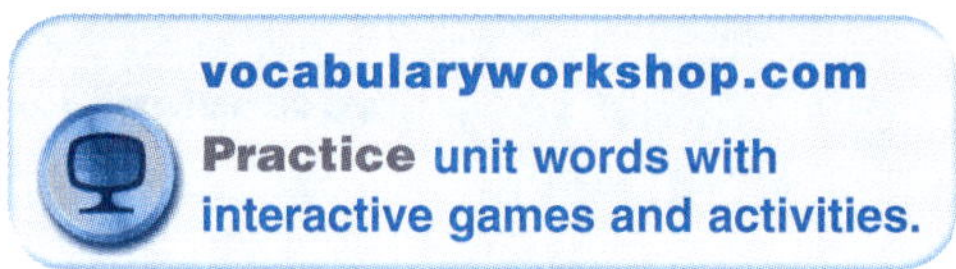

Choose the word whose meaning is suggested by the clue given. Then write the word on the line provided.

1. To cherish your friends is to ___treasure___ them.
a. border b. clasp c. treasure

2. If you are sure about something, you are ___certain___.
a. superb b. certain c. fierce

3. The edge of something is also called its ___border___.
a. border b. journey c. wisdom

4. To ___depart___ from your route is to change it.
a. clasp b. treasure c. depart

5. A knowing person is said to have ___wisdom___.
a. journey b. wisdom c. treasure

6. Something excellent might be described as ___superb___.
a. certain b. fierce c. superb

7. To ___journey___ is to go on a trip.
a. journey b. clasp c. treasure

8. A latch is also called a ___clasp___.
a. border b. wisdom c. clasp

9. A nurse will ___observe___ patients to see how they feel.
a. observe b. treasure c. depart

10. Some wild animals are ___fierce___.
a. certain b. superb c. fierce

The **journey** through the desert was long and hot.

Synonyms

*Choose the word that is most nearly the **same** in meaning as the word or phrase in **dark print**. Then write your choice on the line provided.*

1. **notice** her face
   a. observe b. border c. journey observe

2. **buckle** your seat belts
   a. depart b. clasp c. treasure clasp

3. **travel** wherever you want
   a. border b. journey c. treasure journey

4. gain more **knowledge**
   a. clasp b. treasure c. wisdom wisdom

5. step over the **edge**
   a. journey b. clasp c. border border

6. a **definite** opinion
   a. fierce b. certain c. superb certain

Antonyms

*Choose the word that is most nearly **opposite** in meaning to the word or phrase in **dark print**. Then write your choice on the line provided.*

1. **disregard** his ideas
   a. treasure b. border c. clasp treasure

2. an **ordinary** meal
   a. fierce b. certain c. superb superb

3. chose to **stay**
   a. border b. treasure c. depart depart

4. an **easygoing** manner
   a. fierce b. superb c. certain fierce

Completing the Sentence

Choose the word from the box that best completes each item below. Then write the word on the line provided. (You may have to change the word's ending.)

border	**certain**	**clasp**
depart	**fierce**	**journey**
observe	**superb**	
treasure	**wisdom**	

Traveling to a Foreign Country

■ When you plan to ____journey____ to a foreign country, it is a good idea to learn how it is different from where you live.

■ Be sure to ____observe____ all the rules of the country you are visiting. You might get into trouble if you don't obey them!

■ The rules may change again if you decide to cross the ____border____ to visit another country.

■ Make ____certain____ you know the train schedules.

■ That way, you will always know when trains arrive and ____depart____.

Soccer

■ We have a ____superb____ soccer team. Our coach thinks it's the best team she has ever had. We have very good players, and they score many goals each game.

■ Our coach has a lot of experience. She has much ____wisdom____ to share with us. She knows that encouraging us to have fun and to get along with each other also helps us to win.

■ A player forgot to fasten the ____clasp____ on the back of his shin guard, so it fell off during the game.

■ Soccer games can be very intense. The competition can be ____fierce____! Still, we were always ready to take on the other teams. We finished this season on top.

■ Our team will always ____treasure____ the trophy we won.

For teaching suggestions, see page T30.

Word Study • *Suffixes -ly, -ful, -less*

A **suffix** is a word part that is added to the end of a **base word** to make a new word.

Look at the base words and suffixes in this chart. The suffix *-ly* usually means "in a certain way." You can add the suffix *-ly* to *superb* (page 59) to make the word *superbly*. *Superbly* means "in a superb or wonderful way."

Base Word		Suffix		New Word		Meaning
superb	+	**ly**	=	superb**ly**	→	in a superb or wonderful way
hope	+	**ful**	=	hope**ful**	→	full of hope
care	+	**less**	=	care**less**	→	without care

The suffix *-ful* means "full of." The suffix *-less* means "without." Look at the chart for examples of words with the suffixes *-ful* and *-less*.

PRACTICE ***Write the missing suffix. Then write the meaning of the new word.***

Base Word		Suffix		New Word		Meaning
1. use	+	less	=	useless	→	of no use
2. quick	+	ly	=	quickly	→	in a quick way
3. harm	+	ful	=	harmful	→	full of harm
4. thought	+	less	=	thoughtless	→	without thought

APPLY ***Complete each sentence with a word that contains the suffix -ly, -ful or -less. Choose from the words in the boxes above.***

5. When it was my turn to play, I ran quickly onto the field.

6. My camera was useless after I got sand in it.

7. Some snakebites can be harmful to people.

8. My sister skated superbly in the contest.

Write ***The suffixes -ful and -less are opposites. Choose words with the suffix -ful or -less from the boxes above. Write the opposite of each word.***

Example: hope**ful**/hope**less**

Vocabulary for Comprehension

*Read the following passage in which some of the words you have studied in Units 4–6 appear in **dark print**. Then answer the questions on page 65.*

Nellie Bly: Star Reporter

Elizabeth Cochrane (1867–1922) always wanted to be a writer. She had big ideas and plenty of spirit. Elizabeth struggled before getting a chance at writing. Her break came when she sent a letter to a newspaper complaining about an article that it printed. The letter **captured** the attention of the paper's editor, who soon hired her. Elizabeth changed her name to Nellie Bly and started writing for the paper. In her job, she used her many **talents** to get important stories.

In 1887, Nellie moved to New York City, where she got a job working for a big newspaper. As Nellie grew more popular, her story ideas grew more daring. Once she pretended to be sick so she could **observe** the horrible conditions in a hospital. Another time, she **plunged** off a ferryboat into a river! She wanted to see how long it would take rescue workers to come to her aid.

In 1889, Nellie **convinced** her boss to send her on a trip around the world. She wanted to beat the record described in a book called *Around the World in Eighty Days*. From all over the world, Nellie sent back stories of her adventures and travels. When she completed the trip in just seventy-two days, she became world famous. Her **journey** was a huge success! Not only did Nellie beat the record, but she also proved that women could be brave and tough too.

In 1895, Nellie got married and left reporting. She returned more than twenty years later to report for the *New York Evening Journal*.

Fill in the circle next to the choice that best completes the sentence or answers the question.

1. This passage is mostly about
   - (a) what Nellie did as a reporter.
   - (b) when Nellie changed her name.
   - (c) why Nellie was popular.
   - (d) where Nellie traveled.

2. In this passage, **captured** means
   - (a) lost.
   - (b) caught.
   - (c) missed.
   - (d) discussed.

3. Another word for **talents** is
   - (a) adventures.
   - (b) hobbies.
   - (c) articles.
   - (d) skills.

4. In this passage, **observe** means
   - (a) to pretend.
   - (b) to change.
   - (c) to watch.
   - (d) to rescue.

5. You can tell from this passage that Nellie Bly is
   - (a) tired.
   - (b) afraid.
   - (c) unhappy.
   - (d) brave.

6. The meaning of **plunged** is
   - (a) climbed.
   - (b) jumped.
   - (c) crawled.
   - (d) walked.

7. Another word for **convinced** is
   - (a) beat.
   - (b) departed.
   - (c) persuaded.
   - (d) traveled.

8. The meaning of **journey** is
   - (a) trip.
   - (b) newspaper.
   - (c) world.
   - (d) train.

Write Your Own

During the seventy-two days that Nellie traveled around the world, she wrote about the many exciting adventures she experienced. Picture yourself on a similar journey around the world. On a separate sheet of paper, write a letter to your family back home that describes an adventure you have had during your travels. Use at least three words from Units 4–6.

Classifying

Choose the word from the box that goes best with each group of words. Write the word on the line provided. Then explain what the words have in common. The first one has been done for you.

bitter	**certain**	**exclaim**
gloomy	**patient**	**pause**
~~**restless**~~	**superb**	
swift	**wander**	

1. thoughtless, careless, worthless, restless

The words have the same suffix.

2. wander, walk, skip, run

The words describe ways of moving.

3. happy, cheerful, sad, gloomy

The words describe a person's state of mind.

4. quick, rapid, speedy, swift

The words are synonyms.

5. unsure, doubtful, possible, certain

The words describe degrees of certainty.

6. clause, laws, thaws, pause

The words rhyme.

7. doctor, nurse, aide, patient

The words name people in a place of medical care.

8. exclaim, whisper, declare, shout

The words describe ways of speaking.

9. poor, decent, fine, superb

The words describe quality in order from worst to best.

10. bitter, sour, salty, sweet

The words describe how things taste.

REVIEW UNITS 1–6

Completing the Idea

Complete each sentence so that it makes sense. Pay attention to the word in ***dark print.*** Accept answers that show an understanding of the vocabulary.

1. When it rains, my parents **insist** that I ______.
2. With a quick **glance** over my shoulder, I ______.
3. When a stream is **shallow**, ______.
4. Students in our school **unite** to ______.
5. Water is a precious **resource** because ______.
6. When I came to the narrow **passage**, I ______.
7. When the weather is **mild**, I ______.
8. The **active** baby ______.
9. When I can't **endure** the summer heat, I ______.
10. Whenever I set a **goal** for myself, I ______.
11. When the **fierce** wind blew, ______.
12. I spoke in a **harsh** tone when I ______.
13. On rainy days, I **prefer** to ______.
14. You can **ruin** a painting if ______.
15. To **trace** the picture, I ______.

Writing Challenge

Check that vocabulary is used correctly and that each sentence is written correctly.

Write two sentences using the word ***faint.*** *In the first sentence, use* ***faint*** *as a verb. In the second sentence, use* ***faint*** *as an adjective.*

1. ______
2. ______

REVIEW UNITS 1–6

Introducing the Words

Read the following report about a bell that is part of American history. Notice how the highlighted words are used. These are the words you will be learning in this unit.

The Liberty Bell

(Report)

The Liberty Bell is far from perfect. It never rings, and it has a huge crack. Yet it is a well-known symbol of the United States. To people from coast to coast, it means freedom. Why?

The Liberty Bell has a rich history. It was made in England and sent to Philadelphia in 1752. The bell cracked when it was first tested. Some people accused the makers of doing a poor job when making it. Rather than return it, the city of Philadelphia decided to fix it. The city's leaders hired two clever metalworkers. The men melted the bell down and made another bell, imitating the original. Then the new bell was hung in a tower. It was used to call lawmakers together.

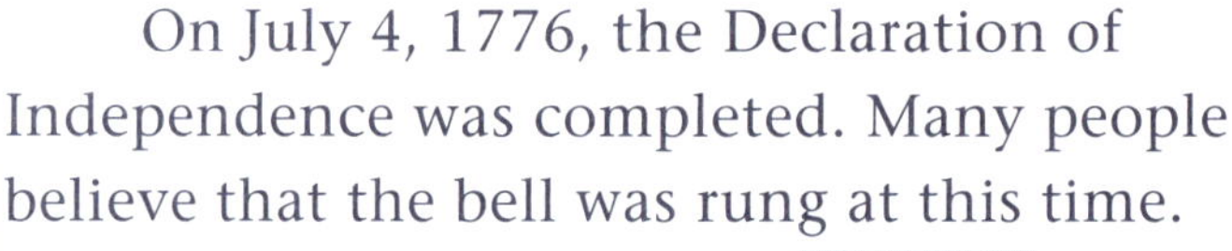

On July 4, 1776, the Declaration of Independence was completed. Many people believe that the bell was rung at this time. However, experts who have explored its history say that the event never happened. In fact, some think that the steeple where the bell was hung was in a delicate condition. It was not strong enough to hold a ringing bell.

Liberty Bell

Here is one story about the ringing of the bell on that day. In the 1840s, a writer named George Lippard wrote a tale about a bell ringer who wanted to ring the bell when the Declaration of Independence was completed. When the time came, he rang the bell in triumph. The sound was heard all over Philadelphia. Many Americans read and loved the story. From then on, the Liberty Bell was a symbol of independence.

Listen to this passage at vocabularyworkshop.com.

The Liberty Bell on one of its journeys

In 1846, the Liberty Bell was rung to honor the birthday of George Washington. He was the country's first president and another symbol of independence. The bell's clear sound pierced the air, but the ringing also had another effect. It widened a crack that had been forming. By noon, the ringing sounded terrible. Since that time, the bell has been silent.

Liberty Bell Center in Philadelphia

Just because the Liberty Bell no longer rang, it did not lose its importance as a symbol of freedom. Beginning in the late 1800s, the Liberty Bell was displayed across the country and was seen by many people. The Liberty Bell reminded Americans of their past and of how they had worked together for freedom.

Today, the Liberty Bell hangs in a glass building in Philadelphia. In the past, hearing its ring was a rare event, and now it does not ring at all. Still, it sings a song of freedom for all Americans.

Definitions

You were introduced to the words below in the passage on pages 68–69. Study the spelling, pronunciation, part of speech, and definition of each word. Write the word on the line in the sentence. Then read the synonyms and antonyms.

Remember

A **noun** *(n.)* is a word that names a person, place, or thing.

A **verb** *(v.)* is a word or words that express action or a state of being.

An **adjective** *(adj.)* is a word that describes a noun or pronoun.

1. accuse (ə kyüz′)

(v.) to say that someone or something has done wrong; blame

Please don't ___accuse___ *me of being lazy!*

SYNONYM: tattle
ANTONYMS: praise, absolve

2. clever (kle′ vər)

(adj.) having or showing a quick mind; bright, smart

The ___clever___ *student answered every question correctly.*

SYNONYMS: skillful, cunning, sharp, intelligent
ANTONYMS: dull, dumb, unintelligent, stupid, slow

3. coast (kōst)

(n.) the land near the sea or ocean

California is on the Pacific ___coast___ *of the United States.*

(v.) to move along without any power or effort; to slide down a slope

Our sleds will ___coast___ *down the hill.*

SYNONYMS: (n.) seashore, seaside, waterfront, beach; (v.) glide, ride

4. delicate (del′ i kət)

(adj.) easily broken or damaged; requiring care or skill

Do not touch that ___delicate___ *teacup, please!*

SYNONYMS: dainty, fragile, weak, frail
ANTONYMS: sturdy, hard, coarse, rough

5. explore (ik splôr′)

(v.) to travel; to discover; to look into or study something

I would like to ___explore___ *the new neighborhood.*

SYNONYMS: examine, investigate, analyze, search, research

6. imitate (i' mə tāt)

(v.) to copy someone's movements or expressions; to appear like something else

I love to imitate *the actor's funny face.*

SYNONYMS: mimic, resemble, repeat, reproduce

7. pierce (pērs)

(v.) to make a hole or opening; to run into or through something, as with a pointed tool or weapon

Use scissors to pierce *the plastic wrap.*

SYNONYMS: stab, perforate, enter, penetrate

8. rare (râr)

(adj.) not often found, seen, or happening; unusually valuable or good; not fully cooked

It is rare *for a pitcher to hit many home runs.*

SYNONYMS: infrequent; unusual, uncommon
ANTONYMS: frequent; ordinary, usual, common, normal

9. symbol (sim' bəl)

(n.) something that stands for something else; a written sign that is used to represent an operation or a calculation

The Statue of Liberty is a symbol *of freedom.*

SYNONYMS: mark, note, token, emblem

10. triumph (trī' əmf)

(n.) an important success or win; a feeling of happiness that comes from winning

Winning the battle was a triumph *for them.*

(v.) to succeed

The basketball team will triumph *in the end.*

SYNONYMS: (n.) victory, achievement; (v.) overcome, conquer
ANTONYMS: (n.) loss, defeat; (v.) lose

Match the Meaning

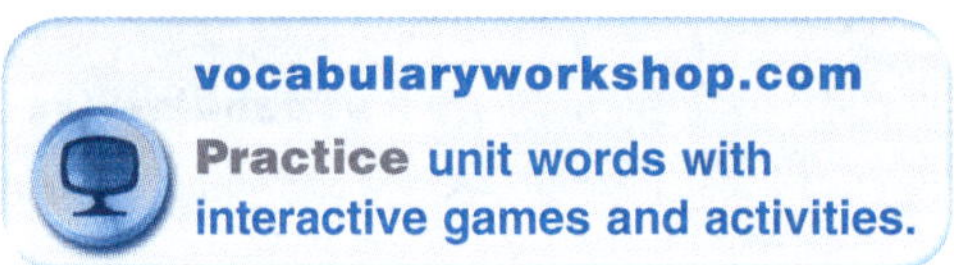

Choose the word whose meaning is suggested by the clue given. Then write the word on the line provided.

1. A strip of land along the water is called a ______coast______.
a. triumph b. symbol c. coast

2. Smart people may also be described as ______clever______.
a. rare b. clever c. delicate

3. To ______explore______ is to go to a new or unknown place.
a. imitate b. explore c. accuse

4. When you ______accuse______ people, you are saying they are doing something wrong.
a. explore b. pierce c. accuse

5. Very unusual objects are said to be ______rare______.
a. rare b. clever c. delicate

6. To ______imitate______ people is to copy them.
a. triumph b. imitate c. coast

7. A ______triumph______ might also be called a victory.
a. triumph b. symbol c. coast

8. A pin might ______pierce______ a balloon.
a. triumph b. pierce c. accuse

9. Something that is easily broken is ______delicate______.
a. clever b. rare c. delicate

10. The mathematical ______symbol______ for addition is the plus sign.
a. coast b. triumph c. symbol

The hikers were excited to **explore** a cave they had never been in before.

Synonyms

*Choose the word that is most nearly the **same** in meaning as the word or phrase in **dark print**. Then write your choice on the line provided.*

1. the beauty of the **seashore**
   a. symbol   b. triumph   c. coast   coast

2. **investigate** the caves
   a. imitate   b. explore   c. pierce   explore

3. **mimic** my voice
   a. pierce   b. imitate   c. accuse   imitate

4. **stab** the meat
   a. explore   b. coast   c. pierce   pierce

5. **blame** the dog
   a. accuse   b. pierce   c. triumph   accuse

6. a **sign** of freedom
   a. symbol   b. coast   c. triumph   symbol

Antonyms

*Choose the word that is most nearly **opposite** in meaning to the word or phrase in **dark print**. Then write your choice on the line provided.*

1. a **dumb** thing to do
   a. delicate   b. clever   c. rare   clever

2. **sturdy** glass plates
   a. clever   b. delicate   c. rare   delicate

3. a surprising **defeat**
   a. triumph   b. coast   c. symbol   triumph

4. a **common** complaint
   a. clever   b. delicate   c. rare   rare

Completing the Sentence

Choose the word from the box that best completes each item below. Then write the word on the line provided. (You may have to change the word's ending.)

accuse	**clever**	**coast**
delicate	**explore**	**imitate**
pierce	**rare**	
symbol	**triumph**	

Holidays

- Holidays give people a chance to be creative and to think of ____clever____ costumes.
- On Halloween this year, I'm going to dress up as my favorite singer. I will ____imitate____ her.
- When children visit, we put our glasses on high shelves. Glasses are ____delicate____ and break easily.
- May Day is an important holiday in England. It is ____rare____, however, for Americans to celebrate that holiday.
- It is always good to ____explore____ new ways of making the holidays fun.

Politics

- Candidates have to work very hard to get votes. If they ____coast____ along instead of working hard, they will probably not win the election.
- Unfortunately, it is common for candidates in a race to ____accuse____ each other of not telling the truth.
- Some politicians speak so loudly that their voices almost ____pierce____ the air.
- The ____symbol____ for the Republican Party is the elephant. The sign of the Democratic Party is the donkey.
- Usually, the candidate who loses the race congratulates the winner on his or her ____triumph____.

Word Associations

Circle the letter next to the choice that best completes the sentence or answers the question. Pay special attention to the word in dark print.

1. If you **accuse** me, you might say,
- a. "It's all your fault."
- b. "Thanks for your help."
- c. "I'll take the blame."
- d. "You are in the clear."

2. It's **rare** to find a
- a. four-wheeled car.
- b. four-legged cat.
- c. four-room apartment.
- d. four-leaf clover.

3. Which tool is used to **pierce**?
- a. a paintbrush
- b. a wrench
- c. a drill
- d. a ruler

4. A **delicate** object would be very easy to
- a. break.
- b. build.
- c. carry.
- d. copy.

5. To **imitate** a kangaroo, you might
- a. read and write.
- b. dance and sing.
- c. hop and wear a pouch.
- d. chirp and spread your arms like wings.

6. A race car could be a **symbol** of
- a. music.
- b. speed.
- c. food.
- d. hate.

7. If you live along the **coast** of Texas, you are probably
- a. a long way from the water.
- b. far from home.
- c. on a mountain top.
- d. near the water.

8. I **explore** if I go to a place I
- a. visit every day.
- b. know inside and out.
- c. have never been to before.
- d. think is no fun.

9. If you **triumph**, you are the
- a. loser.
- b. quitter.
- c. fighter.
- d. winner.

10. It takes a **clever** dog to
- a. bark at strangers.
- b. learn to "shake hands."
- c. chase cats and squirrels.
- d. chew on bones.

For teaching suggestions, see page T31.

Word Study • Homophones

Homophones are words that sound alike but have different spellings and meanings. For example, *symbol* (page 71) and *cymbal* are homophones. A *symbol* is something that stands for something else. A *cymbal* is a round, metal instrument that makes a crashing sound.

Read this sentence: *We used a picture of a **cymbal** as a **symbol** of our drum group*. Notice how the sentence illustrates the meaning of each homophone.

Look at the chart to find the spellings and meanings of other homophones.

brake	a stopping device
break	to split into pieces; to damage or make no longer usable
sew	to stitch together or mend using a needle and thread
sow	to plant or scatter seeds in the ground
heal	to make well
heel	the back part of the foot below the ankle

PRACTICE *Underline the homophone that completes each sentence.*

1. My mother had to (**sew, sow**) my costume for the school play.
2. The driver had to use the emergency (**brake, break**) to stop the car.
3. My broken elbow will take three months to (**heal, heel**).
4. The farmer will (**sew, sow**) corn in his field.
5. Please be careful not to (**brake, break**) my new computer game!
6. I developed a sore (**heal, heel**) from my tight sneakers.

APPLY *Use each homophone pair in a sentence. Write the sentence on the line provided. Be sure to use the correct meaning of each word.*
Accept answers that provide the correct context for each word.

7. **sew, sow** ______________________________
8. **brake, break** ______________________________
9. **heal, heel** ______________________________

Make up a riddle for one of the words in the homophone pairs below. Ask a partner to guess the word and spell it.

ate/eight **berry/bury**

Example: I am a juicy, little fruit. What am I? (a berry)

For teaching suggestions, see page T36.

Shades of Meaning • Idioms 1

In the passage "The Liberty Bell" on pages 68–69, you read this sentence: *To people from* ***coast*** *to coast, it means freedom*. Here, the word *coast* means "land near the sea or ocean."

An **idiom** is an expression that has a special meaning. You cannot figure out its meaning from the individual words. Here is an example: *Before we brought in Mom's surprise, we checked and made sure that the* ***coast was clear***. Here, the idiom *coast was clear* has nothing to do with land near the ocean. Instead, it means "there was no one around."

PRACTICE ***Read each sentence. Figure out the meaning of each idiom in dark print. Write the number of the sentence next to the meaning of the idiom.***

1. I thought writing the report would be difficult, but it was a **piece of cake**.
2. To win a race, you must be ready to start running **at the drop of a hat**.
3. "If you can't say something nice, **bite your tongue**!"
4. I was **under the weather** for a few days, but now I am well.

3 don't speak

1 easy

2 right away, instantly

4 sick

APPLY ***Read each sentence. Figure out the meaning of the idiom in dark print. Write the meaning on the line provided.***

Accept reasonable answers. Possible answers are given.

5. Mom loves Mittens more than she loves our other cats. She says, "He's the **apple of my eye**!" her favorite
6. A wave destroyed my sand castle, but I **went back to square one** and built another one. started over
7. My piano teacher **bends over backwards** to make sure I understand each lesson. tries very hard, puts in extra effort
8. Dad gets up **at the crack of dawn** each day to watch the morning news on television. very early in the morning

UNIT 8

Introducing the Words

Read the following journal article about an army from the past. Notice how the highlighted words are used. These are the words you will be learning in this unit.

The Terracotta Army

(Journal Article)

In 1974, workmen who were digging a well in northwestern China discovered an ancient secret. They uncovered the first of many life-size clay soldiers in a tomb. These soldiers were made of a kind of clay called terracotta. Over time, workers at the tomb exposed more than 8,000 warriors and horses.

The terracotta warriors and horses have been standing in the tomb for more than 2,000 years. Who were these statues supposed to be? What were they doing in the ground? Scientists have been unlocking the mystery for more than thirty years now.

About 2,200 years ago, an emperor named Qin Shi Huang Di (CHĒN SHĒ HWÄŋ dē) ruled the land now called China. To gain control, he fought wars all over the land, even in the remote areas.

When Qin lived, it was the custom to bury a ruler with things he might need after he died. Qin had many enemies, so he felt he needed an army to protect his tomb. That's why the warriors look as if they are prepared to fight.

The terracotta warriors are extremely lifelike. You can see strands of hair that cling to the neck. Every statue has a different face, hairstyle, and expression.

Emperor
Qin Shi Huang Di

Listen to this passage at vocabularyworkshop.com.

Qin was not timid about making the tomb grand. Scientists believe it took 36 years to build. At least 700,000 people worked to complete it. Also, Qin wanted to take with him everything he had when he was alive. He made sure his body would be surrounded by silks, pearls, and gems.

Qin also had statues of acrobats, singers, musicians, and dancers to entertain him. All these people would have performed for the emperor.

There were also statues of pigs, dogs, horses, and sheep in the tomb. At one time, the horses had leather straps with shiny bronze metal. The bronze still shines, but the leather decayed long ago.

The statues were painted in reds, blues, greens, and purples. When scientists took one statue out into the dry climate, the paint disappeared. Horrified, they looked for ways to save the colors in the other statues.

The emperor Qin accomplished a lot during his rule. He began using money for trading. He improved the systems for writing and for using weights and measures. The name *China* probably came from the word *Qin*.

Scientists have learned a lot about how emperors lived by exploring Qin's tomb. Unfortunately, vandals, people who set out to destroy things on purpose, had disturbed part of Qin's tomb. Some things were also damaged by water or fire. Scientists have worked to piece together what was once there.

Today, scientists are still uncovering more treasures from the tomb. With each discovery, we find out more and more about life in China so long ago.

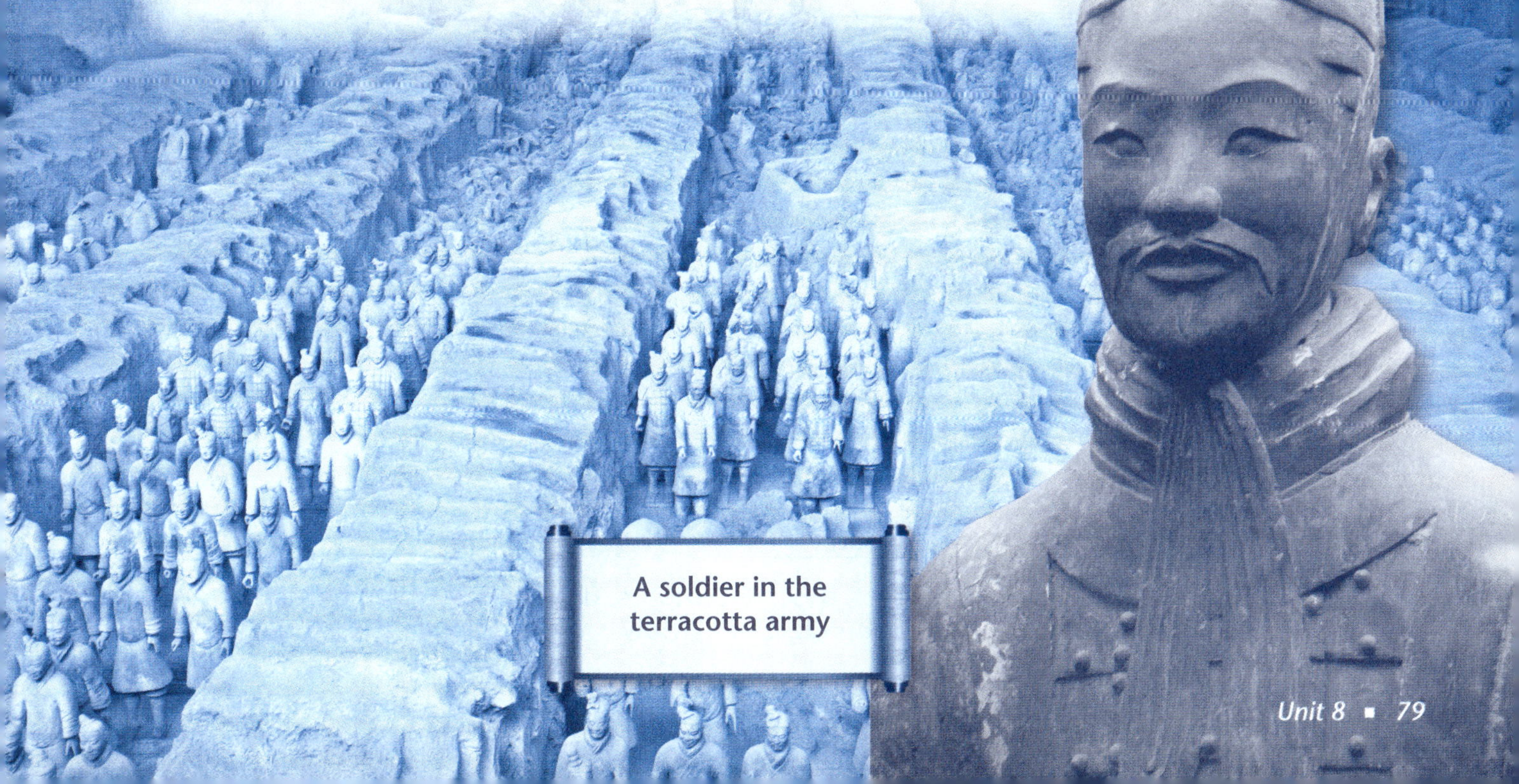

A soldier in the terracotta army

Definitions

You were introduced to the words below in the passage on pages 78–79. Study the spelling, pronunciation, part of speech, and definition of each word. Write the word on the line in the sentence. Then read the synonyms and antonyms.

Remember

A **noun** *(n.)* is a word that names a person, place, or thing.

A **verb** *(v.)* is a word or words that express action or a state of being.

An **adjective** *(adj.)* is a word that describes a noun or pronoun.

1. ancient (ān′ shənt)

(adj.) very old; early in history

The fossil remains are ancient.

SYNONYMS: antique, old-fashioned
ANTONYMS: new, recent

2. climate (klī′ mət)

(n.) the usual weather conditions of a place

I don't like that moist, hot climate.

SYNONYMS: atmosphere, environment, temperature

3. cling (kliŋ)

(v.) to hold on firmly; to have a strong attachment to or feeling for something or someone

As a child, I used to cling *to my mother.*

SYNONYMS: stick, attach, grasp
ANTONYM: release

4. custom (kus′ təm)

(n.) a common practice; the way people do things year after year

Eating turkey and stuffing is a custom *celebrated by many people on Thanksgiving.*

SYNONYMS: tradition, habit

5. decay (di kā′)

(v.) to slowly decline or fall into ruin

The salt water caused the dock to decay.

(n.) the slow decline of something; a wearing away

Go to the dentist twice a year to try to avoid tooth decay.

SYNONYMS: (v.) rot, spoil, decompose, disintegrate; (n.) weakening
ANTONYMS: (v.) flourish, bloom, thrive

6. disturb (di stûrb′)

(v.) to make upset or uneasy

We tried not to ___disturb___ *their sleep.*

SYNONYMS: interrupt, stop, disrupt, alarm
ANTONYMS: calm, soothe

7. expose (ik spōz′)

(v.) to uncover or open to view; to make something known

I promise not to ___expose___ *their secrets.*

SYNONYMS: show, reveal, disclose, display
ANTONYMS: cover, hide, disguise, mask

8. perform (pər fôrm′)

(v.) to carry out a task; to act or entertain

The couple was asked to ___perform___ *the play on Wednesday.*

SYNONYMS: sing, dance; achieve, fulfill, do, function

9. remote (ri mōt′)

(adj.) far removed in distance or time, out of the way; unlikely; very slight

We drove to a ___remote___ *cabin in the woods.*

SYNONYMS: faraway, distant, secluded
ANTONYMS: near, nearby, open

10. timid (ti′ məd)

(adj.) lacking courage or confidence

I was too ___timid___ *to talk to the new teacher.*

SYNONYMS: cautious, shy, meek
ANTONYMS: bold, brash, daring, determined, confident

Match the Meaning

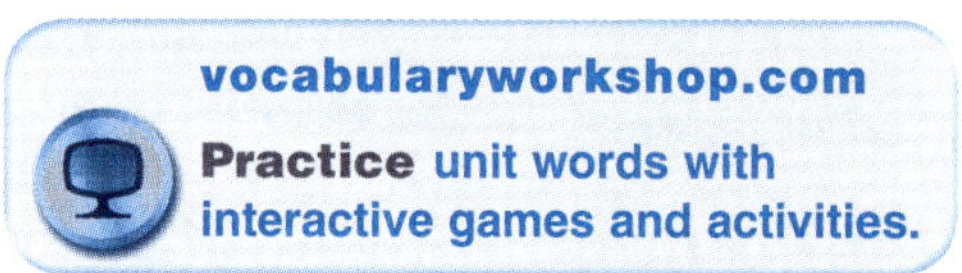

Choose the word whose meaning is suggested by the clue given. Then write the word on the line provided.

1. To interrupt a class is to ___disturb___ it.
a. cling b. decay c. disturb

2. A(n) ___remote___ place is far away.
a. ancient b. timid c. remote

3. Something very old is considered ___ancient___.
a. timid b. ancient c. remote

4. The ___climate___ of a region refers to its weather patterns.
a. custom b. climate c. decay

5. To ___cling___ is to hold on tightly.
a. cling b. perform c. expose

6. If you ___expose___ something, you uncover it.
a. decay b. perform c. expose

7. A(n) ___timid___ person lacks confidence and courage.
a. timid b. remote c. ancient

8. To put on a show is to ___perform___.
a. cling b. perform c. disturb

9. A ___custom___ is an event that is repeated regularly.
a. climate b. decay c. custom

10. The decline of something means its ___decay___.
a. climate b. custom c. decay

The tropical **climate** in the Caribbean Islands makes them a popular vacation spot.

Synonyms

*Choose the word that is most nearly the **same** in meaning as the word or phrase in **dark print**. Then write your choice on the line provided.*

1. **fulfill** your duties
   a. cling b. perform c. decay — perform

2. meat that has **spoiled**
   a. clung b. decayed c. disturbed — decayed

3. **hold** on to the wall
   a. cling b. decay c. expose — cling

4. the city's **weather**
   a. decay b. custom c. climate — climate

5. a family's **tradition**
   a. custom b. climate c. decay — custom

6. news that **upsets**
   a. clings b. performs c. disturbs — disturbs

Antonyms

*Choose the word that is most nearly **opposite** in meaning to the word or phrase in **dark print**. Then write your choice on the line provided.*

1. **new** coins
   a. ancient b. remote c. timid — ancient

2. a **nearby** road
   a. timid b. ancient c. remote — remote

3. a **bold** reaction
   a. remote b. ancient c. timid — timid

4. **cover** the wound
   a. cling b. expose c. perform — expose

Completing the Sentence

Choose the word from the box that best completes each item below. Then write the word on the line provided. (You may have to change the word's ending.)

ancient	climate	cling
custom	decay	disturb
expose	perform	
remote	timid	

Gorillas and Their Environment

- Many gorillas live in jungles and tropical rain forests.
- The ___climate___ of a tropical rain forest is very wet, with very high temperatures.
- A young gorilla will ___cling___ to its mother's back when traveling in the jungle.
- Female gorillas may seem more ___timid___ than males, but in fact they are just as brave.
- Gorillas sleep for a few hours after they eat. It is wise not to ___disturb___ them while they sleep!

Our Theater

- Welcome to our theater! I know it looks old and in a state of ___decay___, but I promise you that it will stand up just fine!
- This theater was once a beautiful place. Just push back the curtains to ___expose___ the lovely murals on the wall.
- This evening, we will ___perform___ a show for you.
- Every year, it is our ___custom___ to put on a show celebrating different countries.
- This play is based on an ___ancient___ Egyptian myth. It is a very old story of how the planet Earth was born.
- I know the chances that I'll become a great star are ___remote___. If that does happen, however, I will be happy to share my secrets of success!

Word Associations

Circle the letter next to the choice that best completes the sentence or answers the question. Pay special attention to the word in dark print.

1. Which is **ancient**?
   a. a computer
   b. a bicycle
   c. a puppy
   d. a mummy

2. A **custom** is something you
   a. do on a regular basis.
   b. don't like to do.
   c. are forced to do.
   d. don't do at all.

3. To **expose** house plants to light, you might put them
   a. near a window.
   b. in a closet.
   c. under the bed.
   d. in the basement.

4. A **timid** person might try to
   a. show off.
   b. make a speech.
   c. be a hero.
   d. shy away from a group.

5. When an apple starts to **decay**, it
   a. tastes sweet and juicy.
   b. goes brown and mushy.
   c. is fresh and crispy.
   d. needs to be washed.

6. People who study the **climate** of a place pay attention to
   a. its people.
   b. its weather.
   c. its traffic.
   d. its cities.

7. If I **disturb** you, I should say,
   a. "Have you read a good book?"
   b. "Will you come to my party?"
   c. "Excuse me for bothering you."
   d. "Please take a bath."

8. To **perform** a task, you must
   a. finish it.
   b. stay away from it.
   c. quit before the end.
   d. ask an adult for help.

9. A **remote** cabin would have
   a. many rooms.
   b. many visitors.
   c. few neighbors.
   d. many houses nearby.

10. If you **cling** to an idea, you
    a. hold on to it.
    b. forget it.
    c. ignore it.
    d. change your mind.

For teaching suggestions, see page T31.

Word Study • Context Clues 2

The **context clues** in a sentence can help you figure out the meaning of a word you do not know. There are many types of context clues. You have learned how to look for a definition. You can also look for examples that can help you figure out the meaning of a word.

Example

The stove, dishwasher, and microwave are different kitchen ***appliances.***

The examples are stove, dishwasher, and microwave. These things help you understand that appliances are machines that perform specific jobs.

PRACTICE *Read each sentence. Use context clues to figure out the meaning of the word in* ***dark print.*** *Write the number of each sentence next to the correct meaning.*

1. He showed us **vessels** such as sailboats, canoes, and kayaks.
2. We felt **sorrowful** and upset when we left our new friends.
3. Apple, peach, and cherry **blossoms** all come from blooming fruit trees.
4. The beach was covered with **litter** such as cans, bottles, and wrappers.

4 trash

1 boats

2 unhappy

3 flowers

APPLY *Read each sentence. Underline the words that help you figure out the meaning of the word in* ***dark print.*** *Then write a definition and a new sentence for the word.*

Accept sentences that use the word correctly in context.

5. My **chores** at home are setting the table and walking the dog.

Definition: jobs or work you do for other people

New Sentence: ______

6. The spaceship was an **extraordinary**, or uncommon, sight in the sky.

Definition: strange, unusual

New Sentence: ______

Give examples of things that belong in the same group. Ask your partner to name the group.

Example: **Partner 1**: *hammer, screwdriver, wrench*

Partner 2: tools

For teaching suggestions, see page T36.

Shades of Meaning • Words That Describe People 1

In the passage "The Terracotta Army" on pages 78–79, you read this sentence: *Qin was not **timid** about making the tomb grand.* The sentence tells us that Qin was bold. He was not afraid to say what he wanted the tomb to look like.

All the words in the chart describe people. Learning the words will help you choose the right word to use when you describe people in speaking and writing.

timid	People who are **timid** are shy. They may lack courage or confidence.
friendly	People who are **friendly** are kind and pleasant.
helpful	People who are **helpful** are ready to assist others.

PRACTICE ***Write the word from the chart that best describes the person speaking.***

1. I see that you are new here. What's your name? friendly
2. Let me take out the recycling bin for you. helpful
3. Can I let someone else read my report to the class? timid
4. Would you like me to put away the dishes? helpful
5. I don't want to walk into the party by myself. timid
6. Hi there! Do you want to eat lunch with us today? friendly

APPLY ***Think about a person you know who fits each description. Describe the person. Explain how he or she fits the description.***

Accept answers that students can justify.

7. **friendly** ______________________________

____

8. **helpful** ______________________________

____

9. **timid** ______________________________

____

UNIT 9

Introducing the Words

Read the following passage about a talented sister and brother. Notice how the highlighted words are used. These are the words you will be learning in this unit.

The Talent Show

(Realistic Fiction)

"I can't sing in the talent show without you," Sundara said.

"I can't sing even *with* you," her brother Vijay replied. "I am so bashful. I would probably melt right on the stage."

"That's a silly remark," Sundara said. "You sing really well."

"I'm shy! Give me a break!"

Sundara did not give in. "Please, please, please!" she begged. "You know this talent show benefits the food bank."

"Okay, I'll consider it," Vijay said. "Don't get your hopes up, though!"

Sundara kept trying. "But we could win. You have a terrific voice," she said.

Vijay said, "You know I don't like to compete with other people."

"That's fine," Sundara said. "Just rehearse with me then."

For the next hour, Sundara and Vijay practiced together while their father played the piano. Finally, Vijay agreed to sing with his sister.

The morning of the talent show, Vijay was very nervous. Then at breakfast, everything changed.

"Good morning," Sundara said in a low moan.

"What's wrong?" Vijay asked.

Then Sundara sneezed.

"Get away!" Vijay said. He shielded his face almost as a reflex.

Sundara couldn't speak. She wrote a short note on a pad of paper and showed it to him.

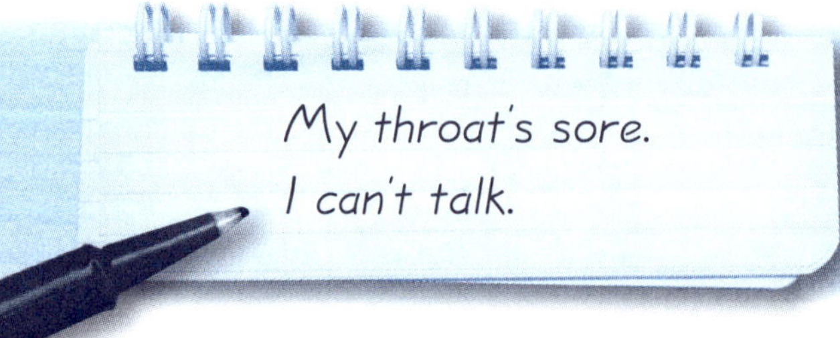

Vijay was suddenly happy. "Too bad," he said. "No duet tonight!" Sundara started scribbling and then thrust another note at him.

Don't think for a ***brief*** *moment that you aren't singing!*

Vijay started to protest. Sundara grabbed the pad again. She wrote:

Stop it! You have the ***ability****. Now just do it—for the food bank!*

Vijay suddenly felt selfish. Of course, he had to sing. It was the right thing to do.

That day, he kept busy to avoid thinking about the show. He practiced the song with his dad first. Then he rode his bike, washed the car, and did some homework. A few hours later, he was onstage. It was his turn to sing.

Before Vijay knew it, the song had ended. As he walked backstage, his mom hugged him and said, "Your song was delightful!"

Ms. Spencer, the show's host, now took the stage. She had two announcements. First, the students had raised over $1,000 for the food bank. Second, the judges had made their decision. Ms. Spencer announced the third-place and second-place winners. Vijay was relieved that his name wasn't called.

Next, Ms. Spencer said, "It's time to announce the first-place winner." She paused and said, "Let's have Vijay Rana come to the stage!" Ms. Spencer handed him a trophy and then asked him to say a word or two.

Vijay said, "Thank you so much. This is a great honor. I want to dedicate this trophy to my sister. After all, I wouldn't be here if it weren't for her!"

Definitions

You were introduced to the words below in the passage on pages 88–89. Study the spelling, pronunciation, part of speech, and definition of each word. Write the word on the line in the sentence. Then read the synonyms and antonyms.

Remember

A **noun** *(n.)* is a word that names a person, place, or thing.

A **verb** *(v.)* is a word or words that express action or a state of being.

An **adjective** *(adj.)* is a word that describes a noun or pronoun.

1. ability (ə bil′ ə tē)

(n.) the power or skill to do something

Lifeguards must have the ___ability___ *to swim well.*

SYNONYMS: talent, capacity, capability
ANTONYMS: inability, powerlessness

2. avoid (ə void′)

(v.) to keep away from

They tried to ___avoid___ *the mud, but they were not successful.*

SYNONYMS: evade, escape, elude
ANTONYM: seek

3. bashful (bash′ fəl)

(adj.) shy, not at ease, especially in a social setting

Why were you so ___bashful___ *at the party?*

SYNONYMS: timid, reserved, awkward, uneasy
ANTONYMS: bold, brash, aggressive, outgoing

4. brief (brēf)

(adj.) short in time, amount, or length

A three-day vacation is too ___brief___ *for me.*

SYNONYMS: quick, fleeting, concise
ANTONYMS: long, lengthy, extended

5. compete (kəm pēt′)

(v.) to try for something, such as a prize; to take part in a game or contest; to play against another or others

In gym, students might ___compete___ *in the 50-yard dash.*

SYNONYMS: strive, rival, contend, challenge

6. consider
(kən sid′ ər)

(v.) to think about or pay attention to

Be sure to consider *your choices carefully.*

SYNONYMS: weigh, analyze, evaluate, ponder, study
ANTONYMS: decline, reject, repel

7. delightful
(di līt′ fəl)

(adj.) very pleasing, wonderful

Going to a carnival is a delightful *experience.*

SYNONYMS: lovely, appealing, enjoyable, agreeable, pleasant, joyful
ANTONYMS: disagreeable, displeasing, unpleasant, joyless

8. honor
(ä′ nər)

(n.) great respect; a sign of respect; a sense of what is right

They sent a card in honor *of my birthday.*

(v.) to respect or value

We should honor *our teachers.*

SYNONYMS: (n. & v.) praise, credit, esteem; (n.) glory, recognition, privilege
ANTONYMS: (n. & v.) disgrace, dishonor; (v.) humiliate

9. reflex
(rē′ fleks)

(n.) an automatic response, usually very quick

My reflex *is to jump at the sight of a spider.*

SYNONYM: instinct

10. remark
(ri märk′)

(n.) a short statement

That was an unkind remark *about their old shoes.*

(v.) to say, mention; give an opinion

Ask them to remark *on the shape of the clouds.*

SYNONYMS: (n. & v.) comment; (n.) observations; (v.) observe, speak, state, mention

Match the Meaning

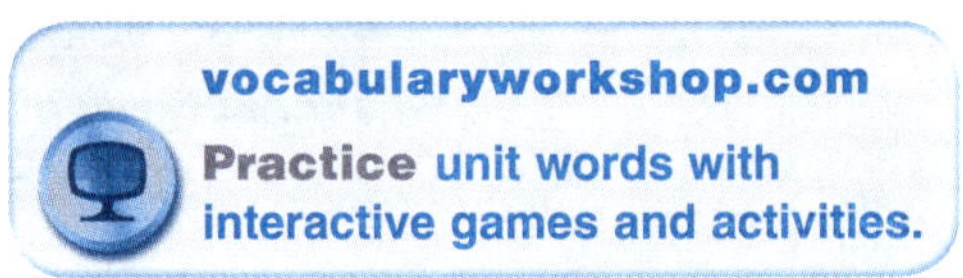

Choose the word whose meaning is suggested by the clue given. Then write the word on the line provided.

1. A quick reaction is a(n) ______reflex______.
a. ability b. reflex c. honor

2. A person who has the skill to do something has the ______ability______ to do it.
a. remark b. honor c. ability

3. When I make a(n) ______remark______, I am commenting on something.
a. remark b. ability c. honor

4. To ______avoid______ something is to stay away from it.
a. avoid b. consider c. compete

5. A ______brief______ speech is a short one.
a. bashful b. brief c. delightful

6. People who are afraid to speak up might be ______bashful______.
a. bashful b. brief c. delightful

7. To ______consider______ taking an action is to think about doing it.
a. compete b. consider c. remark

8. To ______compete______ in a race is to take part in it.
a. avoid b. remark c. compete

9. A person who is well respected receives much ______honor______.
a. ability b. reflex c. honor

10. The long vacation was enjoyable and ______delightful______.
a. delightful b. bashful c. brief

On this obstacle course, the contestants must **avoid** the cones.

Synonyms

*Choose the word that is most nearly the **same** in meaning as the word or phrase in **dark print**. Then write your choice on the line provided.*

1. **escape** the bad weather
   a. compete b. consider c. avoid avoid
2. **strive** for the first place
   a. consider b. compete c. remark compete
3. a **shy** newcomer
   a. bashful b. brief c. delightful bashful
4. a nasty **comment**
   a. honor b. remark c. reflex remark
5. **study** the test results
   a. avoid b. compete c. consider consider
6. a quick **response**
   a. ability b. reflex c. remark reflex

Antonyms

*Choose the word that is most nearly **opposite** in meaning to the word or phrase in **dark print**. Then write your choice on the line provided.*

1. a **lengthy** conversation
   a. brief b. bashful c. delightful brief
2. a **disagreeable** situation
   a. brief b. delightful c. bashful delightful
3. **humiliate** the person
   a. avoid b. honor c. remark honor
4. an **inability** to understand
   a. honor b. ability c. reflex ability

Completing the Sentence

Choose the word from the box that best completes each item below. Then write the word on the line provided. (You may have to change the word's ending.)

ability	**avoid**	**bashful**
brief	**compete**	**consider**
delightful	**honor**	
reflex	**remark**	

My Pets

■ My parents often ______remark______ on how well I take care of my dog and cat, saying that I treat my pets very well.

■ Each of my pets has different ______abilities______. A talent that my cat has is the ability to react and move quickly. She can do that because she has great ______reflexes______.

■ My cat is sometimes ______bashful______. At times, she hides from strangers, the way a shy child might.

■ I love to watch my dog play with other dogs. It's fun to watch the dogs ______compete______ for a big bone or a ball, bumping into each other as each one tries to get the object.

■ Once in a while, I come home from school and am very tired. I'm just not in the mood to play with my dog and cat! On those days, I almost feel like ______avoiding______ my pets.

■ But I always make sure to spend some time with them. Even a ______brief______ amount of time with them is better than no time at all!

■ I love my cat and dog. They are both charming and ______delightful______. It is a(n) ______honor______ to have them as pets!

■ Which animal do you ______consider______ to be the better pet? You have to decide that for yourself!

For teaching suggestions, see page T31.

Word Study • Analogies 1

An **analogy** is a statement that shows how two pairs of words are related. It is usually in the following form: ____ is to ____ as ____ is to ____.

Look at the examples at the right. In Example 1, *bashful* (page 90) and *bold* are antonyms. To complete this analogy, find another pair of words that are antonyms. Answer *b, restless* and *relaxed,* are also antonyms. Here is the complete analogy: *bashful* is to *bold* as *restless* is to *relaxed.*

In Example 2, *remark* (page 91) and *comment* are synonyms. Answer *b, grasp* is to *cling,* completes the analogy: *remark* is to *comment* as *grasp* is to *cling.*

Example 1

Antonyms

bashful is to *bold* as

a. *fast* is to *quick*

b. *restless* is to *relaxed*

Example 2

Synonyms

remark is to *comment* as

a. *throw* is to *catch*

b. *grasp* is to *cling*

PRACTICE *Complete each analogy with the missing word. Write the number of the analogy next to the word that best completes it.*

1. *shatter* is to *break* as *wander* is to	3 *foolish*
2. *honor* is to *respect* as *harm* is to	2 *hurt*
3. *gentle* is to *rough* as *wise* is to	4 *short*
4. *damp* is to *wet* as *brief* is to	1 *roam*

APPLY *Complete each analogy with a word from the box. Then write whether the words in both pairs are synonyms or antonyms.*

ancient	depart	reject
reveal	truthful	

5. *freeze* is to *boil* as *hide* is to reveal — antonyms

6. *strong* is to *weak* as *recent* is to ancient — antonyms

7. *wash* is to *clean* as *leave* is to depart — synonyms

8. *remember* is to *forget* as *accept* is to reject — antonyms

9. *fair* is to *just* as *honest* is to truthful — synonyms

Speak *Create an analogy using a word from Units 7–9. Have a partner complete the analogy. Talk about the relationship between the words.*

Vocabulary for Comprehension

*Read the following passage in which some of the words you have studied in Units 7–9 appear in **dark print**. Then answer the questions on page 97.*

Pants as Good as Gold

I'm so glad I left New York for California. Most people came here to make their fortunes mining gold, but not me. I came to start my own business. I am not a **timid** man! I am not afraid to try new things. In New York, my family sold dry goods. I was confident that I would be successful doing the same in California. Most people would be busy looking for gold. I would have few dry goods merchants to **compete** with.

When I arrived in 1853, I opened my business and named it after myself, Levi Strauss. I sold goods to the small stores where miners bought supplies. My business has grown. I have moved several times to bigger locations.

In 1872, big became huge. I got a letter from a tailor named Jacob Davis. He had a **clever** idea. Davis attached metal rivets to pants at the places where they stretch and pull. The rivets **performed** an important job. They made the pants stronger and last longer.

That made me think. I had often heard miners **remark** that their pants wore out too quickly. Most pants are just too **delicate** for digging for gold! So when Davis asked for my help, I agreed to join him. I knew that many miners would want these sturdy work pants.

Now I am proud when I see miners wearing denim pants with rivets. I like to hear them say their pants are both long lasting and comfortable. I intend to keep making these extraordinary pants. Who would have thought that pants would be as good as gold?

The rivets in the new design meant pants didn't wear out quickly.

Fill in the circle next to the choice that best completes the sentence or answers the question.

1. This passage is mostly about
- (a) Strauss's journey out West.
- (b) how Strauss got rich from making pants.
- (c) why people looked for gold.
- (d) miners in California.

2. The meaning of **timid** is
- (a) bold.
- (b) silent.
- (c) not have courage.
- (d) slow to decide.

3. Strauss would have few merchants to **compete** with because
- (a) most people would be looking for gold.
- (b) his family sold dry goods in New York.
- (c) he named his business after himself.
- (d) the merchants sold few supplies.

4. Another word for **clever** is
- (a) strong.
- (b) slow.
- (c) smart.
- (d) strange.

5. In this passage, **performed** means
- (a) carried out a task.
- (b) entertained.
- (c) made.
- (d) punched with holes.

6. The meaning of **remark** in this passage is
- (a) to question.
- (b) to wonder.
- (c) to do again.
- (d) to make a statement.

7. **Delicate** most nearly means
- (a) sturdy.
- (b) weak.
- (c) fancy.
- (d) small.

8. You can figure out that Strauss
- (a) missed his family.
- (b) wanted to dig for gold.
- (c) made friends easily.
- (d) was proud of his success.

Write Your Own

The pants that Levi Strauss and Jacob Davis made led to the many different kinds of blue jeans in stores today. Think about the effect of Strauss and Davis's creation. On a separate sheet of paper, describe how their creation affects us today. Use at least three words from Units 7–9.

UNIT 10

Introducing the Words

Read the following fairy tale about an unusual test that a princess must pass. Notice how the highlighted words are used. These are the words you will be learning in this unit.

The Princess and the Pea

(Fairy Tale)

Once upon a time, there was a rich, handsome prince. He was also a man of great wit and charm. Many maidens tried to conquer his affection. Often, they pretended to be princesses! It had all become very frustrating. The prince would only marry a true princess.

One day, the prince was hunting in the woods. Suddenly, he saw a maiden on the brink of a cliff. She was crying softly.

"What is wrong, dear lady?" he asked.

"I wandered off from my royal party and am lost," she said.

"Are you a princess?"

"Of course!" she snapped. "What do you intend to do to help me?"

Before he could answer, the wind blew fiercely. A loud clap of thunder shook the forest. The fury of the storm made it impossible to speak. The prince helped the maiden onto his horse and took her back to his castle.

By the time they reached the castle, the maiden felt a chill. Her cloak was wet, and her teeth were chattering. The prince's servants brought hot soup. Then one of them handed the young woman a fresh gown with patterns of polka dots and stripes.

The maiden shrieked. "A princess can't wear this! I must have velvet!"

So the servant brought her a velvet gown. The maiden said, "I wish to sleep now."

The prince thought, "She acts like royalty, but is she an actual princess? I must find out."

The young woman was led up to a tower. Twenty mattresses were placed one on top of the other. The top mattress was covered with a quilt

made with vibrant patches of color. A pea was placed under the mattress at the very bottom of the pile. The maiden climbed a ladder to the top and got into bed.

The next morning, the prince entered the tower.

The maiden said, "I must apologize for my behavior yesterday. I was fortunate to have been saved from the storm. I am grateful for your help."

"How did you sleep, dear lady?" the prince asked.

The maiden said, "I hate to complain, but I slept very poorly! There is something hard under the bed!"

"So you are a princess! Will you marry me?"

"I don't think so," she said. "You couldn't tell that I was a princcss."

"Many maidens have tried to fool me. I had to put you to the test. You felt the pea under the twenty mattresses. Only a real princess would be so delicate. Wouldn't you prefer someone who could truly judge your royal upbringing?"

The princess softened. After they got to know one another, she agreed to marry him. They lived happily ever after, and the princess never again slept with a pea under her mattress.

Definitions

You were introduced to the words below in the passage on pages 98–99. Study the spelling, pronunciation, part of speech, and definition of each word. Write the word on the line in the sentence. Then read the synonyms and antonyms.

Remember

A **noun** *(n.)* is a word that names a person, place, or thing.

A **verb** *(v.)* is a word or words that express action or a state of being.

An **adjective** *(adj.)* is a word that describes a noun or pronoun.

1. actual (ak′ chü wəl)

(adj.) happening in fact or reality

The actual *cost was far less than we guessed it would be.*

SYNONYMS: real, true, factual, genuine, authentic, existing
ANTONYMS: false, untrue, unreal, nonexistent

2. brink (briŋk)

(n.) the edge, especially of a high, steep place

The hiker stood at the brink *of the cliff.*

3. chill (chil)

(n.) an unpleasant feeling of coldness; coolness

I felt a chill *as I skated on the pond.*

(v.) to make or become cold

Should we chill *the dessert?*

SYNONYMS: (n.) nip; (v.) cool, refrigerate
ANTONYMS: (n. & v.) heat; (n.) warmth; (v.) defrost; warm

4. conquer (kän′ kər)

(v.) to defeat or take over; to master or overcome

The army hoped to conquer *the enemy quickly.*

SYNONYMS: win, beat, overpower, overthrow
ANTONYMS: surrender, yield, submit, relinquish

5. fortunate (fôr′ chə nət)

(adj.) having or bringing good luck; lucky

We were fortunate *to have no rain during spring break.*

SYNONYMS: blessed, happy, successful, favorable
ANTONYMS: unfortunate, unlucky, unfavorable

6. fury
(fyůr′ ē)

(n.) strong anger, rage

A bad temper often leads to a state of ___fury___.

SYNONYMS: wrath, fierceness, violence, force, power

7. intend
(in tend′)

(v.) to plan to do something; to have a goal or purpose

I hope you ___intend___ *to do your homework.*

SYNONYMS: plan, mean, aim, expect, propose

8. pattern
(pat′ ərn)

(n.) the way that shapes and colors are put together; a model or guide for making something; a design that is repeated

The striped ___pattern___ *is the same in each candy cane.*

(v.) to make or follow according to a model or design

I hope to ___pattern___ *my behavior after someone I look up to.*

SYNONYMS: (n. & v.) style, form; (n.) system, order, arrangement, sequence, standard; (v.) imitate, match

9. vibrant
(vī′ brənt)

(adj.) full of life, energy, or activity

Your personality is lively and ___vibrant___.

SYNONYMS: lively, energetic, spirited, dynamic, vivid, bright, striking
ANTONYMS: lifeless, dull, ordinary, unremarkable

10. wit
(wit)

(n.) the talent to describe things or people in a funny or unusual way; the ability to think clearly; a clever and amusing person

A teacher with ___wit___ *often knows how to keep the students' attention in class.*

SYNONYMS: humor, intelligence, cleverness

Match the Meaning

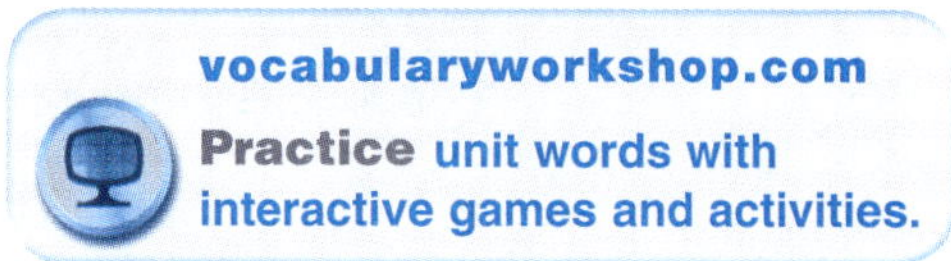

Choose the word whose meaning is suggested by the clue given. Then write the word on the line provided.

1. A ______pattern______ is a design that repeats.
a. wit b. brink c. pattern

2. Something that is true or real is ______actual______.
a. actual b. vibrant c. fortunate

3. You might look over the ______brink______ of a riverbank to look for fish.
a. brink b. chill c. fury

4. A funny person is also sometimes called a ______wit______.
a. pattern b. wit c. brink

5. When you make something cold, you ______chill______ it.
a. conquer b. pattern c. chill

6. Something ______vibrant______ is full of life.
a. actual b. vibrant c. fortunate

7. If you are ______fortunate______, you have good luck.
a. actual b. fortunate c. vibrant

8. To overcome a problem is to ______conquer______ it.
a. conquer b. chill c. intend

9. A very angry person might show ______fury______.
a. brink b. pattern c. fury

10. To ______intend______ to complete a project is to plan to finish it.
a. chill b. conquer c. intend

The woman had to **conquer** her fear of heights before skydiving.

Synonyms

*Choose the word that is most nearly the **same** in meaning as the word or phrase in **dark print**. Then write your choice on the line provided.*

1. hang over the **edge**
   a. fury b. brink c. pattern brink

2. the tiger's **rage**
   a. wit b. chill c. fury fury

3. showing great **intelligence**
   a. brink b. wit c. pattern wit

4. a gorgeous **design**
   a. pattern b. chill c. fury pattern

5. **plan** to see us
   a. intend b. chill c. conquer intend

Antonyms

*Choose the word that is most nearly **opposite** in meaning to the word or phrase in **dark print**. Then write your choice on the line provided.*

1. an **unreal** event
   a. vibrant b. actual c. fortunate actual

2. **warm up** the dessert
   a. chill b. conquer c. pattern chill

3. an **unlucky** person
   a. actual b. vibrant c. fortunate fortunate

4. **surrender** the territory
   a. conquer b. pattern c. intend conquer

5. a **dull** story
   a. actual b. fortunate c. vibrant vibrant

Completing the Sentence

Choose the word from the box that best completes each item below. Then write the word on the line provided. (You may have to change the word's ending.)

actual	**brink**	**chill**
conquer	**fortunate**	**fury**
intend	**pattern**	
vibrant	**wit**	

Books

- I read every book the same way. My reading ___pattern___ is to find a book, put my feet up, and turn to the first page.
- I like reading biographies because I know that I am reading the ___actual___ facts of a person's life.
- I love authors who put ___wit___ into their stories and make me laugh out loud.
- Some mystery books are so good that reading them can send ___chills___ up my spine.
- The books that I enjoy most are those that are fun to read and have a ___vibrant___ writing style.
- My favorite author is Roald Dahl. I like *James and the Giant Peach* so much that I ___intend___ to read it again.

Water, Water Everywhere

- One way that people have tried to ___conquer___ the endless flow of rivers is to build dams, levees, and reservoirs.
- Scientists stand at the ___brink___ of a cliff to observe the flow of the river below.
- People who live in areas of high rainfall are ___fortunate___. They are lucky that they never have to worry about getting enough water.
- There is nothing that compares with the ___fury___ of a hurricane.

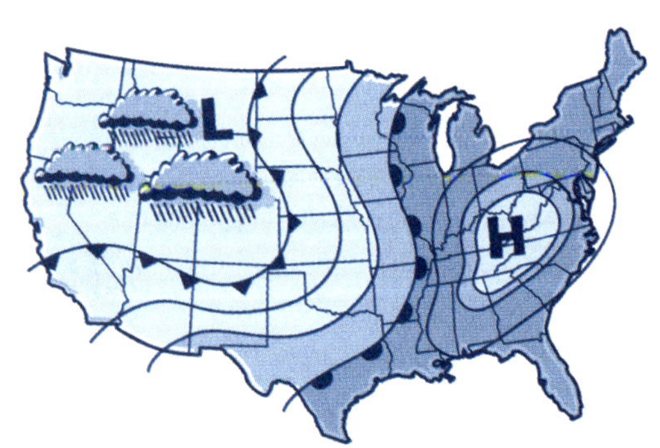

Word Associations

Circle the letter next to the choice that best completes the sentence or answers the question. Pay special attention to the word in dark print.

1. A story of **actual** events is about
a. made-up events.
b. events that never happened.
c. real events.
d. aliens or robots.

2. "I **intend** to go bowling" means
a. I never want to bowl.
b. I plan to try bowling.
c. I'm afraid to try bowling.
d. I don't know what bowling is.

3. If the Bugs **conquer** the Bees, you can say that
a. the Bugs win.
b. the Bees win.
c. the Bugs lose.
d. it's a tie game.

4. A **vibrant** poem is one that
a. always rhymes.
b. sounds like all the others.
c. is exciting.
d. is boring.

5. One way to **chill** a drink is to
a. add ice cubes to it.
b. boil it for five minutes.
c. sprinkle salt into it.
d. pour it into a jar.

6. A song with **wit** might make you
a. cry.
b. laugh.
c. forget the words.
d. cover your ears.

7. Which comment shows **fury**?
a. "What a tasty dessert!"
b. "Sweet dreams, dear."
c. "That's a beautiful sweater!"
d. "Wait till I give them a piece of my mind!"

8. We stood at the **brink** of the cliff
a. to enjoy the view.
b. to eat lunch.
c. to get out of the storm.
d. to fly a kite.

9. You'd probably feel **fortunate** if
a. you got caught in the rain.
b. you scraped your knee.
c. you found a $10 bill.
d. you lost your wallet.

10. A dress with a **pattern** has a
a. long zipper.
b. repeating design.
c. shiny belt.
d. roomy pocket.

For teaching suggestions, see page T32.

Word Study • Prefixes *un-, de-, over-*

You have learned that a **prefix** is a word part that is added to the beginning of a **base word** to make a new word.

Look at the prefixes and base words in this chart. The prefix *un-* means "not." You can add *un-* to *fortunate* (page 100) to make the word *unfortunate*. *Unfortunate* means "not fortunate."

Prefix	Base Word		New Word		Meaning
un	+ fortunate	=	**un**fortunate	→	not fortunate
de	+ frost	=	**de**frost	→	remove frost or ice
over	+ flow	=	**over**flow	→	beyond the top

The prefix *de-* often means "remove." The prefix *over-* means "too much" or "beyond." Look at the chart for examples of words with the prefixes *de-* and *over-*.

PRACTICE ***Write the missing prefix or base word. Then write the meaning of the new word.***

Prefix		Base Word		New Word		Meaning
1. un	+	safe	=	unsafe	→	not safe
2. over	+	time	=	overtime	→	extra time
3. de	+	plane	=	deplane	→	get off the plane
4. un	+	certain	=	uncertain	→	not sure

APPLY ***Complete each sentence with a word that contains the prefix un-, de-, or over-. Choose from the words in the boxes above.***

5. During a thunderstorm, it is unsafe to be outside.

6. I took the turkey out of the freezer to defrost it.

7. The worker got paid for overtime after working extra hours this week.

8. The passengers on Flight 24 will deplane at City Airport.

Add the prefix un-, de-, or over- to each word below to make a new word. Then write a sentence for each new word. You may use a dictionary if you need help.

value **happy** **eat**

For teaching suggestions, see page T37.

Shades of Meaning • Idioms 2

In the passage "The Princess and the Pea" on pages 98–99, you read this sentence about the prince: *He was also a man of great* ***wit*** *and charm.* In this sentence, the word *wit* means "being clever when using words or ideas."

An **idiom** is an expression with a special meaning. You cannot figure out its meaning from the individual words. Here is an example: *So many answers on the test looked right that the girl was* ***at her wit's end***. Here, the idiom *at her wit's end* doesn't refer to clever words or ideas. Instead, it tells how the girl feels. *At her wit's end* means "so upset that she does not know what to do." Below are some idioms that express how we think or feel.

PRACTICE ***Read each sentence. Figure out the meaning of each idiom in dark print. Write the number of the sentence next to the meaning of the idiom.***

1. I feel **tongue-tied** when I begin an oral report, but I start to relax as I speak.	3 interested in a way that makes you excited and nervous
2. I have been **on top of the world** since I won the spelling contest.	1 having problems expressing yourself because you are nervous
3. I was **on the edge of my seat** every time our team got close to scoring a point.	4 doubts about a decision you have made
4. I wanted to ride the roller coaster, but I had **second thoughts** when I saw how big it was.	2 feeling wonderful or very happy about something

APPLY ***Read each sentence. Figure out the meaning of each idiom in dark print. Write the meaning on the line provided.***

Accept reasonable answers. Possible answers are given.

5. I had **my heart set** on going to the street fair until it rained.

to really want to do something

6. My brother looked **down in the mouth**, but he wouldn't tell me what was wrong.

sad and unhappy, not smiling

7. Mom promised to **keep an open mind** as I told her how I wanted to decorate my room.

listen to all the facts before forming an opinion

UNIT 11

Introducing the Words

Read the following journal article about a shipwreck that was found hundreds of years after it was lost at sea. Notice how the highlighted words are used. These are the words you will be learning in this unit.

Treasure Among Diamonds

(Journal Article)

In March 1533, a ship named *Bom Jesus* sailed from Lisbon, Portugal. It was headed for India. At the time, Portugal was in its full glory as a rich and powerful nation. Its kings and queens sent ships to trade in faraway places.

It was a tradition to celebrate when a ship sailed. Flags waved in the harbor. Castles displayed colorful banners. In this way, people waved good-bye to the crew of the *Bom Jesus*.

Gold coins were found in the *Bom Jesus* wreckage.

Listen to this passage at vocabularyworkshop.com.

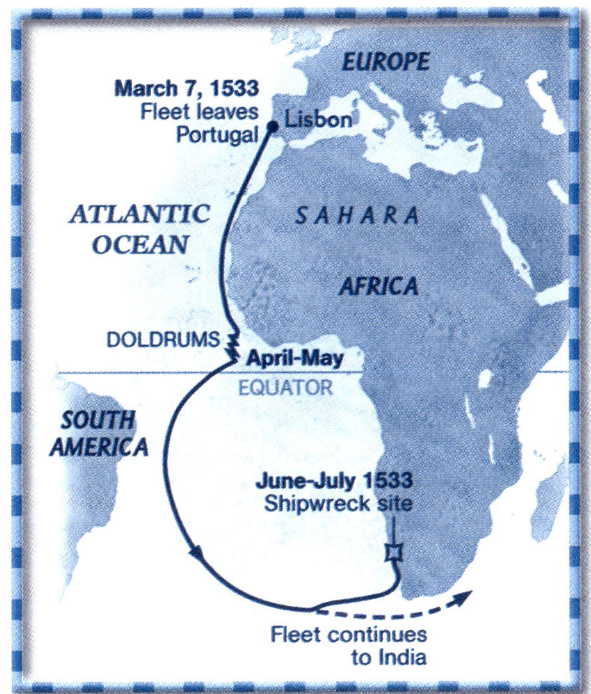

This map shows the journey of the *Bom Jesus.*

After leaving Lisbon, the ship approached the Atlantic Ocean. It was carrying a magnificent load of gold and copper for trading. Pieces of these metals would be traded for rare spices such as pepper and cloves. Later, the spices could be sold for a lot of money.

In those days, ship travel was not for the meek or easily frightened sailor. Danger was always near. Storms could arise. Ships could split apart on rocks. From 1525 to 1600, twenty-one ships bound for India were lost at sea.

Four or five months after leaving Lisbon, the *Bom Jesus* was approaching the tip of Africa. Suddenly, a wild storm pushed the ship toward the shore. The ship struck rocks. All that was on board spilled into the sea. The *Bom Jesus* sank out of sight.

Hundreds of years later, diamonds were discovered in the African country of Namibia. The discovery happened to take place near the rocks where the *Bom Jesus* had sunk. Now a company had opened a diamond mine at the site.

In 2008, a mine worker found an oddly shaped piece of copper on the beach. He took it to the mine company's geologist. The geologist, a scientist who studies the earth, recognized the piece. It was an ingot, a block of copper. He knew it would have been traded for spices long ago.

The geologist also knew that if there was a copper ingot, there was a good chance that a shipwreck was nearby. He described the findings to scientists who searched for shipwrecks. However, since the diamond-mining company owned the beach, the mine owners had to approve any plan for a search.

The response of the mine owners was prompt. They agreed that scientists could look for the ship's wreckage. However, they would only give the searchers ten weeks. Also, the owners would be watchful to make sure no diamonds disappeared from the beach. That meant examining each shipwreck item before it was removed from the site.

The scientists believed that the ship was the *Bom Jesus*. Their guess turned out to be right. By the end of their search, they had uncovered 50 pounds of gold. They found 22 tons of copper ingots. They discovered cannons, swords, guns, and ivory. A wooden part of the ship was recovered, too. All these treasures helped to tell the story and revive the memory of people who sailed the sea so long ago.

Definitions

You were introduced to the words below in the passage on pages 108–109. Study the spelling, pronunciation, part of speech, and definition of each word. Write the word on the line in the sentence. Then read the synonyms and antonyms.

Remember

A **noun** *(n.)* is a word that names a person, place, or thing.

A **verb** *(v.)* is a word or words that express action or a state of being.

An **adjective** *(adj.)* is a word that describes a noun or pronoun.

1. approach (ə prōch′)

(v.) to come close to; to begin to deal with; to make a request

We watched the brand new train ___approach___ *the station.*

(n.) the act of coming close to; a way to deal with something or someone; a way of reaching a place

The ___approach___ *of spring makes many people giddy.*

SYNONYMS: (v. & n.) access; (v.) near; undertake; (n.) manner, method, technique, attitude, style; entrance, avenue
ANTONYMS: (v.) leave, avoid, retreat

2. approve (ə prüv′)

(v.) to have a high opinion of; to give permission

My parents ___approve___ *of my loyal friends.*

SYNONYMS: accept, admire; agree to, endorse, authorize
ANTONYMS: reject, condemn, disapprove

3. glory (glôr′ ē)

(n.) great honor or praise given by others; great beauty

Can anything match the ___glory___ *of a sunset?*

SYNONYMS: fame; splendor, magnificence
ANTONYMS: shame, disgrace, dishonor; ugliness

4. magnificent (mag ni′ fə sənt)

(adj.) very grand and fine; remarkably beautiful or outstanding

The Taj Mahal in India is a ___magnificent___ *building.*

SYNONYMS: superb, majestic, striking, splendid, glorious, impressive
ANTONYMS: ordinary, plain, simple, modest, poor

5. meek
(mēk)

(adj.) not courageous or strong

I felt meek *and did not speak loudly enough.*

SYNONYMS: mild, gentle, quiet; weak, timid
ANTONYMS: strong, courageous, brave, bold, outgoing, outspoken, aggressive

6. prompt
(prämpt)

(adj.) on time; done quickly and without delay

They answered the invitation in a prompt *manner.*

(v.) to move someone to action; to remind someone what to do or what to say

I had to prompt *my friend to make the call.*

SYNONYMS: (adj.) early, punctual, timely; fast, quick; (v.) cause, make, urge, encourage, motivate, cue
ANTONYMS: (adj.) slow, late, tardy, delayed; (v.) discourage, deter

7. revive
(ri vīv′)

(v.) to bring or come back to life

The nurse tried to revive *the patient.*

SYNONYMS: resuscitate, renew, restore
ANTONYMS: deaden, impair, kill

8. tradition
(trə di′ shən)

(n.) a custom, belief, or idea that has been passed down over time

Celebrating with a Fourth of July parade is a tradition *in many towns and cities.*

SYNONYMS: pattern, practice, ritual

9. watchful
(wäch′ fəl)

(adj.) always noticing what is happening, aware

A scout must be silent and watchful.

SYNONYMS: alert, observant, vigilant
ANTONYMS: sleepy, unaware, oblivious

10. wreckage
(re′ kij)

(n.) what is left of something that has been destroyed

The wreckage *of the car was taken away.*

SYNONYMS: ruins, remains, remnants, destruction

Match the Meaning

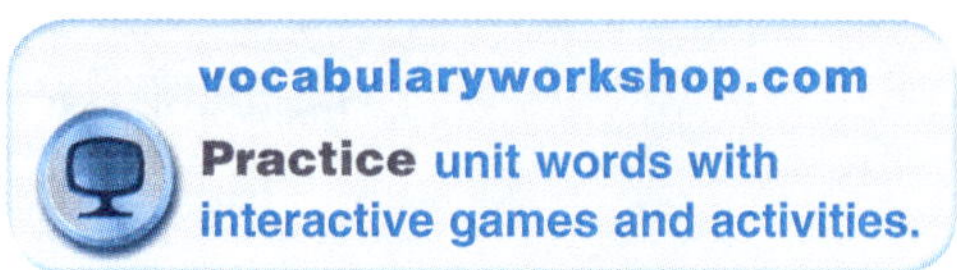

Choose the word whose meaning is suggested by the clue given. Then write the word on the line provided.

1. A ___magnificent___ object might also be described as splendid.
a. meek b. magnificent c. prompt

2. When you give an okay to a job, you ___approve___ it.
a. revive b. approach c. approve

3. To lack courage is to be ___meek___.
a. watchful b. meek c. magnificent

4. A(n) ___approach___ to a highway brings you close to it.
a. wreckage b. glory c. approach

5. The remains of an explosion are often called ___wreckage___.
a. wreckage b. approach c. glory

6. A(n) ___tradition___ is a custom that is passed down.
a. approach b. tradition c. glory

7. To ___revive___ someone is to bring that person back to life.
a. approve b. approach c. revive

The cat kept a **watchful** eye on the bird.

8. To be ___watchful___ is to be awake and alert.
a. watchful b. prompt c. magnificent

9. People who are ___prompt___ are known to be on time.
a. magnificent b. watchful c. prompt

10. Those who want great honor may want a lot of ___glory___.
a. glory b. tradition c. wreckage

Synonyms

*Choose the word that is most nearly the **same** in meaning as the word or phrase in **dark print**. Then write your choice on the line provided.*

1. resuscitate the patient
a. approach b. approve c. revive revive

2. a family **ritual**
a. wreckage b. approach c. tradition tradition

3. near the finish line
a. approach b. revive c. approve approach

4. give **praise** to the winner
a. glory b. approach c. wreckage glory

5. endorse the new test
a. approach b. revive c. approve approve

6. clean up the **ruins**
a. glory b. wreckage c. tradition wreckage

Antonyms

*Choose the word that is most nearly **opposite** in meaning to the word or phrase in **dark print**. Then write your choice on the line provided.*

1. a **simple** gown
a. meek b. magnificent c. prompt magnificent

2. a **strong** reaction to the insult
a. watchful b. meek c. magnificent meek

3. a **sleepy** guard
a. magnificent b. prompt c. watchful watchful

4. discourage the decision
a. prompt b. glory c. tradition prompt

Completing the Sentence

Choose the word from the box that best completes each item below. Then write the word on the line provided. (You may have to change the word's ending.)

approach	**approve**	**glory**
magnificent	**meek**	**prompt**
revive	**tradition**	
watchful	**wreckage**	

Ancient Rome

■ The Roman gods received much ___glory___ and honor because they were believed to have incredible powers and strengths.

■ No expense was spared in building the ___magnificent___ temples where these gods were honored.

■ The destruction of Rome resulted in the ___wreckage___ of these temples. Today we see only their ruins.

■ It would not be a good idea to ___revive___ the ancient Roman custom of having gladiators fight lions in coliseums.

■ The Spanish custom of bullfighting is modeled after that early Roman ___tradition___.

School Lunch

■ Our teachers do not ___approve___ of bad manners in the cafeteria.

■ They are ___watchful___ of us as we carry our trays to our tables. They want to make sure there are no accidents and that no child gets hurt.

■ In the rush to get in line for the hot lunch, ___meek___ children often end up being the last to get their food.

■ Today, our class was the first class to ___approach___ the doors of the cafeteria. That put us at the beginning of the line.

■ Students who are ___prompt___ and finish their lunch on time get to go outside for recess.

Word Associations

Circle the letter next to the choice that best completes the sentence or answers the question. Pay special attention to the word in dark print.

1. If you **approve** of the restaurant, it is likely that you will
a. hate the food you order.
b. like the food you order.
c. argue with the waiter.
d. argue over the bill.

2. In a quarrel, a **meek** child might
a. make strong arguments.
b. refuse to give in.
c. yell and scream.
d. not speak up at all.

3. A **magnificent** hotel would have
a. lumpy beds and broken chairs.
b. fancy rooms and a grand lobby.
c. small, plain guest rooms.
d. poor guest service.

4. You might see **wreckage** after
a. the street cleaners come.
b. you mow the lawn.
c. a building is torn down.
d. you go to the movies.

5. **Prompt** guests will probably be
a. angry.
b. annoying.
c. on time.
d. delayed.

6. It is an old **tradition** in our school to have
a. a field day every June.
b. teachers in the classroom.
c. windows in every room.
d. a telephone number.

7. As I **approach** the lake, it
a. appears to be farther away.
b. is harder to see.
c. seems smaller.
d. appears to be closer.

8. To **revive** an old car, you must
a. make it run again.
b. call an ambulance.
c. learn to drive.
d. sell it.

9. A **watchful** clerk
a. chats with customers.
b. daydreams a lot.
c. doesn't notice much.
d. pays close attention.

10. One **glory** of nature is a
a. muggy night.
b. rainbow.
c. dust storm.
d. mosquito bite.

For teaching suggestions, see page T32.

Word Study • Suffixes *-ness, -er, -or*

You have learned that a **suffix** is a word part that is added to the end of a **base word** to make a new word.

Base Word	Suffix	New Word		Meaning
prompt	+ **ness**	= prompt**ness**	→	the state of being on time
teach	+ **er**	= teach**er**	→	someone who teaches
act	+ **or**	= act**or**	→	someone who acts

Look at the base words and suffixes in this chart. The suffix *-ness* usually means "a state of being." You can add the suffix *-ness* to *prompt* (page 111) to make the word *promptness*. *Promptness* means "the state of being on time."

The suffixes *-er* and *-or* mean "someone who does." Look at the chart for examples of words with the suffixes *-er* and *-or*.

PRACTICE *Write the missing base word or suffix. Then write the meaning of the new word.*

	Base Word	Suffix	New Word		Meaning
1.	paint	+ er	= painter	→	someone who paints
2.	kind	+ ness	= kindness	→	the state of being kind
3.	invent	+ or	= inventor	→	someone who invents
4.	great	+ ness	= greatness	→	the state of being great

APPLY *Complete each sentence with a word (or words) that contains the suffix* -ness, -er, *or* -or. *Choose from the words in the boxes above.*

5. My favorite actor is performing in the new play.

6. The painter will display his paintings in the museum.

7. When our neighbors helped us with the gardening, we thanked them for their kindness.

8. When I arrived on time for class, my teacher looked at the clock and praised my promptness.

Continue the chart in Practice. List more words with the suffixes -ness, -er, *and* -or. *Write the meaning of each new word.*

For teaching suggestions, see page T37.

Shades of Meaning • Words That Describe People 2

In the passage "Treasure Among Diamonds" on pages 108–109, you read this sentence: *In those days, ship travel was not for the **meek** or easily frightened sailor.* The word *meek* tells the reader that only very daring sailors could endure such trips.

When you describe a person, it is important to use words that give your reader or listener a picture of the person. Look at the words in the chart. They all can be used to describe a person.

aloof	If someone is **aloof**, that person is not very warm or friendly toward other people. The person does not become involved.
bold	If someone is **bold**, that person is not afraid to do things that involve risk or danger.
meek	If a person is **meek**, that person is gentle and mild in manner. The person is likely to do what other people say.

PRACTICE *Write the word from the chart that best describes each kind of person.*

1. My friend does everything her sister tells her to do. meek
2. The newcomer didn't care to join in any conversations. aloof
3. The student spoke out in support of the unpopular class president. bold
4. Our new neighbor showed no interest in helping to plan the block party. aloof

APPLY *Think about a person you know who fits each description. Describe the person. Explain how he or she fits the description.*
Accept answers that students can justify.

5. **aloof** ______________________________

6. **bold** ______________________________

7. **meek** ______________________________

Introducing the Words

Read the following folktale about a clever tiger's promise. Notice how the highlighted words are used. These are the words you will be learning in this unit.

The Tiger's Promise

(Korean Folktale)

Long ago, a tiger roamed in the area of a small village. The people were terribly frightened. They put up signs that read, "Watch out for the tiger!" The warnings were punctuated with large exclamation points.

However, the signs didn't do much good. The tiger remained in the area, and everyone was afraid to go outside. The villagers decided it would be better to try to prevent attacks by trapping the tiger. They dug a deep hole and covered it with branches. Sure enough, the tiger fell in and couldn't get out.

The next day, a young man heard a barely audible cry. He looked down into the hole and saw the tiger weeping quietly.

"What's wrong?" the young man asked.

"Woe is me!" said the tiger. "I fell into this hole. If I were a bird, I could fly out. If I were a snake, I could glide away through a tunnel. I am neither of these animals, so I am trapped. Please help me get out!"

The young man was kind, but he was not a fool. He said, "I can't help you—you'll eat me."

"Not true!" the tiger said. "Help me, and I'll return the favor to you someday." Meanwhile, his stomach rumbled with hunger.

The young man lowered a log into the hole. The tiger used it to climb out. When he reached the top, he said, "Hello, breakfast!"

"Wait!" the young man said. "You promised."

"You were foolish to believe that," the tiger said with scorn. "Now I'm afraid I will have to consume you."

A skinny ox was grazing nearby. The young man called out to him. "Kind ox, do you think it's fair for the tiger to eat me?"

The ox looked up from his meal. He said, "As a representative of all the beasts that spend their lives working, I would say it is quite fair. People have done nothing but take advantage of oxen since the origin of humankind. Just look at me—I should be stout and well rested, but instead I am lean and always tired."

Just then a small rabbit hopped by.

The now desperate young man said, "Please, Rabbit, what do you think? I helped the tiger out of the hole. Now he wants to eat me."

The rabbit said to the young man and the tiger, "Show me how this happened."

The young man removed the log from the hole. The tiger, anxious to eat his meal, jumped into the hole.

The tiger said, "You see, I was here and . . ."

". . . there you will stay!" Rabbit said. He turned to the young man. "And you, young man, think twice before you rescue another tiger. A tiger *never* keeps a promise!"

Definitions

You were introduced to the words below in the passage on pages 118–119. Study the spelling, pronunciation, part of speech, and definition of each word. Write the word on the line in the sentence. Then read the synonyms and antonyms.

Remember

A **noun** *(n.)* is a word that names a person, place, or thing.

A **verb** *(v.)* is a word or words that express action or a state of being.

An **adjective** *(adj.)* is a word that describes a noun or pronoun.

1. audible (ô′ də bəl) (adj.) capable of being heard

The music was audible *down the street.*

SYNONYMS: loud, clear, distinct
ANTONYMS: inaudible, faint, indistinct

2. consume (kən süm′) (v.) to eat or drink, especially in large amounts; to use up; to destroy

We plan to consume *an early dinner.*

SYNONYMS: devour; deplete, waste

3. glide (glīd) (v.) to move smoothly and easily

I watched the speed skater glide *around the rink.*

SYNONYMS: slide, coast, cruise, sail

4. origin (ôr′ ə jən) (n.) the cause or beginning

The origin *of chocolate is the cacao bean.*

SYNONYMS: start, source, root, ancestry
ANTONYMS: end, finish, death

5. prevent (pri vent′) (v.) to stop from happening

Waterproof boots prevent *feet from getting wet.*

SYNONYMS: bar, block, prohibit, restrain, obstruct
ANTONYMS: allow, permit, encourage

6. punctuate (puŋk′ chü wāt)

(v.) to mark printed or written materials with periods, commas, and other signs; to give importance to

Be careful how you ___punctuate___ *your sentences.*

SYNONYMS: emphasize, accentuate

7. representative (rep ri zen′ tə tiv)

(n.) a typical example; someone who acts for another

She was the company's ___representative___ *at the meeting.*

(adj.) having to do with elected members; being a typical example

That painting is ___representative___ *of pop art.*

SYNONYMS: (n.) type; agent, spokesperson, delegate; (adj.) elected, chosen; typical
ANTONYMS: (adj.) atypical, unrepresentative

8. scorn (skôrn)

(n.) a feeling that something or someone is worthless or inferior; an expression of that feeling

It is not right to treat those who are less fortunate with ___scorn___.

(v.) to act with contempt toward an object or a person; to make fun of

I wish they did not ___scorn___ *my old bicycle.*

SYNONYMS: (n. & v.) ridicule; (n.) disrespect, mockery; (v.) mock, sneer, dismiss; ANTONYMS: (n.) admiration, praise; (v.) approve, embrace

9. stout (staůt)

(adj.) large and heavy in build; physically strong and sturdy; having courage or determination

The ___stout___ *old maple stood in the meadow.*

SYNONYMS: fat; brave, bold, courageous
ANTONYMS: cowardly, timid; weak; thin

10. woe (wō)

(n.) great sorrow or suffering; trouble

I felt such ___woe___ *when my poor dog died.*

SYNONYMS: sadness, unhappiness, misery, grief; misfortune, suffering
ANTONYMS: happiness, joy; luck

Match the Meaning

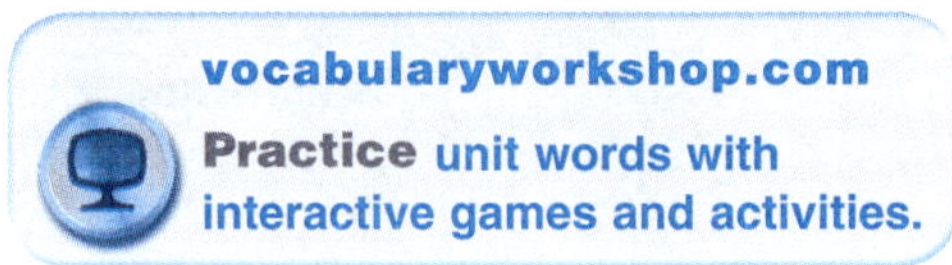

Choose the word whose meaning is suggested by the clue given. Then write the word on the line provided.

1. To ____punctuate____ is to emphasize.
a. consume b. glide c. punctuate

2. When people feel ____woe____, they feel sadness.
a. woe b. scorn c. representative

3. If you ____consume____ something, you use it up.
a. glide b. consume c. prevent

4. The source of a story is its ____origin____.
a. woe b. origin c. representative

5. When a sound can be heard, it is ____audible____.
a. audible b. representative c. stout

6. To ____glide____ is to move along without much effort.
a. consume b. punctuate c. glide

7. When you sneer at something, you show ____scorn____ for it.
a. origin b. woe c. scorn

8. If you try to ____prevent____ something, you are trying to stop it from happening.
a. prevent b. consume c. glide

9. Something that is ____stout____ might also be called sturdy.
a. audible b. representative c. stout

10. A(n) ____representative____ statement is a typical one.
a. audible b. representative c. stout

I felt deep **woe** when I lost my favorite jacket.

Synonyms

*Choose the word that is most nearly the **same** in meaning as the word or phrase in **dark print**. Then write your choice on the line provided.*

1. the **root** of their unhappiness
a. scorn b. woe c. origin origin

2. **cruise** along peacefully
a. consume b. prevent c. glide glide

3. **emphasize** my remarks
a. glide b. prevent c. punctuate punctuate

4. showed terrible **disrespect**
a. scorn b. origin c. woe scorn

5. a **loud** screech
a. audible b. stout c. representative audible

6. **deplete** your energy
a. scorn b. consume c. glide consume

Antonyms

*Choose the word that is most nearly **opposite** in meaning to the word or phrase in **dark print**. Then write your choice on the line provided.*

1. was overcome with **joy**
a. scorn b. origin c. woe woe

2. an **atypical** example
a. audible b. stout c. representative representative

3. a **cowardly** heart
a. stout b. audible c. representative stout

4. **allow** the discussion
a. prevent b. consume c. punctuate prevent

Completing the Sentence

Choose the word from the box that best completes each item below. Then write the word on the line provided. (You may have to change the word's ending.)

audible	**consume**	**glide**
origin	**prevent**	**punctuate**
representative	**scorn**	
stout	**woe**	

Astronauts in Space

■ Astronauts looking down on Earth from space can see oceans and land, but no sounds from our planet are ____audible____.

■ In a spaceship, the astronauts' bodies ____glide____ around smoothly because there is no gravity pulling them down.

■ Astronauts must ____consume____ their food from freeze-dried packets.

■ Even though this food is not very tasty, astronauts must eat in order to ____prevent____ weakness.

Opera

■ The ____origin____ of the term *opera* is the Italian phrase *opera in musica*, meaning "work in music."

■ There are many styles of opera. Therefore, we cannot say that any one opera is ____representative____ of the musical form.

■ People used to think that opera singers needed to have bodies that are ____stout____ and strong. However, many opera singers who have powerful voices are actually quite slim.

■ Many operas deal with touching human stories. Often, a character feels ____scorned____ by a loved one. This situation leads to songs that show strong feelings of ____woe____.

■ Moments of great drama can be ____punctuated____ by trumpets blaring.

For teaching suggestions, see page T32.

Word Study • Homographs 1

Homographs are multiple-meaning words that have more than one dictionary entry. Homographs are spelled the same but have different meanings. Each entry word is followed by a small raised number.

pound[1]	a unit of measure for weight
pound[2]	to hit hard again and again

The word *pound* is a homograph. Look at the box above to see how *pound* might appear in a dictionary.

Look at the chart for other homographs and their meanings.

bank[1]	a place in which money is saved or used for business purposes
bank[2]	the land, often sloping, along the edge of a river or creek
left[1]	relating to the particular side of a person's body
left[2]	went away from
ring[1]	something shaped like a circle
ring[2]	to make the sound of a bell

PRACTICE *Complete each sentence with a homograph from the chart. Then write the number of the homograph whose meaning is shown.*

2 **1.** We found a good place to fish along the bank.

1 **2.** The friends hold hands and form a ring around the pole.

2 **3.** He left the house early this morning to go to work.

2 **4.** The camper will ring the dinner bell at 5 o'clock each day.

1 **5.** I plan to put my baby-sitting money in the bank.

1 **6.** She keeps her keys in her left pocket.

APPLY *Complete each sentence using words from the chart above.*

7. The guard at the bank where I keep my money always stands to the left of the safe.

8. Dad wanted to buy the ring at the jewelry store, but he realized that he left his wallet at home.

Write a sentence using a word from the charts above. Have your partner tell which meaning of the word fits your sentence.

Vocabulary for Comprehension

Read the following passage in which some of the words you have studied in Units 10–12 appear in dark print. Then answer the questions on page 127.

REVIEW UNITS 7–12

A Mountain Hike

Adam gazed at the huge, **magnificent** mountain ahead of him. He **intended** not only to hike to the top but also to camp out there overnight. Although Adam was excited, he was nervous. He had never hiked this far before. He was worried about wild animals, too. What if a bear entered his tent? Adam knew it was important for hikers always to be **watchful**. "I'll have to be aware of my surroundings at all times," Adam said to himself.

His camp counselor's whistle interrupted his thoughts. "Let's get going!" Grace told all ten campers. Adam was determined to **conquer** the challenge. He walked at a brisk pace to keep up with his friends. At first, the trail was flat, so the hike seemed easy. Before long, the group had completed one mile. Grace called for a water break. "The next couple of miles may get harder," she said, "but you can do it!"

Adam was determined. "Nothing will **prevent** me from completing this hike," he thought, "except a bear!" As the hike continued, Adam felt the trail get steeper. His breathing became heavier, too. After a while, Adam was afraid he would need to stop. Just then he heard Grace say, "Here we are!" The group had reached the top of the mountain. Adam realized that he could put aside his worries. He knew now that he could do anything he put his mind to. He also realized that he was so hungry he could **consume** a bear!

Fill in the circle next to the choice that best completes the sentence or answers the question.

1. This passage is mostly about
- (a) how Adam felt during a hike.
- (b) what to take on a hike.
- (c) when Adam completed one mile of the hike.
- (d) why Adam went on a hike.

2. The meaning of **magnificent** is
- (a) fun.
- (b) ordinary.
- (c) grand.
- (d) poor.

3. Intended most nearly means
- (a) planned.
- (b) agreed.
- (c) worried.
- (d) considered.

4. Another word for **watchful** is
- (a) sleepy.
- (b) alert.
- (c) careless.
- (d) simple.

5. The meaning of **conquer** is
- (a) avoid.
- (b) forget.
- (c) overcome.
- (d) begin.

6. To **prevent** means
- (a) to allow.
- (b) to encourage.
- (c) to beg.
- (d) to stop.

7. At the end of the story, Adam was
- (a) disappointed that he didn't finish the hike.
- (b) sorry that he came on the trip.
- (c) scared to sleep overnight on the mountain.
- (d) relieved that he had completed the hike.

8. In this passage, **consume** means to
- (a) race.
- (b) eat.
- (c) scare.
- (d) buy.

Write Your Own

In this story, Adam battled fear and nervousness, but he eventually met his goal and completed a long hike. Imagine how you would feel if you were in a similar situation. On a separate sheet of paper, tell a story (real or made up) in which you deal with a fear in order to complete a challenge. Use at least three words from Units 10–12.

Classifying

Choose the word from the box that goes best with each group of words. Write the word on the line provided. Then explain what the words have in common.

ancient	**bashful**	**chill**
climate	**cling**	**delightful**
fortunate		**rare**
representative		**symbol**

1. lucky, fortunate, blessed

The words are synonyms.

2. reserved, bashful, friendly, outgoing

The words name types of personality traits.

3. ancient, old, recent, brand-new

The words describe age.

4. ring, wing, sting, cling

The words rhyme.

5. president, senator, governor, representative

The words name leaders elected by the people.

6. heat, warm, chill, freeze

The words show how to change an object's temperature.

7. symbol, symbolic, symbolize

The words belong to the same family.

8. rare, medium, well-done

The words describe degrees of doneness.

9. lovely, pleasant, charming, delightful

The words are synonyms.

10. temperature, rainfall, humidity, climate

The words have to do with weather conditions.

Completing the Idea

Complete each sentence so that it makes sense. Pay attention to the word in dark print. Accept answers that show an understanding of the vocabulary.

1. One place I would like to **explore** is ________________.
2. Life on a **remote** island is likely ________________.
3. When I feel scared, my **reflex** is to ________________.
4. My favorite shirt has a **pattern** of ________________.
5. A kite is able to **glide** freely if ________________.
6. It bothers me when people **accuse** me of ________________.
7. Mom wants to **revive** our old car because ________________.
8. My favorite superhero has the **ability** to ________________.
9. The citizens showed **scorn** for the mayor because he ________________.
10. It is a **tradition** in my family to ________________.
11. The concert was so loud that it was **audible** ________________.
12. Please don't **disturb** me when I am ________________.
13. A **vibrant** person might ________________.
14. If you are not **prompt**, then ________________.
15. Many people felt much **woe** after ________________.

Writing Challenge

Check that vocabulary is used correctly and that each sentence is written correctly.

Write two sentences using the word ***coast****. In the first sentence, use* ***coast*** *as a noun. In the second sentence, use* ***coast*** *as a verb.*

1. ________________
2. ________________

REVIEW UNITS 7–12

UNIT 13

Introducing the Words

Read the following news article about one of the world's leading sports events. Notice how the highlighted words are used. These are the words you will be learning in this unit.

The Winter Olympics

(News Article)

Every four years, countries from all over the world compete in the Winter Olympics. This competition is all about snow and ice. Opponents race and jump on skis. They fly 90 miles an hour down a track on bobsleds. Snowboarders jump and twist on courses of packed snow. Figure skaters make fantastic jumps and create beautiful arches in their backs as they twirl on the ice.

Athletes go to the Games with great hopes. All yearn to become champions. Some come back home with medals. Others don't win anything. All come back with one thing in common: They have had the experience of being an Olympic athlete.

A Brief History of the Olympic Games

The first Olympic Games took place about three thousand years ago in ancient Greece. The earliest competition was a modest event. The racers ran a short distance on foot—only 210 yards! Later, more races were added. Events in wrestling, jumping, and throwing were also added. Then the Romans conquered Greece, and the Olympic Games eventually disappeared.

In 1896, the first modern Olympics were held. The first Games were the summer Games, but people were already talking about a winter event. In 1924, the first winter Games were held.

The five rings in the Olympic flag represent the five continents.

Snowboarding is a breathtaking sport.

The Modern Winter Olympics

Many changes have come about in the past nine decades of Winter Olympic competition. At first, professional athletes were not allowed to participate. In 1988, an agreement was signed that granted professionals the right to compete. Some of the first professional winter Olympic athletes played on ice hockey teams.

Today, technology helps with the grave responsibilities that come with judging Olympic events. Such technology can clarify who wins and who loses. In skiing and skating, a race can be won by fractions of a second. Today, computers make it easier to determine who wins and by how much. Also, judges may review an event on video. Doing so can help them decide if a first-place finish is valid.

Going for the Gold

In individual competition, the top three finishers of an event each earn a medal. The first place medal is gold. The second place is silver, and the third place is bronze. Today, an authentic gold medal is only part gold. Solid gold medals are too expensive to make.

After each event, the top three finishers stand on a platform. Each country's flag is raised. The gold medal winner listens to his or her country's national anthem. Tears may follow. It is an emotional occasion. At that moment, the athlete has been declared the best in his or her sport.

Definitions

You were introduced to the words below in the passage on pages 130–131. Study the spelling, pronunciation, part of speech, and definition of each word. Write the word on the line in the sentence. Then read the synonyms and antonyms.

Remember

A **noun** *(n.)* is a word that names a person, place, or thing.

A **verb** *(v.)* is a word or words that express action or a state of being.

An **adjective** *(adj.)* is a word that describes a noun or pronoun.

1. arch (ärch)

(n.) a curved structure that serves as an opening and as a support

The door to the castle had an ___arch___ *over it.*

(adj.) main; playful, mischievous

Surprisingly, the ___arch___ *enemies joined forces.*

SYNONYMS: (n.) archway, curvature, semicircle; (adj.) chief, principal; sly

2. authentic (ô then′ tik)

(adj.) being the real thing; worthy of belief, true

These are ___authentic___ *diamonds.*

SYNONYMS: actual, genuine; sincere
ANTONYMS: fake, false, counterfeit, inauthentic

3. clarify (klar′ ə fī)

(v.) to say clearly or make easier to understand

The teacher tried to ___clarify___ *the assignment.*

SYNONYMS: explain, simplify
ANTONYMS: bewilder, complicate, obscure

4. declare (di klâr′)

(v.) to state strongly; to make a formal or an official statement

I was too shy to ___declare___ *my feelings.*

SYNONYMS: announce, assert, proclaim
ANTONYM: deny

5. grant (grant)

(v.) to permit or allow; to admit that something is true

The leader decided to ___grant___ *their request.*

(n.) something that is given

They received a ___grant___ *to study other cultures.*

SYNONYMS: (v. & n.) award; (v.) give; allow, concede; (n.) gift, present
ANTONYMS: (v.) refuse, disallow

6. grave
(grāv)

(n.) a hole in the ground where something is buried

The ___grave___ *of President Ulysses S. Grant is in New York City.*

(adj.) very important and requiring much attention; serious

The climbers were in ___grave___ *danger.*

SYNONYMS: (n.) tomb; (adj.) critical, significant; solemn, somber
ANTONYMS: (adj.) insignificant, unimportant; cheerful, joking, lighthearted, merry

7. modest
(mä′ dəst)

(adj.) not thinking too highly of oneself, not boastful; proper in speech, dress, or behavior; not extreme or large

We were surprised at how ___modest___ *the famous singer was.*

SYNONYMS: reserved, humble; simple; moderate
ANTONYMS: bold, conceited, proud, self-assured, vain; excessive, grand

8. opponent
(ə pō′ nənt)

(n.) someone who is set against another, as in a contest, game, argument, or fight

In the sport of fencing, each ___opponent___ *challenges the other with a special kind of sword.*

SYNONYMS: foe, rival, enemy, competitor, challenger
ANTONYMS: ally, partner, helper, friend, teammate

9. valid
(va′ ləd)

(adj.) supported by facts or evidence, true

Your report presents many ___valid___ *arguments.*

SYNONYMS: convincing, persuasive, sound
ANTONYMS: false, invalid, unconvincing

10. yearn
(yûrn)

(v.) to long for

I ___yearn___ *for our vacation.*

SYNONYMS: desire, wish, want, crave, need, pine, hunger, thirst

Match the Meaning

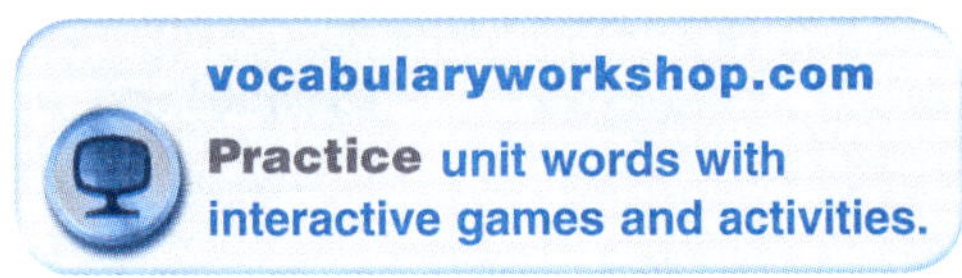

Choose the word whose meaning is suggested by the clue given. Then write the word on the line provided.

1. The person you are playing against is your ____opponent____.
a. arch b. opponent c. grave

2. To want something very much is to ____yearn____ for it.
a. declare b. yearn c. clarify

3. An object that is ____authentic____ is real and not a copy.
a. grave b. authentic c. modest

4. When you make a strong statement, you ____declare____ something.
a. declare b. arch c. grant

5. A ____grave____ expression is a serious one.
a. modest b. valid c. grave

6. To allow something to happen is to ____grant____ it permission to happen.
a. clarify b. yearn c. grant

7. A(n) ____arch____ has a curved shape.
a. opponent b. grave c. arch

8. When you ____clarify____ what you say, you make it easier to understand.
a. declare b. clarify c. grant

9. A(n) ____valid____ argument is said to be true and correct.
a. valid b. modest c. arch

10. A(n) ____modest____ amount is a small amount.
a. authentic b. grave c. modest

The puppy made the girl **yearn** for a pet.

Synonyms

Choose the word that is most nearly the ***same*** *in meaning as the word or phrase in* ***dark print****. Then write your choice on the line provided.*

1. a frightening **foe**
   a. grant　　b. arch　　c. opponent　　opponent

2. **pine** for a banana
   a. clarify　　b. yearn　　c. declare　　yearn

3. a **solemn** event
   a. grave　　b. arch　　c. valid　　grave

4. **announce** the winner
   a. yearn　　b. clarify　　c. declare　　declare

5. **concede** the favor
   a. grant　　b. arch　　c. clarify　　grant

6. a **mischievous** smile
   a. authentic　　b. modest　　c. arch　　arch

Antonyms

Choose the word that is most nearly ***opposite*** *in meaning to the word or phrase in* ***dark print****. Then write your choice on the line provided.*

1. **fake** coins
   a. arch　　b. authentic　　c. modest　　authentic

2. a **false** statement
   a. modest　　b. valid　　c. grave　　valid

3. a **vain** gymnast
   a. valid　　b. authentic　　c. modest　　modest

4. **complicate** the math lesson
   a. clarify　　b. declare　　c. yearn　　clarify

Completing the Sentence

Choose the word from the box that best completes each item below. Then write the word on the line provided. (You may have to change the word's ending.)

arch	**authentic**	**clarify**
declare	**grant**	**grave**
modest	**opponent**	
valid	**yearn**	

Baseball

■ A good baseball announcer will ___clarify___ the complicated rules of the game.

■ It is the job of the umpire at home plate to ___declare___ whether a pitch is a ball or a strike.

■ It's always nice to find major league players who are ___modest___ and do not like to brag about themselves.

■ All players ___yearn___ to play a good game. Of course, they want to beat their ___opponents___.

■ That is certainly a ___valid___ goal, but no team can win all the time, no matter how hard the players try.

Museums

■ We saw designs of Greek temples in the museum and learned that the ___arches___ above the doorways can have a point at the top.

■ We also learned that the paintings in the museum are not fake but ___authentic___.

■ Many museums offer ___grants___ to students that allow them to study how the artworks were made.

■ Some students even dig up old ___graves___ in ancient cities to learn about people who lived in the past.

Word Associations

Circle the letter next to the choice that best completes the sentence or answers the question. Pay special attention to the word in dark print.

1. You need to **clarify** rules that
   a. are easy to follow.
   b. are not important.
   (c.) are complicated.
   d. nobody cares about.

2. People usually have **grave** looks on their faces when they are
   a. at a circus.
   (b.) at a funeral.
   c. at a brunch.
   d. at a party.

3. Your **opponent** probably wants
   a. to help you.
   b. to feed you.
   c. to lose to you.
   (d.) to beat you.

4. Which forms a natural **arch**?
   (a.) a horseshoe
   b. an octopus
   c. a monkey
   d. a brick

5. A **valid** fishing license
   a. is no longer legal.
   b. is impossible to get.
   (c.) is in effect now.
   d. says that fish are real.

6. An **authentic** Japanese coin
   a. is not real.
   (b.) comes from Japan.
   c. is made in America.
   d. can be used in America.

7. What might you say when you **grant** my request?
   (a.) "You may have your wish."
   b. "I won't ever agree to it."
   c. "That is not allowed."
   d. "I will never do anything for you."

8. An actor might **yearn** most for
   a. an old costume.
   (b.) a leading role.
   c. a broken leg.
   d. a bad performance.

9. A **modest** piece of cake would be
   a. huge.
   b. salty.
   (c.) small.
   d. chocolate.

10. You **declare** something if you
   a. are just waking up.
   b. are in the middle of a deep sleep.
   c. feel unsure about that thing.
   (d.) feel strongly about that thing.

For teaching suggestions, see page T33.

Word Study • Compound Words

A **compound word** is a word made by joining two smaller words. You can use what you know about the two smaller words to figure out the meaning of the larger word.

For example, the word *gravestone* is a compound word. It is made up of the smaller words *grave* (page 133) and *stone*. *Gravestone* means "a stone used to mark a grave."

PRACTICE *Find the two words that make up each compound word. Write the words. Then write the meaning of the compound word.*

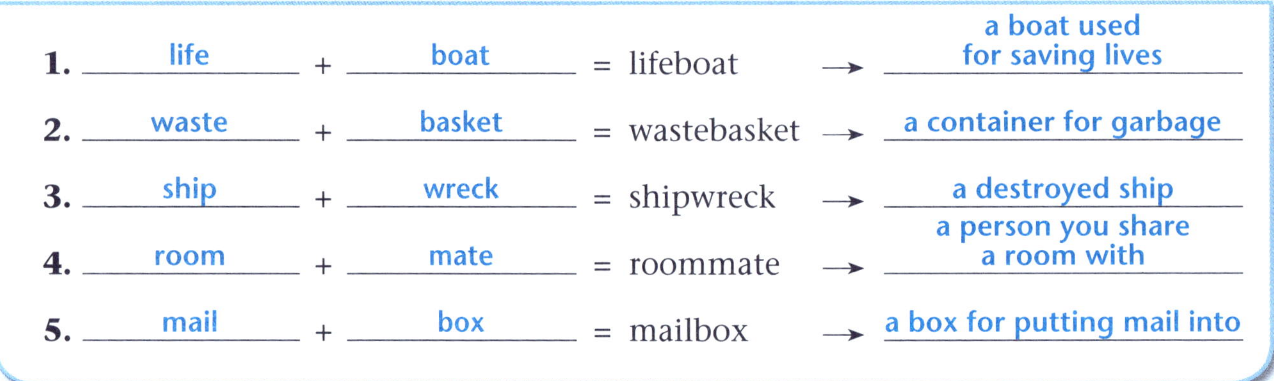

1. life + boat = lifeboat → a boat used for saving lives
2. waste + basket = wastebasket → a container for garbage
3. ship + wreck = shipwreck → a destroyed ship
4. room + mate = roommate → a person you share a room with
5. mail + box = mailbox → a box for putting mail into

APPLY *Complete each sentence with a compound word. Form the compound word by joining two words from the box.*

board	fall	foot	hand	hold
key	land	made	slide	water

6. We stopped at the edge of the river to admire the waterfall.
7. I got scared when I spilled water on the keyboard of my laptop.
8. I stepped onto the foothold as I climbed the rock wall.
9. My costume was special because it was handmade.
10. All the flooding caused a landslide in the nearby hills.

Use all the smaller words shown on this page to make as many new compound words as you can. Trade your list with a partner. Count how many new words you got altogether.

For teaching suggestions, see page T37.

Shades of Meaning • Word Choice

declare, mutter, admit

In the passage "The Winter Olympics" on pages 130–131, you read this sentence: *At that moment, the athlete has been* ***declared*** *the best in his or her sport.* The word *declared* is a specific word. It tells you that something has been officially announced or made known.

Words may have similar meanings, but no two words have exactly the same meaning. Look at the words in the chart. They all involve speaking. Notice how the words differ in meaning.

declare	When you **declare** something, you say it officially or formally.
mutter	When you **mutter** something, you say it so people can barely hear you. You usually mutter if you are unhappy or complaining.
admit	When you **admit** something, you tell the truth and confess.

PRACTICE ***Write the word from the chart that best replaces say in each sentence.***

1. I think I heard him **say**, "I'm really tired of waiting here." mutter
2. It pleases me to **say** that the park is now open to the public! declare
3. I'm sorry to **say** that I was the one who broke the window. admit
4. It wasn't nice to **say** to yourself during the concert that you disliked the songs. mutter

APPLY ***Decide how you would speak in each situation. Be prepared to explain your answers.***
Accept answers that students can justify.

5. You broke your friend's new game by accident when he or she wasn't looking. Do you **admit** or **mutter** what you have done? Write what you would say.

6. You are tired of being called by your nickname, which you think you've outgrown. Would you **admit** or **declare** that it is time for people to use the name you want to go by? Write what you would say.

Introducing the Words

Read the following biography about a pioneer of the air. Notice how the highlighted words are used. These are the words you will be learning in this unit.

Amelia Earhart 1897–1937

(Biography)

Surely, no one in Amelia Earhart's family would have predicted that she would one day fly an airplane. Young Amelia showed no interest in airplanes. She was, on the other hand, interested in women who did admirable things. She collected newspaper articles about women who were engineers and lawyers. In the 1920s, it was unusual for females to have such careers.

Years later, people would read about Earhart herself. Her devotion to flying would one day make her famous.

Earhart's interest in flying was kindled by an exciting experience she had as a young woman. She had gone to an air show. At one point, Earhart heard a distant hum and looked up. A small red airplane

Some of the planes Earhart flew are now at the Air and Space Museum in Washington, DC.

Listen to this passage at vocabularyworkshop.com.

was heading straight toward her and a friend. The plane flew so close that it blew Earhart's hair out of place. She was thrilled.

When Earhart was twenty-three, she flew on her first airplane. A year later, she took her first flying lesson. Six months after that, she bought an airplane.

In 1928, Earhart got a phone call. The man on the line wanted her to be the first woman to fly across the Atlantic Ocean. Was she interested? Earhart didn't have to think twice. An automatic reply of "Yes!" flew out of her mouth.

Two men flew the plane. Earhart made history just by being a passenger. That flight gave her an idea, though: Why couldn't she be the first woman to pilot the same route? In 1932, she achieved her goal. She became the first woman to fly a plane across the Atlantic.

In 1931, Earhart married George Putnam. As she became more famous, she flew more often. Putnam supported Earhart's passion for flying. He didn't mind the long separations that the trips caused. His support helped her try new things.

In 1935, she achieved her next goal. She flew across the Pacific Ocean alone. This flight was 2,408 miles long and would exhaust anyone. Yet Amelia was determined. At one point during the flight, the weather was dreary and cold. To warm herself, she opened a thermos of hot chocolate. She later told people that it was a special moment. There she was, sipping hot chocolate as she flew alone over the middle of the Pacific Ocean!

Amelia Earhart set many world records in aviation.

In 1937, Earhart planned another trip. No other woman had flown around the world yet. She wanted to be the first! She hoped that this stunt would be her last. Sadly, it did become her final trip. Somewhere over the Pacific Ocean, Amelia Earhart's airplane disappeared.

No one knows for sure what happened. She might have crashed in the ocean or on an island. Whatever occurred, Amelia Earhart has a place in history. Today, she is a symbol of courage and adventure.

Definitions

You were introduced to the words below in the passage on pages 140–141. Study the spelling, pronunciation, part of speech, and definition of each word. Write the word on the line in the sentence. Then read the synonyms and antonyms.

Remember

A **noun** *(n.)* is a word that names a person, place, or thing.

A **verb** *(v.)* is a word or words that express action or a state of being.

An **adjective** *(adj.)* is a word that describes a noun or pronoun.

1. admirable (ad′ mə rə bəl) (adj.) deserving praise

The murals they painted on the wall are ___admirable___.

SYNONYMS: excellent, superior, wonderful, praiseworthy, first-rate
ANTONYMS: inferior, mediocre, second-rate

2. automatic (ô tə ma′ tik) (adj.) done without thought or will; done by a machine, not by a human

Blinking is an ___automatic___ *response.*

SYNONYMS: involuntary, instinctive, unconscious, mechanical
ANTONYMS: deliberate, conscious, voluntary

3. devotion (di vō′ shən) (n.) loyalty and affection

They showed their ___devotion___ *to their religious faith by attending services on a regular basis.*

SYNONYMS: attachment, commitment, dedication, faith, allegiance
ANTONYMS: disloyalty, faithlessness

4. distant (dis′ tənt) (adj.) far away; not friendly

The ___distant___ *cabin was difficult to get to.*

SYNONYMS: remote, apart, removed, separated; reserved, unapproachable, unfriendly, cold
ANTONYMS: near, close, adjacent, neighboring; accessible, warm

5. dreary (drir′ ē) (adj.) gloomy or dismal; without cheer, comfort, or enthusiasm

The rain did not stop at all during the ___dreary___ *afternoon.*

SYNONYMS: depressing, bleak
ANTONYMS: cheery, exciting, vibrant, lively, merry

6. exhaust
(ig zôst′)

(v.) to use up; to wear out

Don't ___exhaust___ *yourself shopping at the mall.*

(n.) the escape of gas from an engine

The ___exhaust___ *from the bus made me choke.*

SYNONYMS: (v.) tire, fatigue, weaken, consume, deplete, drain, empty
ANTONYMS: (v.) refresh, enliven, fill, quicken

7. kindle
(kin′ dəl)

(v.) to get a fire going; to stir up or to start something

We tried to ___kindle___ *a campfire.*

SYNONYMS: ignite, burn, light; awaken, excite
ANTONYMS: extinguish; discourage, dampen, smother, deaden

8. predict
(pri dikt′)

(v.) to guess what is going to happen

No one can ___predict___ *the future.*

SYNONYMS: forecast, foretell, foresee, anticipate, expect

9. separation
(se pə rā′ shən)

(n.) the act or condition of being apart

They met again after a ___separation___ *of ten years.*

SYNONYMS: disconnection, detachment, rift, break, division
ANTONYMS: connection, attachment, unification

10. stunt
(stunt)

(v.) to stop or slow down the growth of

The scientist worked to ___stunt___ *the growth of the weed.*

(n.) an act that shows great strength, bravery, or skill, often to get attention

Harry Houdini, the great magician and escape artist, was known to perform a daring escape ___stunt___.

SYNONYMS: (v.) block, hamper, suppress, restrain; (n.) feat, performance, achievement
ANTONYMS: (v.) encourage, promote

Match the Meaning

vocabularyworkshop.com
Practice unit words with interactive games and activities.

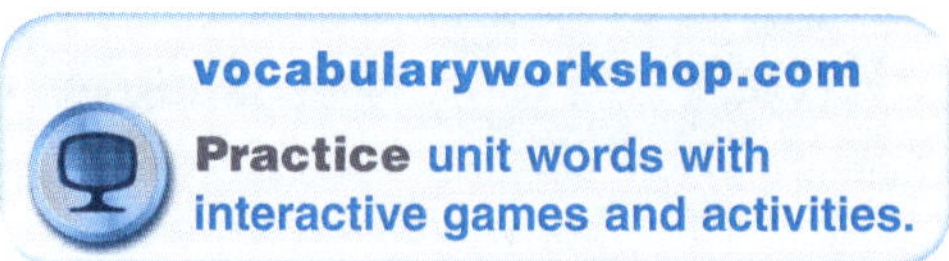

Choose the word whose meaning is suggested by the clue given. Then write the word on the line provided.

1. To ______predict______ is to make a guess about what will happen.
a. kindle b. stunt c. predict

2. Something ______admirable______ might be described as excellent.
a. automatic b. distant c. admirable

3. A feat that displays much skill is a(n) ______stunt______.
a. devotion b. stunt c. exhaust

4. Something far away is ______distant______.
a. admirable b. automatic c. distant

5. A(n) ______automatic______ reaction is one that happens without thought.
a. admirable b. dreary c. automatic

6. To show ______devotion______ is to show loyalty.
a. devotion b. separation c. stunt

7. A(n) ______separation______ from people might also be a detachment from them.
a. exhaust b. devotion c. separation

8. A(n) ______dreary______ afternoon can also be considered gloomy.
a. distant b. dreary c. automatic

9. To light a fire is to ______kindle______ it.
a. predict b. kindle c. stunt

10. The fumes that come from an engine are called ______exhaust______.
a. separation b. material c. exhaust

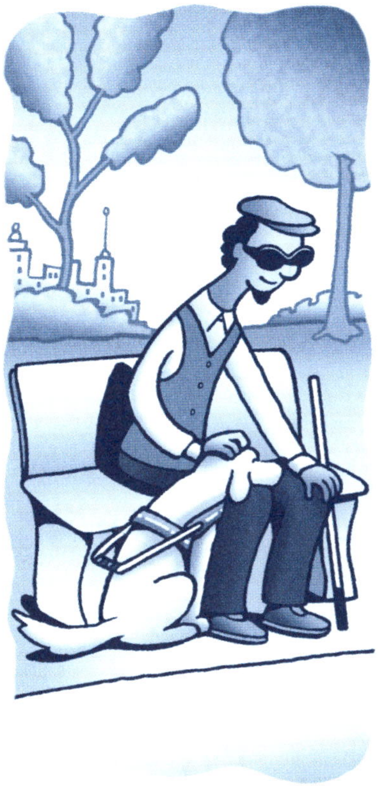

The guide dog showed complete **devotion** to the man.

Synonyms

*Choose the word that is most nearly the **same** in meaning as the word or phrase in **dark print**. Then write your choice on the line provided.*

1. **tire out** the workers
   a. exhaust b. kindle c. predict exhaust

2. **forecast** the weather
   a. kindle b. exhaust c. predict predict

3. **hamper** your progress
   a. kindle b. exhaust c. stunt stunt

4. an **excellent** way with animals
   a. automatic b. admirable c. distant admirable

5. an **involuntary** thought
   a. automatic b. admirable c. dreary automatic

Antonyms

*Choose the word that is most nearly **opposite** in meaning to the word or phrase in **dark print**. Then write your choice on the line provided.*

1. a long **attachment**
   a. devotion b. separation c. stunt separation

2. a **cheery** scene
   a. admirable b. automatic c. dreary dreary

3. **extinguish** the flame
   a. kindle b. stunt c. exhaust kindle

4. a soldier's **disloyalty**
   a. stunt b. separation c. devotion devotion

5. a **close** relative
   a. admirable b. distant c. automatic distant

Completing the Sentence

Choose the word from the box that best completes each item below. Then write the word on the line provided. (You may have to change the word's ending.)

admirable	**automatic**	**devotion**
distant	**dreary**	**exhaust**
kindle	**predict**	
separation	**stunt**	

Winter

■ Many people find the long, cold winter to be ____dreary____.

■ It helps the mood to ____kindle____ a fire and warm up by the fireplace.

■ Winter sports can also help a person's frame of mind. It can be fun to ice skate for hours, even if it ____exhausts____ you!

■ Sometimes, however, the winter seems as if it will never end. Spring seems to be a ____distant____ dream.

My Friend, the Gardener

■ I have a friend who is an ____admirable____ gardener. Everything he plants grows beautifully.

■ The ____devotion____ he shows to every detail of his garden is impressive.

■ He's always happy when the weather forecasters ____predict____ rain. That is because he knows that if it doesn't rain, the plants' growth will be ____stunted____ by lack of water.

■ When he goes away, he turns on an ____automatic____ sprinkler that will water his garden in his absence.

■ If you want my friend to be happy, make sure there is never too long a ____separation____ between him and his garden!

Word Associations

Circle the letter next to the choice that best completes the sentence or answers the question. Pay special attention to the word in dark print.

1. To show **devotion** to learning,
   a. come late to class.
   b. do your homework.
   c. forget to study.
   d. skip school.

2. If you seem **distant** to someone,
   a. you are warm.
   b. you are cold.
   c. you are friendly.
   d. you are happy.

3. You might see daring **stunts** at the
   a. computer.
   b. hardware store.
   c. grocery store.
   d. circus.

4. If you feel **exhausted**, you might
   a. jog a few miles.
   b. paint a picture.
   c. take a nap.
   d. learn to skate.

5. A long **separation** would be
   a. a lot of time to wait.
   b. a little time to wait.
   c. something to look forward to.
   d. something you probably wouldn't notice.

6. It's an **admirable** trait to be
   a. polite.
   b. grumpy.
   c. selfish.
   d. boring.

7. On a dark and **dreary** Saturday afternoon, you might feel
   a. excited.
   b. gloomy.
   c. honored.
   d. hopeful.

8. You can **predict** the score for
   a. last night's ball game.
   b. yesterday's ball game.
   c. tomorrow's ball game.
   d. last week's ball game.

9. Which of these things would you use to **kindle** a fire?
   a. water
   b. soda
   c. plastic
   d. matches

10. Which of the following is done **automatically**?
   a. driving
   b. eating
   c. drinking
   d. breathing

For teaching suggestions, see page T33.

Word Study • Homographs 2

You have learned that **homographs** are multiple-meaning words that have separate entries in a dictionary. Homographs have a small raised number after them in the dictionary.

exhaust[1]	to use up or wear out
exhaust[2]	the escape of gas from an engine

The word *exhaust* (page 143) is a homograph. Look at the box above to see how *exhaust* would appear in a dictionary.

Look at the chart for other homographs and their meanings.

bear[1]	to support or carry; to last through something
bear[2]	a large, furry mammal with a short tail
shed[1]	a small shelter
shed[2]	to drop or throw off
fine[1]	high quality
fine[2]	money paid as punishment

PRACTICE ***Complete each sentence with a homograph from the chart. Write the number of the homograph whose meaning is shown.***

2 **1.** A bear may eat both plants and insects.

2 **2.** A snake will shed its skin.

1 **3.** I couldn't bear the weight of my backpack any longer.

2 **4.** Late library books mean you must pay a fine.

1 **5.** The graduation gown was made of very fine cloth.

1 **6.** Dad's tools are kept in the shed.

APPLY ***Complete each sentence using words from the chart above.***

7. I hid in the shed to avoid the prowling bear.

8. Dad couldn't bear to pay the $50 fine.

9. The dog shed its hair on Mom's fine carpet.

Write *Write a sentence that includes a pair of homographs.*

Example: My mother **set** her best **set** of dishes on the table.

For teaching suggestions, see page T38.

Shades of Meaning • Word Choice

predict, suspect, wonder

In the passage "Amelia Earhart" on pages 140–141, you read this sentence: *Surely, no one in Amelia Earhart's family would have* ***predicted*** *that she would one day fly an airplane.* When people predict, they make a guess about what will happen in the future. They are not certain of the outcome.

When you know something for sure, you are certain about it. When you don't know something for sure, there are words that can describe your level of understanding. The chart below shows some of these words.

predict	When you **predict**, you say what is going to happen based on what you already know.
suspect	When you **suspect**, you believe something is probably true based on clues.
wonder	When you **wonder**, you think about something that you want to know more about.

PRACTICE *Write the word from the chart that best completes each sentence.*

1. I ____suspect____ a deer was here because I see its footprints.

2. As you read, ____predict____ what will happen at the end of the story.

3. I ____wonder____ why the bus driver is late in picking us up.

4. I ____predict____ that it is going to rain tomorrow.

5. We ____suspect____ that a raccoon got into the garbage last night.

APPLY *Answer each question. Use the word in* ***dark print*** *in your answer. Be sure to write complete sentences.*
Accept answers that students can justify.

6. What is something in nature that you **wonder** about?

____

7. What do you **predict** you will be doing at this hour next week?

____

8. What do you **suspect** happened to Amelia Earhart?

____

UNIT 15

Introducing the Words

Read the following magazine article about an underwater wonderland. Notice how the highlighted words are used. These are the words you will be learning in this unit.

The Great Barrier Reef

(Magazine Article)

Dive into the waters of northeastern Australia, and you will find the Great Barrier Reef. This natural wonder runs along the coast like a colorful underwater fence. You will see picturesque structures made of coral. Corals are made up of tiny sea creatures that have clumped together. They are often white, pink, or reddish. Some corals are shaped like fans. Others look like the horns of a deer or moose. Still others look like flowers.

Perhaps you will have the privilege of seeing the reef from an airplane. This sight is equally stunning. You can see islands of coral in the clear, blue-green water.

Reefs keep growing in size. The Great Barrier Reef, which has been forming for millions of years, is about 1,400 miles long.

Life on the reef is abundant. It is home to more than 1,500 kinds of fish. Hiding near the coral are tiny fish that have bodies you can see through. Deadly stonefish stare at divers with fierce eyes. Sea turtles, clownfish, and dolphins also swim in the waters.

Fish like to find nooks and crannies within the reef. There, they can slumber in safety. They must stay hidden because the barrier reef is a hunting ground.

Listen to this passage at vocabularyworkshop.com.

Sharks, stonefish, and manta rays are just a few of the predators that search for food in these waters.

In recent years, scientists have noticed changes in the Great Barrier Reef. They have inquired about how human activities might be affecting it. Money was set aside. Then formal tests were run. The tests showed that the reef is no longer growing.

The scientists believe that the pollution of the air and land are two reasons behind the changes. Rain carries dangerous substances into ocean waters. It also washes chemicals that pollute the land into the ocean. These chemicals harm the reefs, which need clear, clean water to survive.

Another problem might be the warming temperatures. Corals grow in warm oceans. However, if the water is too warm, they die.

The Great Barrier Reef took a long time to form. To save the reef from destruction, the Australian government has passed laws to protect it. Anyone who knowingly breaks these laws will be penalized. In addition, scientists all over the world are putting their ideas together. Before long, they might conceive more ways to protect this natural treasure.

Definitions

You were introduced to the words below in the passage on pages 150–151. Study the spelling, pronunciation, part of speech, and definition of each word. Write the word on the line in the sentence. Then read the synonyms and antonyms.

Remember

A **noun** *(n.)* is a word that names a person, place, or thing.

A **verb** *(v.)* is a word or words that express action or a state of being.

An **adjective** *(adj.)* is a word that describes a noun or pronoun.

1. abundant (ə bun′ dənt)

(adj.) large or more than enough; plentiful

There was an abundant *amount of food at the restaurant.*

SYNONYMS: bountiful, generous
ANTONYMS: limited, meager, sparse, scarce

2. barrier (bar′ ē ər)

(n.) something that blocks or bars movement or passage

The mountains acted as a barrier *to the wind.*

SYNONYMS: wall, obstacle, barricade, roadblock, obstruction, restraint
ANTONYMS: entrance, passageway

3. conceive (kən sēv′)

(v.) to start something; to think up or begin to understand

I began to conceive *a plan on how to get all my work done.*

SYNONYMS: form, formulate, develop, devise, imagine, think

4. formal (fôr′ məl)

(adj.) following strict rules or customs; requiring fancy clothes and fine manners

The club members were required to follow a formal *dress code.*

SYNONYMS: official, conventional, standard; proper, fancy
ANTONYMS: informal, unofficial; casual

5. inquire (in kwīr′)

(v.) to ask about

The detective has begun to inquire *about the crime.*

SYNONYMS: investigate, question, examine, explore, interrogate

6. penalize (pē′ nəl īz) (v.) to punish

Our teacher will ___penalize___ *us for incomplete work.*

SYNONYMS: discipline, chasten
ANTONYM: reward

7. picturesque (pik chə resk′) (adj.) charming, quaint

The little town is so ___picturesque___.

SYNONYMS: beautiful, pretty, lovely, striking, vivid, scenic, delightful
ANTONYMS: ugly, drab, dull, grim, unpleasant, distasteful

8. predator (pre′ də tər) (n.) one that destroys or devours others; an animal that stalks and eats other animals

A snake is a ___predator___ *of mice and other rodents.*

SYNONYMS: thief, bandit
ANTONYMS: prey, victim

9. privilege (priv′ lij) (n.) a special right, benefit, or permission

The players who arrived first got the ___privilege___ *of choosing the nicest uniforms.*

SYNONYMS: advantage, honor

10. slumber (slum′ bər) (v.) to sleep lightly

The baby will ___slumber___ *for a while after lunch.*

(n.) a sleep or light sleep

The cat lay in ___slumber___ *for most of the afternoon.*

SYNONYMS: (v. & n.) nap, doze, rest, snooze
ANTONYMS: (v.) awake, arouse, stir; (n.) awareness

Match the Meaning

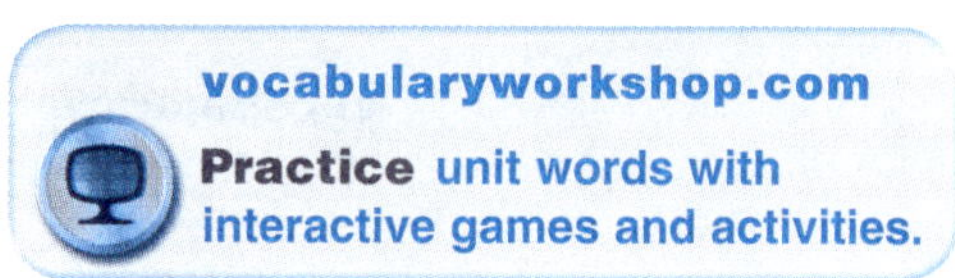

Choose the word whose meaning is suggested by the clue given. Then write the word on the line provided.

1. A ___barrier___ blocks the way or does not allow passage.
a. barrier b. privilege c. slumber

2. To ___penalize___ is to give a punishment or penalty.
a. conceive b. slumber c. penalize

3. An invitation to a(n) ___formal___ party might request that you dress in a fancy way.
a. formal b. abundant c. picturesque

4. If you fall asleep, you are said to ___slumber___.
a. penalize b. inquire c. slumber

5. To think of a plan or an idea is to ___conceive___ it.
a. inquire b. conceive c. penalize

6. A ___predator___ is known to attack and eat its prey.
a. predator b. privilege c. barrier

7. When you ___inquire___ about a story, you ask about it.
a. inquire b. slumber c. conceive

The bald eagle is a skilled **predator** because of its sharp eyesight.

8. An amount that is ___abundant___ is large.
a. formal b. abundant c. picturesque

9. An advantage or right can also be known as a ___privilege___.
a. predator b. barrier c. privilege

10. The colorful scene was described by the artists as ___picturesque___.
a. formal b. abundant c. picturesque

Synonyms

*Choose the word that is most nearly the **same** in meaning as the word or phrase in **dark print**. Then write your choice on the line provided.*

1. a sneaky **bandit**
a. privilege b. predator c. barrier predator

2. the **right** to leave
a. predator b. privilege c. slumber privilege

3. a huge **obstacle**
a. barrier b. predator c. privilege barrier

4. **ask** about my test score
a. penalize b. slumber c. inquire inquire

5. **think of** a clever solution
a. conceive b. penalize c. slumber conceive

Antonyms

*Choose the word that is most nearly **opposite** in meaning to the word or phrase in **dark print**. Then write your choice on the line provided.*

1. caused me to **awake**
a. penalize b. inquire c. slumber slumber

2. a **drab** city
a. formal b. abundant c. picturesque picturesque

3. the **meager** number of birthday cards
a. formal b. abundant c. picturesque abundant

4. **reward** the last player remaining in a game
a. conceive b. inquire c. penalize penalize

5. a **casual** invitation
a. abundant b. formal c. picturesque formal

Completing the Sentence

Choose the word from the box that best completes each item below. Then write the word on the line provided. (You may have to change the word's ending.)

abundant	**barrier**	**conceive**
formal	**inquire**	**penalize**
picturesque	**predator**	
privilege	**slumber**	

Etymology

■ When we study the history of a word, or its etymology, we learn of its beginnings and how it has come to be a part of our language.

■ The word ____barrier____, which we use to describe something that bars the way, comes from the French word *barre*. Dancers use a barre to stretch their legs.

■ A pretty scene is ____picturesque____. This word comes from *pictor*, the Latin word for painter.

■ Many English words are the result of the joining of two or more Latin words. For example, ____privilege____ comes from *privus*, the word for "private," and *lex*, the word for "law."

■ The English word ____inquire____, which means "to ask about," comes from the Latin word *quaerere*, which means "to seek."

■ Both the English word ____predator____ and its ancient relative *praedator*, come from the Latin word, which means "to seize or capture."

Skiing

■ I went skiing last week. There was a blizzard the night before, which left a(n) ____abundant____ amount of snow.

■ It was hard to ____conceive____ how I would make it all the way down the steep mountain without falling!

■ Since that was hard to imagine, I decided to try an easier slope. No one would ____penalize____ me for being cautious.

■ Some ski outfits were so fancy that they made skiing seem as if it were a ____formal____ event!

■ At the end of the day, we fell into a peaceful ____slumber____ by the fire.

For teaching suggestions, see page T33.

Word Study • Analogies 2

You have learned that an **analogy** is a statement that shows how two pairs of words are related. The words may be synonyms or antonyms. The words may also show other types of relationships.

Here is an analogy with the word *barrier* (page 152): *barrier* is to *block* as *bridge* is to *connect*. In this analogy, the first word in each pair names an object, and the second word gives a function, or a use, for the object. A *barrier* can be used to *block* off an area, and a *bridge* can be used to *connect* two places separated by water.

The chart at the right shows some types of relationships that analogies can have.

Object/ Function	*barrier* is to *block* as *bridge* is to *connect*
Synonym	*slumber* is to *nap* as *draw* is to *sketch*
Antonym	*formal* is to *casual* as *picturesque* is to *ugly*

PRACTICE *Match the word pairs to form a complete analogy. Write the number of the first pair next to the pair with the same relationship.*

1. *small* is to *tiny* as	1 *thin* is to *lean*
2. *crayon* is to *color* as	3 *leader* is to *follower*
3. *friend* is to *enemy* as	2 *needle* is to *sew*

APPLY *Complete each analogy with a word from the box. Then explain the relationship on the lines provided.*

chop	fly
notice	vibrant

4. *gloomy* is to *cheerful* as *dull* is to vibrant

Relationship: The pairs of words are antonyms.

5. *knife* is to *cut* as *axe* is to chop

Relationship: A knife is used to cut, and an axe is used to chop.

6. *sprint* is to *dash* as *observe* is to notice

Relationship: The pairs of words are synonyms.

7. *car* is to *drive* as *plane* is to fly

Relationship: A car is something to drive, and a plane is something to fly.

With a partner, create an analogy using a word from Units 10–15. Talk about the relationship between the words. Accept answers that demonstrate an understanding of the unit word and the analogy relationship.

Vocabulary for Comprehension

Read the following passage in which some of the words you have studied in Units 13–15 appear in dark print. Then answer the questions on page 159.

An Amazing Creature

The coast of Florida is home to many turtle nests during warm summer months. Turtles nest along ocean beaches in other southern states, too. Loggerheads are one type of turtle that nest on the beach.

A loggerhead can grow to be as long as three feet. Some may weigh as much as 350 pounds or more. These huge creatures spend most of their lives in the ocean. They swim for years at a time. When a loggerhead female is ready to lay eggs, though, she journeys to a **distant** beach. Usually, she returns to the beach where she was born.

On the beach, the female digs a hole in the sand. She lays about 100 eggs inside. She buries the eggs so **predators** cannot find them. Then she returns to the sea. A month or two later, the young turtles are born. They crawl out of the sand, and their **separation** from the sea is over. They immediately make their way to the ocean. The young turtles are only about two inches long.

Loggerhead nests used to be **abundant**. But now they are in **grave** danger. When people build houses on the beach, loggerheads stay away. In addition, bright lights from the houses confuse the turtles, causing them to run in the wrong direction—away from the ocean. As a result, fewer loggerheads are being born or survive than in the past. Scientists worry that these turtles may die out.

Some people want the government to **declare** the loggerhead an endangered species. They also want to protect beaches where loggerheads nest. That way, more loggerheads may be born in the future.

Baby loggerhead turtles heading toward the ocean

Fill in the circle next to the choice that best completes the sentence or answers the question.

1. This passage is mostly about
ⓐ things you see at the beach.
ⓑ animals in Florida.
ⓒ loggerhead turtles and their nests.
ⓓ how sea turtles swim.

2. In this passage, **distant** means
ⓐ far away.
ⓑ near.
ⓒ easy to reach.
ⓓ not friendly.

3. The **predators** in this passage are
ⓐ animals that lay turtle eggs.
ⓑ scientists who study turtles.
ⓒ people who build houses.
ⓓ animals that eat turtle eggs.

4. A **separation** from the sea means
ⓐ having a connection to it.
ⓑ being apart from it.
ⓒ being related to it.
ⓓ having an interest in it.

5. Another word for **abundant** is
ⓐ few.
ⓑ happy.
ⓒ confused.
ⓓ plentiful.

6. The meaning of **grave** is
ⓐ reserved.
ⓑ serious.
ⓒ wonderful.
ⓓ remote.

7. Which of these is not true about loggerhead turtles?
ⓐ They spend most of their lives on land.
ⓑ They lay eggs on the beach.
ⓒ They swim a lot.
ⓓ They can be very big.

8. In this passage, **declare** means
ⓐ to sing.
ⓑ to state quietly.
ⓒ to make a formal statement.
ⓓ to make a complaint.

Write Your Own

Some people worry that loggerhead turtles will die off if their homes are not protected. Think about reasons why the government should help protect the loggerhead. On a separate sheet of paper, write a paragraph that tells the government what it can do to help protect loggerhead turtles. Use at least three words from Units 13–15.

UNIT 16

Introducing the Words

Read the following fantasy about a wild adventure. Notice how the highlighted words are used. These are the words you will be learning in this unit.

Two Troublesome Monkeys

(Fantasy)

Barnie and Chichi were monkeys who lived in the rain forest. They were always getting into trouble. They took advantage of the younger monkeys and stole their bananas. They played tricks on the older monkeys.

One day, the monkey troop held a meeting. Chief Monkey announced, "We've had enough of you, Barnie and Chichi."

"What are you implying?" Chichi asked.

"I'm not implying anything!" Chief Monkey said. "I am saying it clearly. You won't listen to anyone and you are defiant. Go and leave us all in peace!"

Now, Chichi had always wanted to travel. "Great," she said. "I am totally ready."

Barnie had always had ambition. He wanted to be Chief Monkey some day. He thought he might be able to learn things from people, so he agreed with Chichi. The two of them caught the next train into the city.

As soon as they got off the train, they saw a bus marked "City Zoo." "Sounds like fun," said Chichi.

Once inside the zoo, they caused nothing but trouble. They made faces at the giraffes, jumped on the backs of two fearsome tigers, and teased the bears. Soon, all of the animals in the zoo were upset and started screeching. The zookeeper said, "I revoke all of your privileges to visit this zoo! You shouldn't have been allowed inside in the first place! I'm calling the police!"

By this time, the two monkeys were hungry and ready to leave anyway. Barnie spotted a police officer buying a banana at a fruit stand. Chichi grabbed the banana. Barnie stole a mango. Then the two monkeys ran off as fast as they could.

By then, the police were on full alert. The officers finally caught the monkeys. Not long after, the monkeys found themselves sitting in jail.

"Have you noticed how dirty the city air is?" Chichi asked.

"Yes," Barnie said, "they should purify it."

"Have you noticed how small and damp this cell is?"

"It's wretched."

"It's noisy here, too," Chichi remarked. "And the banana I ate wasn't ripe. I think we were better off in the rain forest."

"That idea merits further thought," Barnie said.

At that moment, Chief Monkey appeared outside the jail cell. She said, "I'm here to take you home."

"Great!" Chichi and Barnie exclaimed together.

"There's one condition!"

"We're glad to negotiate!" Chichi said. "We don't really like the city."

"Very well," Chief Monkey said. "Then you will cause no more trouble at home. You'll respect both the young and old monkeys."

"We promise!" the two monkeys said.

And so the two monkeys went back to the rain forest. From then on, they were well behaved. In a few years, Chichi, not Barnie, became Chief Monkey. She kept perfect order within the troop. She knew how to deal with troublesome monkeys. After all, she had been one herself.

Definitions

You were introduced to the words below in the passage on pages 160–161. Study the spelling, pronunciation, part of speech, and definition of each word. Write the word on the line in the sentence. Then read the synonyms and antonyms.

Remember

A **noun** *(n.)* is a word that names a person, place, or thing.

A **verb** *(v.)* is a word or words that express action or a state of being.

An **adjective** *(adj.)* is a word that describes a noun or pronoun.

1. advantage
(əd van′ tij)

(n.) something that puts someone in a better position

The advantage *of sitting up front is being able to see the movie better.*

SYNONYMS: benefit, gain, edge, asset
ANTONYMS: disadvantage, drawback

2. ambition
(am bi′ shən)

(n.) a strong desire for importance or success

My ambition *is to be an excellent artist.*

SYNONYMS: aim, aspiration, goal

3. defiant
(di fī′ ənt)

(adj.) showing strong resistance; willing to challenge or confront

The defiant *team member refused to listen to the coach.*

SYNONYMS: rebellious, disobedient, uncooperative
ANTONYMS: submissive, cooperative, obedient

4. fearsome
(fir′ səm)

(adj.) frightening or alarming

That horror movie was quite fearsome.

SYNONYMS: scary, terrifying, horrifying
ANTONYMS: reassuring, comforting, encouraging

5. imply
(im plī′)

(v.) to suggest something without saying it directly

Their kind remarks imply *that they want me to join in.*

SYNONYMS: hint, indicate
ANTONYMS: declare, state, announce

6. merit
(mer′ ət)

(n.) a quality that deserves praise

The chief merit *of the book is its surprise ending.*

(v.) to be worthy of, deserve

We merit *good grades for our hard work.*

SYNONYMS: (n.) value, virtue, worth, excellence, achievement; (v.) earn, warrant
ANTONYMS: (n.) inferiority, fault

7. negotiate
(ni gō′ shē āt)

(v.) to discuss in order to arrive at an agreement

The United States and Great Britain negotiate *the Treaty of Paris in 1783.*

SYNONYM: debate

8. purify
(pyůr′ ə fī)

(v.) to make clean and free of dirt or pollutants

We need to purify *the dirty water so we can drink it.*

SYNONYMS: cleanse, filter, freshen, refine, sanitize
ANTONYMS: pollute, contaminate, cloud, dirty, muddy, soil

9. revoke
(ri vōk′)

(v.) to cancel by withdrawing or reversing

The judge decided to revoke *his license.*

SYNONYMS: remove, repeal, rescind
ANTONYMS: give, offer, provide, supply

10. wretched
(re′ chəd)

(adj.) very unhappy or unfortunate, miserable; very poor in quality

We felt wretched *about the terrible accident.*

SYNONYMS: depressed, dejected; inferior, dreadful
ANTONYMS: happy, pleased, elated, great, superior

Match the Meaning

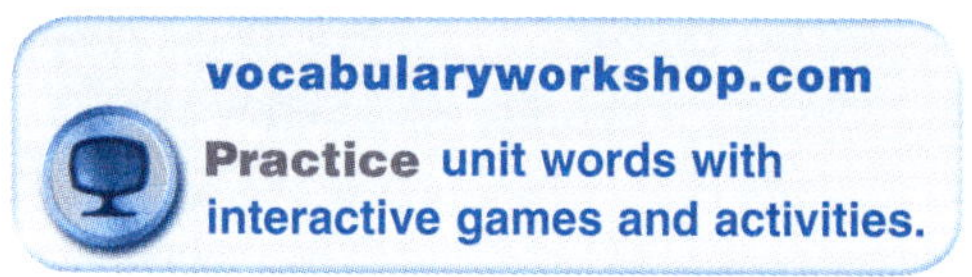

Choose the word whose meaning is suggested by the clue given. Then write the word on the line provided.

1. To refuse to obey authority is to be ___defiant___.
a. fearsome b. wretched c. defiant

2. To have a(n) ___advantage___ is to be in a better position than others are.
a. ambition b. merit c. advantage

3. When you feel really awful, you feel ___wretched___.
a. fearsome b. defiant c. wretched

4. If you ___purify___ water, you make it clean.
a. imply b. purify c. negotiate

5. To ___revoke___ an offer is to take it back.
a. merit b. revoke c. negotiate

6. A(n) ___ambition___ is a wish to achieve or be successful.
a. ambition b. advantage c. merit

7. Something that is ___fearsome___ can also be described as scary.
a. fearsome b. defiant c. wretched

The great white shark is a **fearsome** fish.

8. To ___negotiate___ is to try to reach an agreement.
a. revoke b. purify c. negotiate

9. A job that is well done ___merits___ a reward.
a. implies b. merits c. purifies

10. When you hint at something, you ___imply___ it.
a. imply b. merit c. purify

Synonyms

*Choose the word that is most nearly the **same** in meaning as the word or phrase in **dark print**. Then write your choice on the line provided.*

1. a **terrifying** howl
a. fearsome b. defiant c. wretched fearsome

2. a daring **aspiration**
a. ambition b. advantage c. merit ambition

3. discuss who does the dishes
a. imply b. negotiate c. merit negotiate

4. hint that they are coming
a. revoke b. merit c. imply imply

5. rescind the offer
a. purify b. revoke c. merit revoke

6. a **virtue** worth rewarding
a. merit b. advantage c. ambition merit

Antonyms

*Choose the word that is most nearly **opposite** in meaning to the word or phrase in **dark print**. Then write your choice on the line provided.*

1. an unbelievable **handicap**
a. advantage b. ambition c. merit advantage

2. obedient children
a. fearsome b. wretched c. defiant defiant

3. in **superior** condition
a. fearsome b. wretched c. defiant wretched

4. contaminate the air
a. purify b. negotiate c. revoke purify

Completing the Sentence

Choose the word from the box that best completes each item below. Then write the word on the line provided. (You may have to change the word's ending.)

advantage	ambition	defiant
fearsome	imply	merit
negotiate	purify	
revoke	wretched	

Baking

- Our family has a tradition of baking a cake every Sunday. Now it's my ___ambition___ to be a professional baker.
- If we misbehave, our baking privileges are ___revoked___, and our fun is taken away.
- We use only the best ingredients in our cakes, and we ___purify___ the tap water by using a water filter.
- I like banana cake, but my parents prefer carrot cake. We have to ___negotiate___ which cake to make.
- The cake comes out perfectly! It always ___merits___ compliments and praise.
- I have learned that if we kids ___imply___ that we want a piece of cake, no one will respond. We have to ask for it directly!

Polar Bears

- Polar bears are aggressive and powerful hunters and can be quite ___fearsome___. It is only when people are ___defiant___ and confront a bear that they put themselves in danger.
- Polar bears live in very cold climates. To us, it might seem like a ___wretched___ way to live, but polar bears love the cold and ice. They have the ___advantage___ of a furry coat to keep them warm.

Word Associations

Circle the letter next to the choice that best completes the sentence or answers the question. Pay special attention to the word in dark print.

1. A person who is **defiant** might be
   a. hungry.
   b. sleepy.
   c. weak.
   d. bold.

2. Which **implies** that you are sad?
   a. "I'm not in a very jolly mood."
   b. "I feel like I could eat a horse!"
   c. "I am floating on air!"
   d. "I love fresh fruit."

3. You must **purify** drinking water if it is
   a. cold.
   b. polluted.
   c. fresh.
   d. wet.

4. After a long and **wretched** night without sleep,
   a. you feel great.
   b. you feel rested.
   c. you feel tired.
   d. you want dinner.

5. A **fearsome** dog may make you
   a. bark.
   b. growl.
   c. tremble.
   d. laugh.

6. In summer, it's an **advantage** to
   a. have hot soup.
   b. have mittens.
   c. have a snow suit.
   d. have an air conditioner.

7. A movie that has **merit** is likely to
   a. be in black-and-white.
   b. win an award.
   c. come with free popcorn.
   d. have actors in it.

8. If your free pass is **revoked**, you
   a. may enter without paying.
   b. will not be allowed to pay.
   c. will have to pay to enter.
   d. will have to go home.

9. When people **negotiate**, they expect to
   a. sink or swim.
   b. laugh or cry.
   c. give and take.
   d. dance and sing.

10. Someone with strong **ambition**
    a. tries to be a failure.
    b. tries to be lazy.
    c. tries to be a great success.
    d. doesn't care about anything.

For teaching suggestions, see page T34.

Word Study • Prefixes *dis-*, *mis-*, *im-*

Remember that a **prefix** is a word part that is added to the beginning of a **base word** to make a new word.

Prefix		Base Word		New Word		Meaning
dis	+	advantage	=	**dis**advantage	→	opposite of advantage
mis	+	inform	=	**mis**inform	→	give wrong information
im	+	pure	=	**im**pure	→	not pure or clean

Look at the prefixes and base words in this chart. The prefix *dis-* means "opposite of." You can add *dis-* to *advantage* (page 162) to make the word *disadvantage*. *Disadvantage* means "opposite of advantage."

The prefix *mis-* sometimes means "wrongly." The prefix *im-* sometimes means "not." Look at the chart for examples of words with the prefixes *mis-* and *im-*.

PRACTICE ***Write the missing prefix or base word. Then write the meaning of the new word.***

Prefix		Base Word		New Word		Meaning
1. im	+	polite	=	impolite	→	not polite
2. dis	+	like	=	dislike	→	opposite of like
3. mis	+	use	=	misuse	→	use wrongly
4. mis	+	understand	=	misunderstand	→	understand incorrectly

APPLY ***Complete each sentence with a word that contains the prefix dis-, mis-, or im-. Choose from the words in the boxes above.***

5. If you misuse the MP3 player, it might stop working.

6. The party guest was impolite to leave without thanking the host.

7. When the star player was absent, the team was at a disadvantage.

8. I don't want to misunderstand the directions, so I will listen carefully.

Watch out for words that seem to have prefixes but really do not. For example, when you remove im from imagine, no base word remains. In this example, im is not a prefix. Underline the words below that do not have a prefix. Explain your choices to a partner.

distant **disappear** **mistrust** **mister** **impossible** **imitate**

For teaching suggestions, see page T38.

Shades of Meaning • Words That Describe Behavior

In the passage "Two Troublesome Monkeys" on pages 160–161, you read this sentence: *You won't listen to anyone and you are* ***defiant****!* In the sentence, *defiant* is used to describe Chichi's behavior. Behavior is the way in which a person or animal acts.

Look at the words in the chart. They each describe a particular behavior.

defiant	A person who is **defiant** is willing to challenge or confront others.
charming	A person who is **charming** has the ability to attract and please people.
cunning	A person who is **cunning** is skilled at tricking others.

PRACTICE *Write the word from the chart that best describes each behavior.*

1. The singer wore sunglasses and a large hat so that she would not be noticed. cunning

2. The actor smiled and shook hands with all of his fans. charming

3. The child would not leave the playground. defiant

4. She told a delightful story at the dinner table. charming

5. The thief slipped away quietly as the police arrived. cunning

6. The angry crowd refused to be silent during the speech. defiant

APPLY *Write about a time when you have shown or seen each behavior.*

Accept answers that students can justify.

7. cunning ______

8. charming ______

9. defiant ______

UNIT 17

Introducing the Words

Read the following journal article about an animal that lives near warm bodies of water in Africa. Notice how the highlighted words are used. These are the words you will be learning in this unit.

The Nile Crocodile

(Journal Article)

The Nile crocodile is the largest crocodile in Africa. It is a fearsome animal with huge jaws. It also has large teeth. Its strong body can move quickly.

Habitat

The Nile crocodile lives in the warmer parts of Africa. It must live near water. The animal will die without it. The Nile crocodile might live in tranquil freshwater lakes. It might live in muddy, swampy rivers. It might even live in a ditch. The Nile crocodile sometimes travels as far as 15 miles in search of water.

Nile crocodiles can live for short periods in salt water. Scientists think that at some point, they even swam across the channel that separates Madagascar from Africa. This would explain how this kind of crocodile came to live on Madagascar.

Behavior

The Nile crocodile is a cold-blooded animal. It depends on its surroundings to keep its body warm and cool. To warm up, it lies in the sun to absorb heat. To cool off, it moves into the shade or the water. It also opens its mouth to let heat escape.

Diet

For some crocodiles, waiting in the water for hours for its food might seem tiresome. For the Nile crocodile, however, it's all in a day's work.

Unlike many animals that hunt on land, the Nile crocodile does not target mainly sick, lame, and weak animals. Instead, it waits to attack any animal that comes near. For example, a gazelle, a deerlike animal that moves with grace, might wander over for a drink. Its elegant neck reaches down

Nile crocodile

Listen to this passage at vocabularyworkshop.com.

to the water. At that moment, the Nile crocodile shoots out of the water. It grabs the gazelle with its huge jaws.

A Nile crocodile eats almost anything that it can catch. It enjoys fish. It eats small or large land animals. It will even eat other crocodiles!

Description

Most people don't get close enough to a Nile crocodile to inspect it. However, if you could take a close look, you would see strong feet and legs. The tail is very strong, too. It moves the crocodile through the water quickly. The tail is so powerful, in fact, that it can knock down a large animal.

The eyes and nostrils of this crocodile are on the top of its head. This makes it possible for the crocodile to suspend its body under water and still see and breathe.

Tourists travel in boats to see Nile crocodiles. Both professional and amateur photographers have taken photographs of this fierce animal. Wise visitors know they must stay clear of its tail and mouth. If hungry, a Nile crocodile will take a bite out of almost anything . . . or anyone!

NILE CROCODILE FACTS

- Can weigh over 2,000 pounds
- Can measure 20 feet in length
- Can eat half its weight in one meal
- Can live between 45 and 100 years
- Cannot chew. It tips its head up and swallows the food whole!

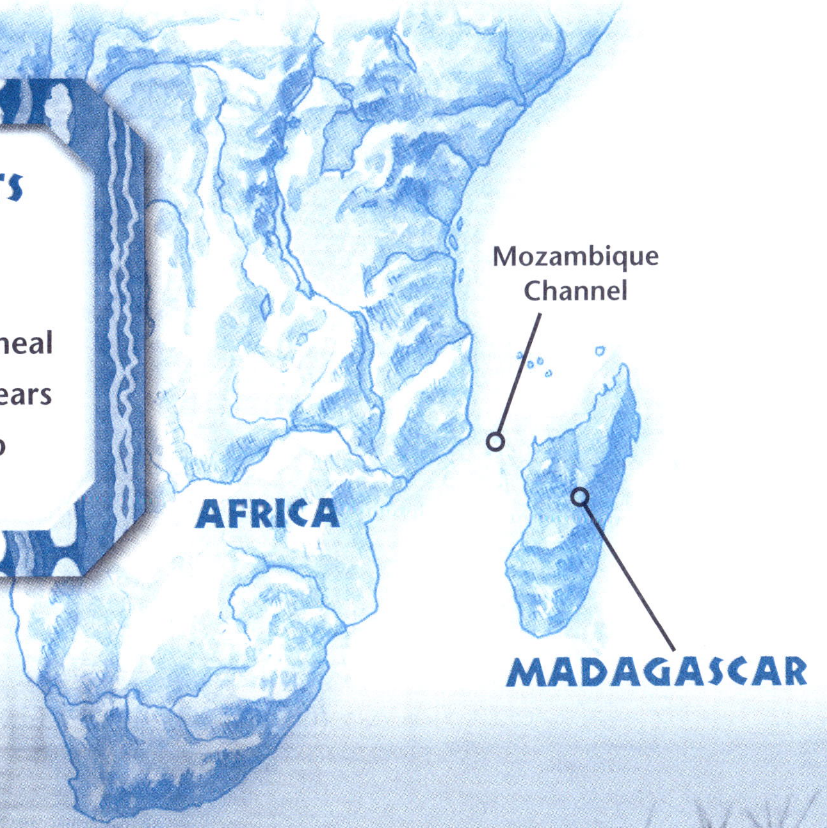

Mozambique Channel

AFRICA

MADAGASCAR

Definitions

You were introduced to the words below in the passage on pages 170–171. Study the spelling, pronunciation, part of speech, and definition of each word. Write the word on the line in the sentence. Then read the synonyms and antonyms.

Remember

A **noun** *(n.)* is a word that names a person, place, or thing.

A **verb** *(v.)* is a word or words that express action or a state of being.

An **adjective** *(adj.)* is a word that describes a noun or pronoun.

1. absorb (əb sôrb′)

(v.) to soak up or take in; to keep the attention of

A sponge can ____absorb____ *every last drop of water.*

SYNONYMS: consume, devour; engage, captivate, engross
ANTONYMS: discharge, emit, secrete

2. amateur (a′ mə tər)

(n.) someone who does something for pleasure and not for money; someone who does not have much experience

The young boy wanted to be a professional singer but sang with his choir as an ____amateur____.

SYNONYMS: beginner, nonprofessional, layman
ANTONYMS: expert, professional, master

3. channel (chan′ əl)

(n.) the deepest part of a river; a body of water that links two larger ones; a long, narrow groove; a band of radio waves; a course of action

Many ships pass through the ____channel____ *between England and France.*

(v.) to make a long, narrow groove; to direct or focus

They began to ____channel____ *through the rock.*

SYNONYMS: (n.) passage, strait, waterway; course, way, direction; (v.) plow, cut; direct, guide

4. elegant (e′ li gənt)

(adj.) showing beauty, high quality, and good taste

The diamond is an ____elegant____ *jewel.*

SYNONYMS: stylish, graceful, exquisite, charming, refined, cultured
ANTONYMS: coarse, crude, inelegant, unfashionable, rough

5. grace (grās)

(n.) ease and beauty of movement; a charming or pleasing quality; a short prayer at meals

The horse galloped with incredible ____grace____.

(v.) to add beauty or honor to

Will she ____grace____ *our party with her presence?*

SYNONYMS: (n.) elegance, loveliness, charm; (v.) enhance, enrich, adorn
ANTONYMS: (n.) clumsiness, inelegance; (v.) disgrace

6. inspect (in spekt′)

(v.) to look over closely

Please ____inspect____ *the clothes for any damage.*

SYNONYMS: examine, check, investigate, probe, scan

7. lame (lām)

(adj.) stiff, sore, or not able to move properly; weak, not satisfactory

I cannot swim because of my ____lame____ *leg.*

SYNONYMS: disabled, limping, weak; feeble, flimsy, unconvincing
ANTONYMS: strong, healthy

8. suspend (sə spend′)

(v.) to hang in order to allow free movement; to stop for a time, interrupt; to bar from a position or privilege

Please ____suspend____ *those streamers from the ceiling.*

SYNONYMS: dangle; postpone, delay, halt; remove, exclude
ANTONYMS: continue, resume, prolong

9. tiresome (tīr′ səm)

(adj.) annoyingly dull or exhausting; unexciting

Scrubbing the kitchen floor can be ____tiresome____.

SYNONYMS: boring, annoying, irritating
ANTONYMS: interesting, exciting, pleasant

10. tranquil (traŋ′ kwəl)

(adj.) free from trouble or disturbance; quiet

The ____tranquil____ *lake is relaxing.*

SYNONYMS: calm, serene, peaceful, composed
ANTONYMS: noisy, disturbed, excited

Match the Meaning

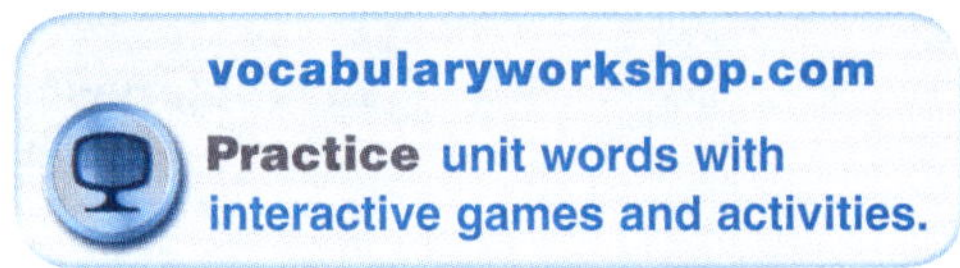

Choose the word whose meaning is suggested by the clue given. Then write the word on the line provided.

1. When you stop an activity for a short while, you ___suspend___ it.
a. absorb b. suspend c. inspect

2. If you are a beginner, you are a(n) ___amateur___.
a. channel b. amateur c. grace

3. An irritating chore can be described as ___tiresome___.
a. elegant b. tranquil c. tiresome

4. To ___absorb___ something is to soak it up.
a. channel b. suspend c. absorb

5. At mealtimes, some families recite ___grace___.
a. grace b. amateur c. channel

6. Something that is ___tranquil___ is peaceful and serene.
a. elegant b. lame c. tranquil

7. To make a groove is to ___channel___.
a. channel b. suspend c. inspect

8. Someone who is ___lame___ may not be able to move quickly.
a. elegant b. lame c. tranquil

9. If you ___inspect___ an object, you look at it closely.
a. absorb b. grace c. inspect

10. When something is high in quality, it is ___elegant___.
a. elegant b. lame c. tiresome

The gown that the movie star wore on the red carpet was **elegant**.

Synonyms

*Choose the word that is most nearly the **same** in meaning as the word or phrase in **dark print**. Then write your choice on the line provided.*

1. boats in the **canal**
a. grace b. amateur c. channel — channel

2. scrutinize my face
a. inspect b. absorb c. suspend — inspect

3. a **boring** task
a. elegant b. tranquil c. tiresome — tiresome

4. an **inadequate** excuse
a. lame b. elegant c. tranquil — lame

5. captivate my attention
a. grace b. absorb c. inspect — absorb

Antonyms

*Choose the word that is most nearly **opposite** in meaning to the word or phrase in **dark print**. Then write your choice on the line provided.*

1. a **master** carpenter
a. channel b. amateur c. grace — amateur

2. the **coarse** fabric
a. elegant b. lame c. tranquil — elegant

3. a **noisy** place
a. tiresome b. tranquil c. lame — tranquil

4. extend the trip
a. absorb b. inspect c. suspend — suspend

5. the comedian's **clumsiness**
a. amateur b. channel c. grace — grace

Completing the Sentence

Choose the word from the box that best completes each item below. Then write the word on the line provided. (You may have to change the word's ending.)

absorb	**amateur**	**channel**
elegant	**grace**	**inspect**
lame	**suspend**	
tiresome	**tranquil**	

Presidents

■ The life of the president of the United States is not a ____tranquil____ one. It is full of activity and excitement.

■ Presidents must be hardworking. They have to ____channel____ all their energy into their job.

■ Some duties of the office are ____tiresome____. It may be tedious to ____inspect____ all the papers that need to be signed, but that's one of the responsibilities of the president!

■ Franklin Delano Roosevelt, who was president from 1933 to 1945, was made ____lame____ by a disease called *polio*. He could not walk without braces.

■ George Washington had to ____suspend____ his life as a farmer to become president. He loved his farm in Virginia almost as much as his country.

First Ladies

■ The wives of American presidents are called *first ladies*. Most of the presidents' wives had experience in politics before they came to the White House. They were not ____amateurs____.

■ Jacqueline Kennedy, who was married to John F. Kennedy, was considered ____elegant____ because she was beautiful and stylish. She was famous for her charm and ____grace____.

■ As first lady, Eleanor Roosevelt spoke out for the needs of the poor and hungry. Her role as first lady ____absorbed____ her full attention.

Both these women were important to our country.

Word Associations

Circle the letter next to the choice that best completes the sentence or answers the question. Pay special attention to the word in dark print.

1. Why do most **amateurs** in competition skate?
a. because it is their job
b. because they are experts
c. to get rich
d. just for the fun of it

2. To **inspect** a bicycle, you can
a. check its tires and gears.
b. read a bicycle magazine.
c. glance at it quickly.
d. lock it in the garage.

3. A **tiresome** task might make you
a. burst into song.
b. feel excited and happy.
c. repeat it as soon as possible.
d. complain of boredom.

4. To **suspend** a glass ornament,
a. take a photo of it.
b. sell it to a museum.
c. hang it from your window.
d. wrap it in soft padding.

5. Which animal runs with **grace**?
a. a walrus
b. a camel
c. a turtle
d. a deer

6. **Elegant** dinners often include
a. paper plates and plastic forks.
b. flowers, candles, and silverware.
c. baby food and bottles.
d. hot dogs and popcorn.

7. A **lame** research paper is probably
a. a good one.
b. a well-done one.
c. a poor one.
d. one you would like to hand in.

8. The English **Channel** is
a. a television program.
b. a wild party spot.
c. a body of water.
d. a city near London.

9. A **tranquil** scene is
a. calm.
b. noisy.
c. busy.
d. exciting.

10. If a book **absorbs** me, I
a. put it back on the shelf.
b. wipe it with a sponge.
c. can't stop reading it.
d. write my name in it.

For teaching suggestions, see page T34.

Word Study • Suffixes *-ion, -ment, -able*

Remember that a **suffix** is a word part that is added to the end of a **base word** to make a new word.

Base Word	Suffix	New Word		Meaning
inspect	+ **ion**	= inspect**ion**	→	act of inspecting
improve	+ **ment**	= improve**ment**	→	result of something improved
break	+ **able**	= break**able**	→	can be broken

Look at the base words and suffixes in this chart. The suffix *-ion* means "the act, state, or result of." You can add the suffix *-ion* to *inspect* (page 173) to make the word *inspection*. *Inspection* means "the act of inspecting."

The suffix *-ment* also means "the act, state, or result of." The suffix *-able* means "can be." Look at the chart for examples of words with the suffixes *-ment* and *-able*.

PRACTICE ***Write the missing base word or suffix. Then write the meaning of the new word.***

Base Word	Suffix	New Word	Meaning
1. connect	+ ion	= connection →	act of connecting
2. enjoy	+ able	= enjoyable →	can be enjoyed
3. agree	+ ment	= agreement →	the result of agreeing
4. respect	+ able	= respectable →	can be respected

APPLY ***Complete each sentence with words that contain the suffix -ion, -ment, or -able. Choose from the words in the boxes above.***

5. In order for the floor plan to pass inspection, the town has to see an improvement in the layout.

6. We made an agreement to handle the breakable glasses with care.

7. A story is more enjoyable when I make a connection between the events in the story and my own life.

Work with a partner. Add the suffix -ion to two of the base words and -ment to the other two. Use each new word in a sentence.

subtract **measure** **develop** **protect**

For teaching suggestions, see page T38.

Shades of Meaning • Words That Describe Appearance

In the passage "The Nile Crocodile" on pages 170–171, you read this sentence: *Its **elegant** neck reaches down to the water.* The word *elegant* describes appearance, or how something looks. In the sentence, *elegant* tells what a gazelle's neck looks like. Look at the chart for other words that describe appearance.

elegant	Someone or something that is **elegant** looks beautiful and graceful.
shabby	When something or someplace looks **shabby**, it looks old and worn out.
tidy	Something or someplace that looks **tidy** is neat and orderly.

PRACTICE *Write the word from the chart that best completes each sentence.*

1. After we organized our books, the bookcase looked ___tidy___.
2. We wore old, ___shabby___ clothes when we painted the doghouse.
3. The movie star looked ___elegant___ in her long gown.
4. The cabin looked ___shabby___ because no one had lived there for a long time.
5. Our teacher always tells us to keep our desks ___tidy___.
6. The dining room looked ___elegant___ after it was decorated for the wedding.

APPLY *Write a sentence to describe how each place looks. Pay attention to the word in **dark print**. Use the word in your sentence.*
Accept answers that students can justify.

7. a **tidy** kitchen

____

8. a **shabby** hotel

____

9. an **elegant** restaurant

____

UNIT 18

Introducing the Words

Read the following textbook entry about a discovery that changed many lives. Notice how the highlighted words are used. These are the words you will be learning in this unit.

Gold! Gold! Gold!

(Textbook Entry)

Gold is the world's most valuable metal. One reason it is so valuable is because there is so little of it. What little there is can be hard to find. Still, many people have been willing to try to find it.

Hints of Gold in California

It was 1848 in California. Pieces of gold the size of peas glistened on the ground. James Marshall, a worker at a sawmill, picked them up. He told John Sutter, the mill owner, about his find. The two men agreed to keep it quiet. They didn't want to create an uproar that would bring people into the area to look for gold.

A storekeeper, Samuel Brannan, discovered their secret. He went to San Francisco, where he boasted about all the gold discovered at Sutter's Mill. At the same time, he invested the money he had. He bought items such as picks and shovels and got ready to sell them in a store near

John Sutter, owner of Sutter's Mill

Sutter's Mill. It was an ideal plan: Miners would need supplies, and he would sell them everything they needed.

The Rush for Gold

What Marshall and Sutter had feared came true. The possibility of finding gold was sufficient encouragement for thousands of people. They sold their homes and left everything behind to search for gold. They came from all over the world. In all, more than eighty thousand people rushed to California.

Miners bent over streams day after day, looking for gold. They dipped metal pans into the rippling water and sifted for gold. They took tools called pickaxes and dug into the earth. The California Gold Rush was on!

Winners and Losers

Some people did become rich. Three German miners located a large supply of gold. Their mine eventually produced gold worth about $561 million today. Another small group, the Murphy brothers, found gold in their first few days of mining. By the end of the year, the gold they found was worth about $37 million in today's dollars.

Other people were not so lucky. Hiram Pierce came from Troy, New York. He paid $25 for a cradle, a tool that separated dirt from gold. By the time he returned home a year or two later, he was broke.

Pierce wrote eloquent descriptions and stories about mining. The work was difficult. Miners had to wade in freezing streams. They moved heavy dirt. They got hurt in accidents.

Many Native Americans were losers in the California Gold Rush, too. When miners became sick with infectious diseases, many Native Americans who lived in the area caught the diseases and died.

Today's Gold

Today, gold is used for many things. There is gold in some computer parts. People wear gold jewelry. Countries collect gold, which helps them protect the value of their money. As long as gold is scarce, it will continue to be the world's most precious metal.

Miners used a cradle to help them separate dirt from gold.

Gold nugget

Definitions

You were introduced to the words below in the passage on pages 180–181. Study the spelling, pronunciation, part of speech, and definition of each word. Write the word on the line in the sentence. Then read the synonyms and antonyms.

Remember

A **noun** *(n.)* is a word that names a person, place, or thing.

A **verb** *(v.)* is a word or words that express action or a state of being.

An **adjective** *(adj.)* is a word that describes a noun or pronoun.

1. boast (bōst)

(v.) to speak proudly of oneself, brag; to take pride in

The team members tend to ___boast___ *whenever they win.*

(n.) talk that is too full of pride in oneself

My ___boast___ *about my grades drove away my friends.*

SYNONYMS: (v.) crow, exaggerate, flaunt, overstate; (n.) self-praise
ANTONYM: (v.) belittle

2. eloquent (el′ ə kwənt)

(adj.) showing the ability to use words clearly and effectively

Martin Luther King, Jr., was an ___eloquent___ *civil rights speaker.*

SYNONYMS: expressive, well-spoken, persuasive, forceful, powerful
ANTONYMS: awkward, tongue-tied

3. glisten (gli′ sən)

(v.) to shine with sparkling light

I like to see the morning dew ___glisten___ *in the sunshine.*

SYNONYMS: sparkle, glimmer, glitter, shimmer, gleam

4. ideal (ī dēl′)

(adj.) considered to be perfect; existing only in the imagination

Today was an ___ideal___ *spring day.*

(n.) a person or thing that is considered to be perfect

My ___ideal___ *is a world without violence.*

SYNONYMS: (adj.) supreme, flawless, exemplary, ultimate; (n.) model, example
ANTONYMS: (adj.) practical, pragmatic, real

5. infectious
(in fek′ shəs)

(adj.) caused or spread by germs; able or tending to spread from one to another

Chicken pox is a highly ___infectious___ *disease.*

SYNONYMS: contagious, catching

6. invest
(in vest′)

(v.) to put money into something that will earn interest or make a profit; to make use of for future benefit

They will ___invest___ *their money in stocks and bonds.*

SYNONYMS: spend, expend, contribute

7. locate
(lō′ kāt)

(v.) to find the position of; to settle into a place

I need to ___locate___ *the highway on the map.*

SYNONYMS: discover, identify, pinpoint, detect, uncover; situate, build, establish

8. ripple
(rip′ əl)

(n.) a small wave

The pebble caused a ___ripple___ *in the pool.*

(v.) to form or cause small waves

A rowboat will ___ripple___ *the surface of the lake.*

SYNONYMS: (n.) vibration; (v.) ruffle, spread

9. sufficient
(sə fi′ shənt)

(adj.) as much as is needed, enough

We have a ___sufficient___ *amount of time to finish our task.*

SYNONYMS: adequate, plenty, ample
ANTONYMS: insufficient, inadequate, deficient, lacking, sparse, scanty

10. uproar
(up′ rôr)

(n.) a state of noisy excitement, confusion

When I entered, I found the room in an ___uproar___.

SYNONYMS: disorder, commotion, disturbance
ANTONYMS: calmness, serenity, tranquility

Match the Meaning

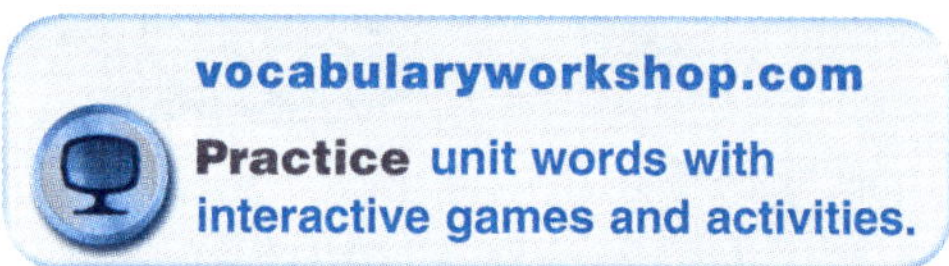

Choose the word whose meaning is suggested by the clue given. Then write the word on the line provided.

1. If you put money into something that will earn more money, you ____invest____ it.

a. invest b. ripple c. boast

2. To brag is also to ____boast____.

a. glisten b. locate c. boast

3. When you find something, you ____locate____ it.

a. locate b. invest c. ripple

4. A well-spoken person can be described as ____eloquent____.

a. ideal b. infectious c. eloquent

5. A(n) ____ripple____ is a small wave.

a. uproar b. ripple c. boast

6. To have a(n)____sufficient____ amount is to have as much as you need.

a. eloquent b. infectious c. sufficient

7. A disease that can be caught by others is said to be ____infectious____.

a. infectious b. sufficient c. ideal

8. Something that is ____ideal____ is considered to be perfect.

a. eloquent b. sufficient c. ideal

9. If you cause a(n) ____uproar____, you create much excitement.

a. uproar b. boast c. ripple

10. When an object shines, it might ____glisten____.

a. locate b. glisten c. invest

The campers used a map and a compass to **locate** the hidden treasure.

Synonyms

*Choose the word that is most nearly the **same** in meaning as the word or phrase in **dark print**. Then write your choice on the line provided.*

1. a **contagious** laugh
a. sufficient b. infectious c. eloquent ___infectious___

2. created a **wave**
a. ripple b. uproar c. boast ___ripple___

3. **shimmer** in the moonlight
a. boast b. glisten c. locate ___glisten___

4. **find** your gloves
a. invest b. glisten c. locate ___locate___

5. **spend** my time
a. boast b. ripple c. invest ___invest___

6. an unnecessary **disturbance**
a. ripple b. uproar c. boast ___uproar___

Antonyms

*Choose the word that is most nearly **opposite** in meaning to the word or phrase in **dark print**. Then write your choice on the line provided.*

1. **belittle** oneself in front of others
a. ripple b. locate c. boast about ___boast about___

2. a **pragmatic** solution
a. ideal b. infectious c. sufficient ___ideal___

3. a **scanty** amount of food
a. eloquent b. infectious c. sufficient ___sufficient___

4. a **fumbling** speech
a. ideal b. eloquent c. infectious ___eloquent___

Completing the Sentence

Choose the word from the box that best completes each item below. Then write the word on the line provided. (You may have to change the word's ending.)

boast	**eloquent**	**glisten**
ideal	**infectious**	**invest**
locate	**ripple**	
sufficient	**uproar**	

Public Speaking

■ It is an art to be a good public speaker. The most ___eloquent___ speakers know how to speak clearly and effectively.

■ The United States can ___boast___ of many political leaders who were and are excellent communicators.

■ The moods and emotions of a speaker can be so ___infectious___ that those same feelings are felt by the audience.

■ Sometimes, a speaker chooses to discuss a topic over which there are differences of opinion. At the end of a powerful speech that addresses such a topic, the room might be in an ___uproar___.

■ When audiences enjoy a speaker, a ___ripple___ of applause often turns into thunderous applause.

Antoni Gaudí

■ Antoni Gaudí was a Spanish architect. He is known for the original and imaginative designs of his buildings. He found the use of bright colors to be a(n) ___ideal___ way to make his buildings stand out.

■ My favorite Gaudí works are those that look like the scales of a dragon. I especially like looking at them when they ___glisten___ in the sunshine.

■ Gaudí's most famous creation is La Sagrada Família, a church ___located___ in Barcelona.

■ Gaudí ___invested___ many years in this project, but it is still not finished after more than 100 years! It seems there will never be ___sufficient___ time to complete it!

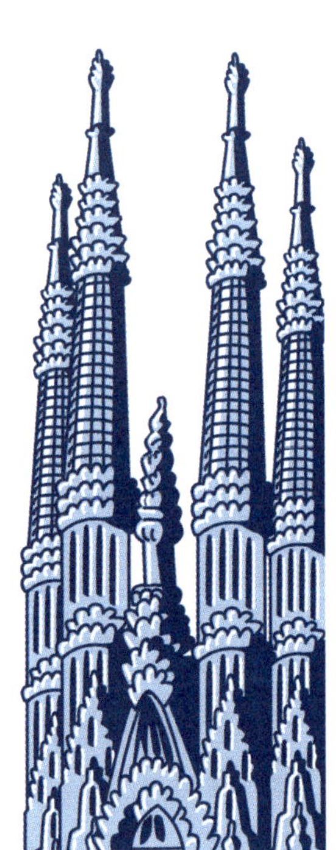

For teaching suggestions, see page T34.

Word Study • Roots *loc, aud*

A **root** is the main part of a word. Roots have meaning, but few roots can stand alone. Sometimes, knowing the meaning of a root can help you figure out the meaning of a word.

loc—place
The root **loc** appears in **locate** (page 183). When you **locate** something, you find its place.
aud—hear
The root **aud** appears in **audible**. When music is **audible**, you are able to hear it.

The chart below gives the meanings of words with the roots *loc* and *aud*.

audience	a group of people gathered to see or hear something
auditorium	a large room or building where people gather to see and hear performances and other events
local	belonging or relating to a certain place, such as a town
location	a place or position

PRACTICE *Complete each sentence with a word that contains the root loc or aud. Choose from the words above.*

1. The car's radio was ___audible___ from the sidewalk.
2. We had to ___locate___ the park on a map.
3. We found a good ___location___ for our picnic.
4. The ___auditorium___ was filled with people waiting for the show.
5. I buy ___local___ fruits because they are fresher.
6. The ___audience___ cheered when the band came onto the stage.

APPLY *Complete each sentence to show you understand the meaning of the word in **dark print**.*
Accept reasonable answers. Possible answers are given.

7. You might go to an **auditorium** to ___listen to a concert___.
8. His voice was barely **audible** because ___he had a sore throat___.
9. A house might be hard to **locate** if ___it is in the woods___.

Work with a partner to list other words that contain the roots loc and aud. Write definitions for the words. Then look in an online or classroom dictionary to check the meanings.

Vocabulary for Comprehension

Read the following passage in which some of the words you have studied in Units 16–18 appear in* dark print*. Then answer the questions on page 189.

Anansi the Hungry Spider

Anansi, a trickster, lived in a poor village where there was little food. Life there was **wretched** for all the animals, including spiders like Anansi.

A giant named Five also lived in the village. Everyone feared Five because she was mean and greedy. Those who spoke her name had to give her all the food they had. Thinking about Five helped hungry Anansi to conceive a plan. Soon he **negotiated** a deal with her. Anansi would help Five get food if she would share the prize with him. But he had to be careful *not* to say her name.

Anansi gathered **sufficient** corn to carry out the plan. He put the corn in five piles. Then, seated on one pile, he called to Rabbit, "Want some corn?" Of course, Rabbit did.

Anansi told him, "Count the piles, and one is yours!"

Rabbit counted, "One, two, three, four, five." As soon as the giant's name, Five, was said, poor Rabbit lost all his food. Anansi cooked the food and shared the feast with Five. For weeks, Anansi would **boast** about his feast.

When his food was no longer abundant, Anansi decided to trick Goose. Goose, however, didn't trust Anansi and **inspected** the situation carefully. As Anansi sat on a pile of corn, Goose counted. "One, two, three, four, ..., and the one you're sitting on!"

Angry Anansi shouted, "That's wrong!"

Goose counted again. "One, two, three, four, ..., and the one you're sitting on!"

By now, Anansi was in an **uproar**. He screamed, "No! It's one, two, three, four, five!" No sooner did Anansi say the word *five* than the giant seized all of Anansi's food. Goose smiled, said grace, and ate the corn. She not only tricked the trickster, she had...how many piles of corn?

Fill in the circle next to the choice that best completes the sentence or answers the question.

1. This passage is mostly about
- (a) a poor village.
- (b) how Anansi tries to trick the animals.
- (c) how Rabbit gets tricked.
- (d) how the giant tricked Anansi.

2. The meaning of **wretched** is
- (a) tricky.
- (b) greedy.
- (c) happy.
- (d) awful.

3. In this passage, **negotiated** means
- (a) discussed.
- (b) announced.
- (c) rejected.
- (d) dismissed.

4. Sufficient most nearly means
- (a) extra.
- (b) enough.
- (c) hardly any.
- (d) none.

5. The meaning of **boast** is
- (a) to complain.
- (b) to lose money.
- (c) to brag.
- (d) to act in a bashful way.

6. Another word for **inspected** is
- (a) examined.
- (b) ignored.
- (c) described.
- (d) modeled.

7. Goose outsmarted Anansi by
- (a) sharing her food with him.
- (b) counting slowly.
- (c) refusing to say the word *five.*
- (d) making her own deal with Five.

8. In this passage, **uproar** means
- (a) a feeling of calmness.
- (b) loud laughter.
- (c) a fight.
- (d) a state of excitement.

Write Your Own

In this story, Anansi learns that he can't fool everyone. Imagine how he felt after Goose tricked him and Five took all of his food. On a separate sheet of paper, write a journal entry from Anansi's point of view that describes how he felt. Use at least three words from Units 16–18.

Classifying

Choose the word from the box that goes best with each group of words. Write the word on the line provided. Then explain what the words have in common.

admirable	**arch**	**channel**
conceive	**dreary**	**fearsome**
formal	**invest**	
purify	**uproar**	

1. channel, lake, pond, river

The words name bodies of water.

2. think, imagine, create, conceive

The words are synonyms.

3. wall, roof, window, arch

The words name parts of a building.

4. fear, fearful, fearless, fearsome

The words belong to the same family.

5. comfortable, reasonable, admirable, considerable

The words end with the same suffix.

6. save, spend, donate, invest

The words describe what to do with money.

7. eerie, leery, weary, dreary

The words rhyme.

8. earthquake, frostbite, headache, uproar

The words are compound words.

9. athletic, casual, dressy, formal

The words name clothing styles.

10. freshen, filter, disinfect, purify

The words describe ways to clean.

REVIEW UNITS 13–18

Completing the Idea

*Complete each sentence so that it makes sense. Pay attention to the word in **dark print**.* Accept answers that show an understanding of the vocabulary.

1. It was difficult to beat our **opponent** because ______.
2. I was awarded the **privilege** of ______.
3. My **ambition** for the future is to ______.
4. We had to **suspend** the game because ______.
5. An **eloquent** speaker might inspire people to ______.
6. Some scientists try to **predict** ______.
7. A referee will **penalize** a player who ______.
8. A **modest** person would not ______.
9. One chore that is **tiresome** is ______.
10. My uncle asked me to **locate** ______.
11. I often **yearn** for ______.
12. When I visit the museum, I want to **inquire** about ______.
13. You can **merit** an allowance by ______.
14. I try to **absorb** new information by ______.
15. The **ideal** time to go for a jog is ______.

Writing Challenge

Check that vocabulary is used correctly and that each sentence is written correctly.

*Write two sentences using the word **stunt**. In the first sentence, use **stunt** as a verb. In the second sentence, use **stunt** as a noun.*

1. ______
2. ______

REVIEW UNITS 13–18

Word List

The following is a list of all the words taught in the units of this book. The number after each entry indicates the page on which the word is first introduced.